BIBLE OVERVIEW

HENDRICKSON PUBLISHERS ROSE PUBLISHING

www.hendricksonrose.com

Bible Overview
© Copyright 2012 Bristol Works, Inc.
Rose Publishing, LLC
P.O. Box 3473
Peabody, Massachusetts 01961-3473 USA
www.hendricksonrose.com

Contributors: Benjamin Galan, MTS, ThM; Jessica Curiel, MA; Shawn Vander Lugt, MA; William Brent Ashby, BT

Cover and layout design by Monty Morgan and Sergio Urquiza

All Scripture quotations, unless otherwise indicated, are taken from the Holy Bible, New International Version® NIV®. Copyright © 1973, 1978, 1984, 2011 by Biblica.™ Used by permission of Zondervan. All rights reserved worldwide.

Library of Congress Cataloging-in-Publication Data

Rose Bible overview / [contributors, Benjamin Galan et al.].
    p. cm.
 Summary: "A quick-reference overview of all 66 biblical books; includes themes, outlines, maps, time lines, charts, and full-color photos"--Provided by publisher.
 ISBN 978-1-59636-569-8 (pbk.)
 1. Bible--Introductions. 2. Bible--Outlines, syllabi, etc. I. Galan, Benjamin.
 BS475.3.R67 2012
 220.6'1--dc23
                    2012030413

Printed in the United States of America
110619VP

CONTENTS

CONTENTS

INTRODUCTION

Reading the Bible is an exciting spiritual, emotional, and intellectual adventure. It is an invitation to walk alongside God's people in Scripture and meet an awe-inspiring God. God invites us to have an intimate relationship with him. Through the Holy Spirit and the Scriptures, we get to know a loving, compassionate, graceful, stern, holy, and just God. Knowing God is a life-long journey. It is not an easy journey—as Israel's journey through the wilderness, for example, shows, or Paul's ministry in the book of Acts. However, God has promised to be with us through the journey: "My Presence will go with you, and I will give you rest" (Ex. 33:14), and "Surely I am with you always, to the very end of the age" (Matt. 28:20).

Whether you travel on your own or with other fellow travelers, *Bible Overview* is a tool to help you in your journey through the Bible. If you are teaching the Bible, *Bible Overview* is a fully **reproducible** book that you can share with those traveling alongside you.

Traveling through the Bible is similar to visiting a foreign, exotic country. Many things are familiar, while many others seem too strange for us to understand them. However, the experience leaves us transformed. Reading the Bible is a transformative experience. Gradually, the Holy Spirit renews our inner beings so we mature and grow in grace before God and other people. Sometimes on this journey we will face opposition and setbacks. Don't be discouraged; remember and be "confident of this, that he who began a good work in you will carry it on to completion until the day of Christ Jesus" (Phil. 1:6).

How Bible Overview Will Help You

- *Bible Overview* provides you with the **background** of each biblical book, so you can become acquainted with the lands and the cultures in the Bible. It's the who, what, where, and when of each book.

- We also explore the **purpose** of the biblical book. This section is similar to a compass that helps you navigate a trek through the mountains. It does not show the final destination, but it helps you get there.

- The **outline** of each book gives you a way to travel through the book, so you can enjoy the richness and beauty of the Scriptures.

- Knowing the major **themes** in each biblical book will also help you grasp the main message of each book. Keeping in mind the main message of the book will help you stay on the path as you travel.

- Recognizing the **key people** in the books of the Bible—particularly in the narrative books—helps us follow the story line. When we can follow the plot of the story, we begin to discern the way God interacts with people and nations. As you read the Bible, focus on the main characters. Humbly learn from their shortcomings, and gratefully recognize the wonderful things that God did in and through them.

- **Key verses** are nuggets of truth in each book that sum up the message of the book, contain important prophecies and words of Jesus, and help us focus our attention squarely on who God is and what he has promised.

- The section **Being God's People** is a reminder that one of the main functions of the Bible is to provide an identity to God's people. It helps us know who we are in Christ: a new creation, God's holy nation, and a royal priesthood (2 Cor. 5:17; 1 Peter 2:9). It helps us know about God's intense love for his creation, his compassion, and his merciful plan of salvation.

- Finally, recognizing that **Jesus is the center** and star of God's revelation, Bible Overview shows the way Jesus is present in each book of the Bible. Like the northern star that has guided sailors for hundreds of years, the light of Jesus guides us so we can understand God's plan of salvation.

How We Got the Bible

To begin this journey, knowing a few important facts about the Bible will give us the proper starting point.

1. God inspired the whole Bible (2 Tim. 3:16–17; 2 Peter 1:20–21).

2. The Bible is made up of 66 different books that were written over 1,000 years, by more than 40 individuals. The Old Testament has 39 books, and the New Testament has 27 books. The Hebrew Bible has the same text as the English Bible's Old Testament. However, the Hebrew Bible has different divisions and arrangements of the books.

3. The Old Testament was written mainly in Hebrew, with some Aramaic. The New Testament was written in a dialect of ancient Greek that merchants and travelers used.

4. The books of the Bible were collected and arranged and recognized as inspired sacred authority by councils of rabbis and councils of church leaders based on careful guidelines.

5. Before the printing press was invented, the Bible was copied by hand. The Bible was copied very accurately, in many cases by special scribes who developed intricate methods of counting words and letters to ensure that no errors had been made.

6. The Bible was the first book ever printed on the printing press with moveable type (Gutenberg Press, 1455, Latin Bible).

7. There is much evidence that the Bible we have today is remarkably true to the original writings. Of the thousands of copies made by hand before the year 1500, more than 5,900 Greek manuscripts from the New Testament alone still exist today. The text of the Bible is better preserved than the writings of Plato or Aristotle.

8. The discovery of the Dead Sea Scrolls confirmed the astonishing reliability of some of the copies of the Old Testament made over the years. Although some spelling variations exist, no variation affects basic Bible doctrines.

9. As the Bible was carried to other countries, it was translated into the common language of the people by scholars who wanted others to know God's Word. By AD 200, the Bible was translated into seven languages; by 500, 13 languages; by 900, 17 languages; by 1400, 28 languages; by 1800, 57 languages; by 1900, 537 languages; by 1980, 1,100 languages; by 2006, 2,426 languages have some portions of the Scripture. Today there are still 2,000 people groups with no Bible in their own language. (Source: *The World Christian Encyclopedia;* Wycliffe, International.)

Reasons to Study the Bible

To know God. God created the heaven and the earth and everyone in it (Gen. 1–3). To know God is to have eternal life (John 17:3).

To enjoy and love God. Meditate on God's character, principles, and promises. Rejoice in his love, care, and forgiveness (Ps. 119:12–18, 160–162; 1 Tim. 6:17).

To know God's Word. The Scriptures were inspired by God. They teach us the truth and show us what is wrong in our lives. They straighten us out (2 Tim. 3:16).

To understand the Word. Jesus is called the Word because he is the ultimate communication from God. He existed from the beginning with God, he is God, and he created everything. He said that those who have seen him have seen the Father (John 1:1–3; 10:30; 12:44, 45; 14:7–9).

To learn direction in life. The Bible shows us what to do (Ps. 119:11).

To find comfort and hope. The Scriptures give us encouragement (Rom. 15:4).

To let God expose our innermost thoughts and desires. God's Word helps us see ourselves as we really are and convicts us of sin so that we repent and change (Heb. 4:12–16).

To become pure and holy. Jesus prayed this for all believers that they would be set apart for God and his holy purposes (John 17:17–23).

To obey the Great Commandment. The more we know God, the more we can love him. The Great Commandment is to love God with all of our being and our neighbor as ourselves (Mark 12:29–31). And Jesus gave us a new commandment to love one another (John 13:34–35).

How to Study the Bible

Plan a study time. Decide on a quiet time and place to study God's Word and make it a daily habit, like eating. Some people get up early to spend time with God. Others study during the day or evening.

Pray. Ask God to help you understand his Word. Pray using your own words or something like this: "Lord, thank you for the Bible so that we will know who you are and what you want for our lives. Please help me understand it and do what you want me to do."

Read and re-read It. The Bible is the most important letter you can ever receive—a message from the God of the universe who made you, loves you, and wants to communicate with you. Open your "love letter" every day. Re-read each chapter and verse several times.

Know the author. Read Genesis to learn about God who created the world. All Scripture is inspired by God. God actually visited earth in the form of man—the man Christ Jesus. Jesus said, "I and my Father are one." Read the Gospel of John to learn about God's plan for you.

Take notes. Write notes about what you read. Use a specific notebook or "spiritual journal" especially for Bible study. You might want to underline key verses or write notes in the margin of your Bible.

Make the Bible your authority. Accept and believe that what the Bible says is true. You may not understand everything in the Bible, but obey and apply what you do understand.

Find a group. "As iron sharpens iron, so one person sharpens another" (Prov. 27:17). God gave his Word to his people. When you share what you are learning with other fellow believers, God will do amazing things. It will also help you to be accountable to someone.

Basic Principles of Bible Study

Look for God's over-all plan. The Old Testament reveals God's loving plan of salvation, from creation to prophecies of the future Messiah (the Savior). The New Testament reveals God's salvation of sinful humanity by the suffering, death, and resurrection of the Messiah, Jesus Christ, and reveals the everlasting kingdom of God.

Find the background of the books. Find out who wrote the books, the reason for writing, and the themes of the books. Ask "Who, What, Where, When, Why, and How?" Usually this information is in the first chapter or in the introduction of the book.

Read verses in context. Read the surrounding chapters and the verses before and after the verse you are studying. Get the whole picture. Don't study verses out of context. Look at the outline of the book.

Get the whole message of God's Word. Take the whole Bible as God's Word. Don't just concentrate on one verse or one idea. See if the teaching is explained more fully in other parts of the Bible. If you are using a study Bible, look at the small cross references in your Bible to help you find other verses on the same subject.

Discover the intended meaning. As you read the Bible, look for the author's intended meaning. What did the author want to say? What did it mean in that culture? What does it mean now? What are the main ideas? If you have questions, write them down, pray for insight, and discuss your ideas with others.

Learn the history and geography. Use a time line to learn about the history of the Bible. Use maps to learn about the geography of where the events took place.

Pay attention to figurative language. Figures of speech are word pictures that help us understand a truth. "Your word is a lamp for my feet, a light on my path" (Ps. 119:105) is a metaphor that helps us picture the Bible enlightening our minds and actions and giving us direction. "As the deer pants for streams of water, so my soul pants for you, my God" (Ps. 42:1) is a simile that compares ideas with the words "like" or "as." Similes occur over 175 times in the Psalms. Jesus used personification when he said if the people did not declare the mighty works they had seen God do, the stones would cry out in praise (Luke 19:40). Hyperbole (exaggeration) is found in Matthew 5:29–30 when Jesus speaks of eyes and hands causing one to stumble.

Know the forms of literature. The Bible contains various forms of literature: history, narrative, poetry and wisdom, prophecy, parables and letters. Recognizing each form will help you interpret the meaning. For example, parables explain a spiritual truth by means of a story or analogy. The parable of the Prodigal Son in Luke 15 does not refer to a specific historical person, but teaches that God is a loving father who joyfully welcomes back prodigal or rebellious children who later repent and return to him.

THE OLD TESTAMENT

Reading the Old Testament

Reading the Old Testament can be an intimidating activity. However, making the effort to read and understand the Old Testament produces great fruit in our lives. In the many stories, poems, prophecies, songs, prayers, wisdom, and instructions of the Old Testament, we see the way God relates to humanity, both his people in particular and the nations in general.

Here are some things to keep in mind when reading the Old Testament:

1. **The Old Testament is as much the Word of God as the New Testament.** Though the Old Testament was compiled over hundreds of years and written by many different authors, it all originated with God. It is his Word to his people. The apostle Peter reminds believers, "We also have the prophetic message as something completely reliable.... No prophecy of Scripture came about by the prophet's own interpretation of things. For prophecy never had its origin in the human will, but prophets, though human, spoke from God as they were carried along by the Holy Spirit" (2 Peter 1:19–21).

2. **The Old Testament helps us understand the New Testament.** The Old Testament deals with events and teachings hundreds—and even thousands— of years before Jesus was born. All of those events and teachings give us the background to all that happened when Jesus was born and during his life. For example, understanding the Old Testament sacrifices sheds light on what Jesus' sacrifice on the cross means. Knowing about the Old Testament prophecies of a coming Messiah helps us see how Jesus is that Messiah (the "Christ") who fulfills God's promises given long ago. The Old Testament laws, customs, and religious traditions help us make sense of Jesus' interactions with the Jewish religious leaders of his day.

3. **God's grace for humanity is seen throughout the Old Testament.** As we read the Old Testament, we begin to understand the gracious and powerful God who created all things. We also understand the need for God's grace as we contemplate human folly and sin. Because of God's grace, rather than destroying humanity, God planned to save us. We see this plan unfold in the pages of the Old Testament. It is not always a straightforward telling of God's plan. Often, we must carefully find God's plan in the stories of people who, just like us today, experience the goodness of creation, the corruption of a good creation, the terrible distorting power of sin, and the sad consequences of our separation from God.

4. **Old Testament people and stories serve as examples for believers today.** The apostle Paul tells us that the things that happened to people in the Old Testament "happened to them as examples and were written down as warnings for us, on whom the culmination of the ages has come. So, if you think you are standing firm, be careful that you don't fall!" (1 Cor. 10:11–12). Even the most faithful people in the Old Testament, like Moses and King David, fell into sin and were disciplined by God. Yet we see in the Old Testament how God continued to redeem and restore his people even after terrible sin and tragedy.

5. **The Old Testament helps us recognize God's actions.** Although we are not of the world, Jesus has sent us to the world to be witnesses of his love, grace, and sacrifice. As long as we are in the world, we must learn to recognize the way God moves and acts in the world, through people, and sometimes in extraordinary ways that do not require people. The more we read the Old Testament, the more we learn to recognize God's ways in the world.

Geography and Cultural Context

The Old Testament covers the life of a people through a large expanse of space and time. From the fertile Delta of the Nile in Egypt, through the barren wilderness of the Sinai peninsula, the rugged terrain of Edom and Moab, to the lands east and west of the Jordan River, to the wealthy Fertile Crescent of the cities between the two mighty rivers the Tigris and the Euphrates, the Old Testament unfolds the story of God and God's people in wonderful, dramatic, and often sad ways. Through it all, however, God's grace shines through, illuminating the plan of the One who would give an answer to the greatest human problem of sin and death.

Knowing the cultures in and around Israel helps us to more fully grasp the meaning of the stories and songs of the Old Testament. Many practices in the Old Testament seem very strange to us. Some of them are beyond our understanding. (For example, the prohibition to eat pork continues to puzzle scholars.) However, many other practices we can understand by looking at the historical and social world of the Old Testament. An important example of this is the concept of royalty and covenants.

The ancient world was very familiar with the concept of royalty. In our day, we have lost the sense of what it was like to have a king. We do not fully understand how difficult it was for people to relate to someone so lofty. "Regular" people did not have contact with royalty. A covenant was often the only way to relate to royalty. There were two main kinds of covenants for that purpose: conditional and unconditional covenants.

■ In conditional covenants, the king claimed complete authority over his subject. In return, the king pledged to offer protection and provision on condition of the subject's loyalty. The subject, on the other hand, pledged loyalty and service to the king, and expected in return the king's protection and favor.

■ Then there are the unconditional covenants. In these, the king pledged a royal favor on behalf of a subject, perhaps to reward a special service to the king. The favor could take different forms; a common form was a royal grant of land.

One of the main metaphors used in the Bible to speak about God is that of the king. God is the Great King, the King of kings. He chose to relate to humans in terms that we could understand. The concept of kingship is an important metaphor to understand our relationship with our Creator.

In the Old Testament we see both kinds of covenants between God the King and his people. For example, the covenant God revealed to Moses on Mount Sinai was conditional. In this covenant, God promised to make Israel his people and he expected Israel to obey and keep the covenant (Ex. 19:5–6). God's covenant with David however was unconditional. God promised to preserve David's descendants upon the throne of Israel (2 Sam. 7:11)—a promise that found its fulfillment in the Messiah Jesus, a descendant of David.

Books of the Old Testament

The Old Testament is made up of thirty-nine books, divided into four main sections.

Pentateuch	Historical Books	Poetry & Wisdom Books	Prophetic Books	
Genesis	Joshua	Job	*Major Prophets:*	*Minor Prophets:*
Exodus	Judges	Psalms	Isaiah	Hosea
Leviticus	Ruth	Proverbs	Jeremiah	Joel
Numbers	1 Samuel	Ecclesiastes	Lamentations	Amos
Deuteronomy	2 Samuel	Song of Songs	Ezekiel	Obadiah
	1 Kings		Daniel	Jonah
	2 Kings			Micah
	1 Chronicles			Nahum
	2 Chronicles			Habakkuk
	Ezra			Zephaniah
	Nehemiah			Haggai
	Esther			Zechariah
				Malachi

Old Testament Time Line

Books of the Bible

|2100 BC | 2000 BC | 1900 BC | 1800 BC |

The period for each book of the Bible shows its historical setting, not the date the book was written. Many dates listed are approximate and may vary according to different scholars.

▶ Genesis

Abraham to the Sojourn in Egypt

Bible History

Some scholars place Abraham's birth at 1952 BC. In this case, biblical events through Joseph would slide to the right 214 years.

Joseph c. 1914-1805

Abraham c. 2166-1991

● Joseph becomes and official in Egypt c. 1884

● Abrahamic Covenant

● Jacob and his family move to Egypt c. 1876

Ishmael c. 2080-1943

Isaac c. 2066-1886

Jacob (Israel) c. 2005-1859

KEY

	TIME SPAN MARKER
●	YEAR MARKER
| |	10 YEARS BETWEEN LINES
C.	CIRCA (ABOUT)

|1200 BC | 1100 BC | 1000 BC | 900 BC | 800 BC |

Books of the Bible

1 Chronicles | 2 Chronicles

1 Samuel | 2 Samuel | 1 Kings | 2 Kings

Psalms, Proverbs, Song of Songs, Ecclesiastes, Job (dates uncertain)

▶ Judges

Era of Judges | United Kingdom Era | Divided Kingdom Era

Bible History

● Kingdom divides into Northern Kingdom (Israel) and Southern Kingdom (Judah) 931

Eli, Priest in Shiloh c. 1100-1060

Judge & Prophet Samuel c. 1060-1020

Prophet Elijah c. 870-845

King Saul c. 1051-1011

Prophet Elisha c. 845-800

King David c. 1011-971

King Solomon c. 971-931

● Solomon's temple (first temple) completed 960

(Kings listed by dates of reign)

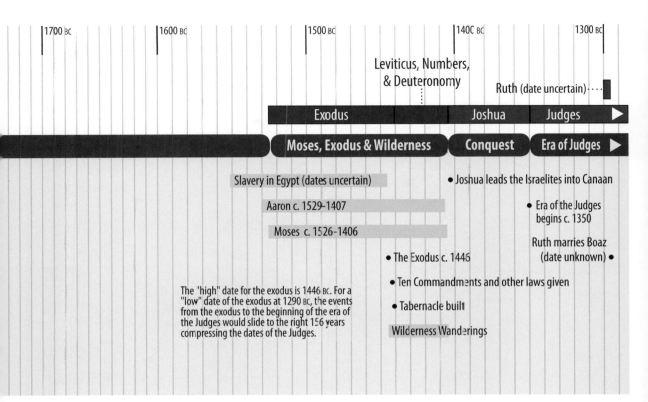
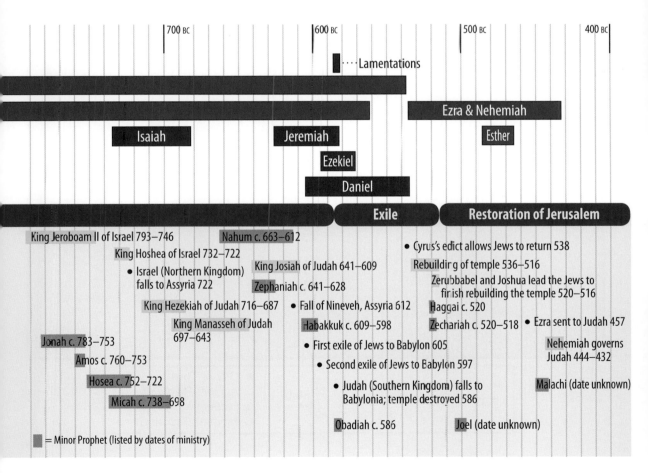

ANCIENT MIDDLE EAST

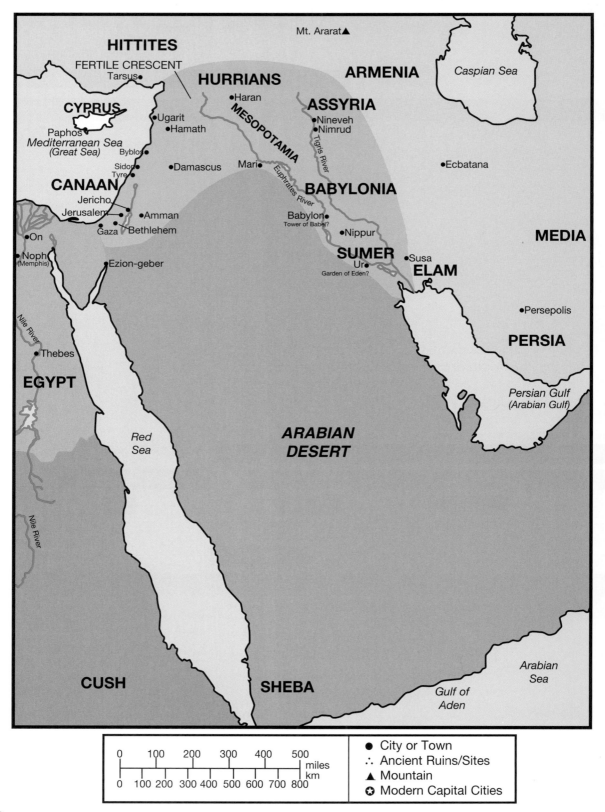

HITTITES

FERTILE CRESCENT
Tarsus

Mt. Ararat ▲

Caspian Sea

HURRIANS

ARMENIA

Haran

ASSYRIA

CYPRUS

MESOPOTAMIA

Nineveh
Nimrud

Paphos
Mediterranean Sea
(Great Sea)

Ugarit
Hamath

Byblos

Damascus

Mari

Ecbatana

Sidon
Tyre

CANAAN

Jericho
Jerusalem

Amman

Gaza Bethlehem

On

Noph
(Memphis)

Ezion-geber

Tigris River

Euphrates River

BABYLONIA

Babylon
Tower of Babel?

Nippur

SUMER
Ur
Garden of Eden?

Susa
ELAM

MEDIA

Persepolis

PERSIA

Thebes

EGYPT

Nile River

Red
Sea

ARABIAN
DESERT

Persian Gulf
(Arabian Gulf)

Nile River

CUSH

SHEBA

Gulf of
Aden

Arabian
Sea

0	100	200	300	400	500

miles

0	100	200	300	400	500	600	700	800

km

● City or Town
∴ Ancient Ruins/Sites
▲ Mountain
✪ Modern Capital Cities

GOD'S INSTRUCTIONS FOR GOD'S PEOPLE

What Is the Pentateuch?

The Pentateuch refers to the first five books of the Bible. The word *Pentateuch* comes from a Greek word that means "five vessels or scrolls." In Hebrew, this section is known as *Torah*. Commonly translated as "law," *torah* is better translated as "instruction." This way, the Torah is not limited to legal sections, but it includes everything in the Pentateuch: genealogies, stories, laws, discourses, and songs.

On one level, the Pentateuch is a collection of books. On a deeper level, the Pentateuch is God's gracious provision for his people. It provides an identity for God's people. It provides the answers to the questions, what does it mean to be God's people, and how can we be God's people? The Pentateuch is God's instructions for a nation learning to be God's people while living in the world.

For this reason, the Pentateuch lays the basis for the rest of the Bible. It explains the origin of the universe, of the nations, and of God's people. It explains the need for God's direct intervention in human history— human sin. The stories show how God acts in the lives of his people.

Pentateuch

Genesis
Exodus
Leviticus
Numbers
Deuteronomy

Who Wrote the Pentateuch?

This is a difficult question. Some scholars argue that Moses wrote the whole of the Pentateuch, and they offer good arguments in favor. Other scholars argue that the collection of books underwent a long writing process, which ended centuries after Moses' life. Still others will grant that Moses wrote a portion of the material. Scholars still debate how much of that material Moses wrote—and how much was written in a long process of editing and rearranging of the material.

The two main arguments for recognizing Moses as the author of the Pentateuch are:

- We know that God ordered Moses to write (Ex. 17:14; 24:3, 4, 7; 32:7–10, 30–34; 34:27; Lev. 26:46; 27:34; Deut. 31:9, 24, 25).

- The Old and New Testaments recognize the Pentateuch as "Moses' Law" (Josh. 8:31, 32; 1 Kings 2:3; Jer. 7:22; Ezra 6:18; Neh. 8:1; Mal. 4:4; Matt. 22:24; Acts 15:21).

However, even supporting Moses as the author, many scholars still recognize that Moses did not write everything in the Pentateuch.

- Moses probably didn't write about his own death (Deut. 34).

- Other passages that use names for cities that don't fit the times (Gen. 11:31; 14:14) or that talk about Moses' humility (Num. 12:3) were probably written by a later author.

- The text itself names ancient sources that were used in the books of the Pentateuch: The Book of the Wars of the Lord (Num. 21:14) and the Book of the Covenant (Ex. 24:7).

Other scholars have taken the idea of ancient sources beyond those two mentioned in the text itself. Although earlier scholars took their critical views too far and with little support, many scholars today continue to see an important history of composition of the books. Despite of how we think the collection was written, the Pentateuch is the Word of God and lays the theological groundwork for the rest of the Scriptures.

Characteristics of the Pentateuch

Literature: Most of the Pentateuch is prose narrative of a high literary quality. That means that besides being divinely inspired books which teach us truths about God and the world he created, the books of the Pentateuch are also beautiful writings. The Pentateuch has two main kinds of literature: stories and laws. The laws—Exodus 20, for example—are framed with stories. The stories help us make sense of the laws, and the laws give boundaries to our lives so we can be God's separate people. This way, we come to understand that the Pentateuch is not about Moses; it is not a Moses biography. Rather, the Pentateuch is about God and God's people.

Main Characters:

- *God:* God is the Pentateuch's main interest. The Pentateuch does not tell us all or most of what there is to know about God. Rather, the importance of everything that happens depends on how it relates to God: God caused or allowed it, it reveals something about God's character—his goodness, holiness, justice, love, compassion—or it helps us understand how God works in and through history.

- *Abraham:* God's calling of Abraham shows God's initiative to rescue humanity from sin and death. The Pentateuch illustrates the beginning of the fulfillment of God's promises to Abraham: Abraham's descendants were many, through Joseph they were a blessing to all the nations of the world, and God remained with them.

- *Israel:* God decided to work his plan of salvation in and through Israel, a chosen people. Israel becomes central in the great drama of salvation.

- *Moses:* Moses was perhaps the most important person in the Old Testament. His life was bound to the life of God's people and to God himself. Learning about Moses means learning about God's people and about God.

- *The Promised Land:* The Promised Land becomes a character in the Pentateuch and the whole of Scripture. The land is the concrete representation of God's promises to Abraham. The relationship of God's people with the land becomes a constant theme in the Pentateuch and beyond.

GENESIS

THE STORY OF BEGINNINGS

Genesis

The name Genesis comes from the Greek word *gignesthai*, which means "to be born" or "to be produced." The Hebrew title of the book is *bereshit*, the first word of the book that is translated as "in the beginning."

Purpose

The book of Genesis is a book about beginnings. It narrates the beginning of all things, of the nations, and of God's people, Israel. Genesis spans many hundreds of years—more years than any other book of the Bible. These years encompass the very beginning of the universe to a time when Abraham's descendants flee to Egypt escaping a famine around the 1800s BC. Genesis tells us about the good beginning of creation, the beginning of all human problems, and the beginning of God's solution to those problems.

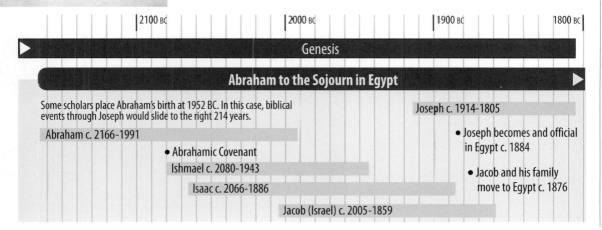

	2100 BC	2000 BC	1900 BC	1800 BC

Genesis

Abraham to the Sojourn in Egypt

Some scholars place Abraham's birth at 1952 BC. In this case, biblical events through Joseph would slide to the right 214 years.

Abraham c. 2166-1991

Joseph c. 1914-1805

- Abrahamic Covenant
Ishmael c. 2080-1943

- Joseph becomes and official in Egypt c. 1884

Isaac c. 2066-1886

- Jacob and his family move to Egypt c. 1876

Jacob (Israel) c. 2005-1859

Outline

1. Origin of the World (1:1–2:3)
   a. Seven days of creation

2. Origin of the Nations—These are the generations of:
   a. The heavens and the earth (2:4–4:26)
      ■ Adam and Eve, and the fall
      ■ Cain and Abel
   b. Adam (5:1–6:8)
      ■ Genealogy from Adam to Noah
   c. Noah (6:9–9:29)
      ■ The flood and God's covenant with Noah
   d. The sons of Noah (10:1–11:9)
      ■ Tower of Babel

3. Origin of Israel—These are the generations of:
   a. Shem (11:10–26)
      ■ Genealogy from Noah's son Shem to Abram's father Terah
   b. Terah (11:27–25:11)
      ■ Call of Abram and the covenant with Abram
      ■ Hagar and her son Ishmael
      ■ Isaac born to Abraham and Sarah
   c. Ishmael (25:12–18)
      ■ Genealogy of Ishmael
   d. Isaac (25:19–35:29)
      ■ Isaac's sons Jacob and Esau
      ■ Jacob and his wives Leah and Rachel
   e. Esau (36:1–37:1)
      ■ Genealogy of Esau
   f. Jacob (37:2–50:26)
      ■ Jacob's twelve sons
      ■ Joseph in Egypt
      ■ Jacob and his family move to Egypt

Origin of a Nation

The book of Genesis is most naturally divided by the repetition of the Hebrew expression *elleh toledot*, which means, "these are the generations" (sometimes translated as "begat"). The word *toledot* is related to a word that means "to father, to give birth." It refers to the origin of a family or a nation.

Abraham's Journey from Ur to Canaan
by József Molnár

Sections of Genesis	Themes	People
Origin of the World (1:1–2:3)	■ Creation ■ Sovereignty ■ Humans as God's image ■ Human responsibility	■ God ■ Human beings
Origin of the Nations (2:4–11:9)	■ Human failure and sin ■ Death ■ Sin and punishment ■ Promise and grace	■ Adam and Eve ■ The Serpent ■ Cain and Abel ■ Noah
Origin of Israel (11:10–50:26)	■ Covenant ■ God' plans of redemption ■ God's people ■ God's work through a family ■ God's work through the nations	■ Abraham and Sarah ■ Hagar ■ Lot ■ Isaac and Rebekah ■ Jacob, Rachel, Leah, Bilhah, Zilpah ■ Jacob's 12 sons ■ Tamar ■ Potiphar

In Genesis we see that:

■ God is the creator of all things, the world, the nations, and Israel. Creation begins a story of relationships. God wants to relate to his creation, especially to humans.

■ Although God created all things good and was pleased with them, humans abused their freedom and, because of sin, broke their relationship with God, with each other, and with nature.

■ However, God's grace extended to humanity. Instead of leaving them in their rebellion and corruption, God promised to act directly to solve the human predicament. He announced the coming of the One who would crush the head of the deceiving serpent (Gen. 3:15). On the cross, Jesus crushed Satan's head.

■ God began his plan of restoration by choosing the family of Abraham to start over. God made a covenant with Abraham. God relates, guides, rescues, and provides for the family he has chosen.

Background

Author: Although the book of Genesis does not name its author, Jewish and Christian tradition has accepted the author of Genesis (and the other four books of the Pentateuch) to be Moses.

Date: Moses would have written Genesis (and the rest of the Pentateuch) between 1446 BC (a possible date of the exodus) and 1406 BC (the date of Moses' death).

Setting: In chapter 12, God calls Abraham to leave his hometown of Ur to travel to the land of Canaan, the Promised Land. The city of Ur, located in southern Iraq, was an important cultural center in the second millennium (2000s) BC. Archaeological remains attest to the glory and importance of the city. Among the documents, many names were found that resemble the names of Abraham's family. As with many cities of the ancient world, Ur was a center for many deities including the main god of the city, the moon god Sin.

The land of Canaan was surrounded by powerful kingdoms: the Mesopotamian kingdoms—Assyria and Babylonia—to the north, and Egypt to the south. The book of Genesis ends with Abraham's descendants no longer living in Canaan, but in northern Egypt in the land of Goshen.

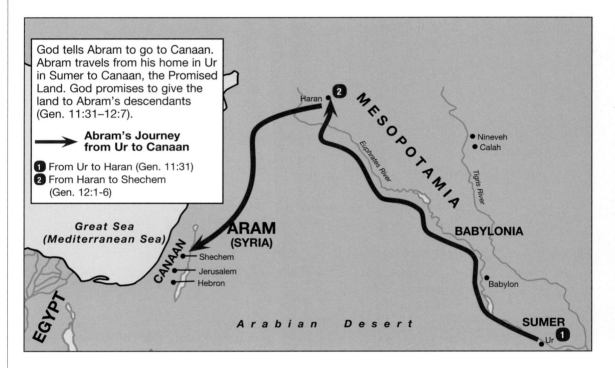

God tells Abram to go to Canaan. Abram travels from his home in Ur in Sumer to Canaan, the Promised Land. God promises to give the land to Abram's descendants (Gen. 11:31–12:7).

→ **Abram's Journey from Ur to Canaan**

❶ From Ur to Haran (Gen. 11:31)
❷ From Haran to Shechem (Gen. 12:1-6)

Key Verses

And I will put enmity between you and the woman, and between your offspring and hers; he will crush your head, and you will strike his heel.—Gen. 3:15

The Lord had said to Abram, "Go from your country, your people and your father's household to the land I will show you. I will make you into a great nation, and I will bless you; I will make your name great, and you will be a blessing. I will bless those who bless you, and whoever curses you I will curse; and all peoples on earth will be blessed through you." —Gen. 12:1

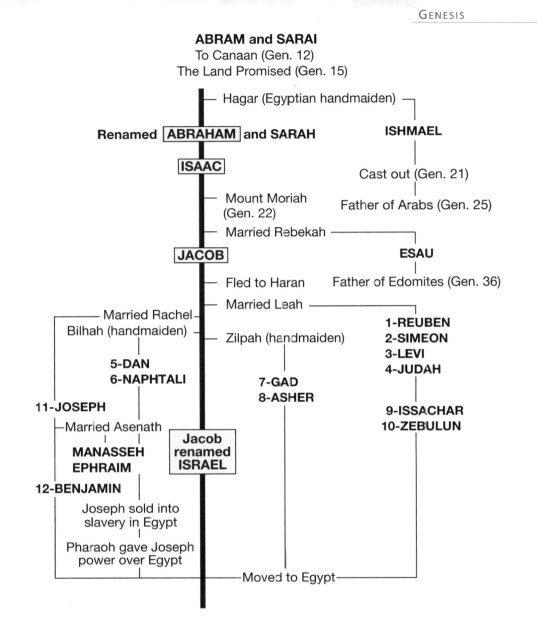

ABRAM and SARAI
To Canaan (Gen. 12)
The Land Promised (Gen. 15)

— Hagar (Egyptian handmaiden) —

Renamed ABRAHAM and SARAH   ISHMAEL

ISAAC

— Mount Moriah   Cast out (Gen. 21)
(Gen. 22)
Father of Arabs (Gen. 25)

— Married Rebekah —

JACOB   ESAU

— Fled to Haran   Father of Edomites (Gen. 36)

— Married Leah —

— Married Rachel —   1-REUBEN
Bilhah (handmaiden) —   2-SIMEON
— Zilpah (handmaiden) —   3-LEVI
                               4-JUDAH
5-DAN
6-NAPHTALI
          7-GAD
          8-ASHER
11-JOSEPH
                               9-ISSACHAR
—Married Asenath   10-ZEBULUN

MANASSEH   Jacob
renamed
EPHRAIM   ISRAEL

12-BENJAMIN

Joseph sold into
slavery in Egypt

Pharaoh gave Joseph
power over Egypt

—Moved to Egypt—

The Royal Standard of Ur
The Bible mentions Ur as Abraham's home (Gen. 11). Archaeological exploration has shown Ur as a powerful cultural center in the time of Abraham (2100s BC). The Royal Standard of Ur (shown here) was discovered in an ancient cemetery in modern Iraq, south of Baghdad.

Being God's People

Then: In Genesis, God reveals himself as the Creator and King, who loves his creation. He plans to redeem humanity through a person and a family, so all the nations, and creation itself, will be blessed. God chose Abraham and his descendants to be blessed and to be a blessing to others. Even though each person—like Isaac, Rebekah, Judah, and even Joseph—had their shortcomings, God still used them to fulfill his promises.

Now: God is on a mission to redeem his creation. As he called people in ancient times to be part of that mission, he continues to call believers today. Hebrews 11:8 tells us that "By faith Abraham, when called to go to a place he would later receive as his inheritance, obeyed and went, even though he did not know where he was going." As in Old Testament times, it still takes faith for us today to let God to lead us where he wants us to go—especially when, like Abraham, we don't know what lies ahead.

Jesus in Genesis

As a book of origins, Genesis shows the origin of humanity's greatest predicament: sin. It also shows that God's mercy promised his own solution to this quandary: "And I will put enmity between you and the woman, and between your offspring and hers; he will crush your head, and you will strike his heel" (Gen. 3:15). In addition, God promised Abraham, "I will make you into a great nation, and I will bless you; I will make your name great, and you will be a blessing. I will bless those who bless you, and whoever curses you I will curse; and all peoples on earth will be blessed through you" (Gen. 12:2–3). All of these promises point to God's final and perfect solution for humanity's fallen state: Jesus, God's own Son.

Nuzi Tablets
Excavations of the ancient city of Nuzi, located southwest of Kirkuk near the Tigris River, revealed over 5,000 baked clay tablets. The tablets contain official documents and letters exchanged between Assyrian kings and Egyptian pharaohs. They reveal many previously unknown customs that agree with the biblical portrayal of the patriarchs. The tablet shown here is from a royal archive and lists the workers on the royal estate and the rations they were given.

©Kim Walton/Walton Image Supply

EXODUS

FROM SLAVERY TO FREEDOM

Israel in Egypt by Edward Poynter

Moses' Name

The Hebrew name Moses sounds like the Hebrew verb for "to draw out." Pharaoh's daughter named the child Moses because "I drew him out of the water" (Ex. 2:10). But the name Moses has an Egyptian meaning as well. It is found in many Egyptian names: Ra-messes, Thut-mose, Ah-mose. The first part of each name is related to an Egyptian deity (Ra, Thut, Ah). The second part of the names (messes/mose) means "boy" or "son." Moses can be an Egyptian name meaning boy, son, or child.

Purpose

Israel is the story of God rescuing his people from slavery and forming them into a nation. While Genesis deals with the beginnings of all things, the book of Exodus focuses more on the origin of God's people. He gives Moses the Law, but this Law is more than just a series of rules of behavior. God's instructions to Israel shape the nation and give boundaries for the safety of the people. It shows Israel what it means to be God's people in the midst of other nations.

In addition, the book connects creation with redemption. In the exodus itself—the redeeming or liberation of Israel from Egypt—God creates a new people, his people. The first five books of the Bible, the Pentateuch, which in the Hebrew Bible is considered the Torah, has the purpose of instructing Israel on what it means to be God's people in the midst of other nations.

Outline

1. Israel in Egypt: God Frees His People (1:1–15:21).
   a. Israel is enslaved in Egypt.
   b. God calls Moses through a burning bush.
   c. The ten plagues upon Egypt and the first Passover.
   d. The exodus and the parting of the Red Sea.

2. Israel on the Way Toward Sinai: God Travels with His People (15:22–18:27).
   a. God provides manna and quail, and water from a rock.

3. Israel at Sinai: God Instructs and Organizes His People (19:1–40:38).
   a. Moses meets with God on Mount Sinai.
   b. The Ten Commandments.
   c. Instructions for the tabernacle.
   d. The people worship the golden calf.
   e. Moses and the people build the tabernacle.

The Code of Hammurabi
This black stele inscribed with about 300 laws claims to have been written by Babylonian King Hammurabi around 1750 BC. Many of the laws inscribed on the stone resemble the style and, to some extent, the content of Moses' laws in the Pentateuch. For example, the law of "an eye for an eye" is found in the Code of Hammurabi and in Exodus 21:24.

Background

Author: Although the book of Exodus does not name its author, Jewish and Christian tradition has accepted the author of Exodus (and the other four books of the Pentateuch) to be Moses.

Date: Moses would have written Exodus (and the rest of the Pentateuch) between 1446 BC (a possible date of the exodus) and 1406 BC (the date of Moses' death).

Setting: There are two main settings in the book of Exodus: Egypt and the wilderness.

To escape famine, Jacob's children had settled in northern Egypt, in Goshen (Gen. 47:5–6). The Israelites lived in Egypt in a time of Egyptian prosperity and political power. However, later generations became slaves to the Egyptian pharaohs (Ex. 1).

After the Israelites left Egypt in the event known as the exodus, they traveled in the wilderness on their way to Sinai. Traditionally, many people believe that Mount Sinai is found the southern part of the peninsula. However, some scholars believe that the mountain might be found in the northern part or, even, outside of the peninsula (one possible location for ancient Median).

Clash of the Gods

In Egypt, pharaohs were considered to be divine beings. When Moses came to Pharaoh to ask for the release of God's people, God and a false god, Pharaoh, clashed in a battle of wills and power. God showed his supremacy through the plagues. One way to understand the plagues is that they were direct attacks against the false gods of Egypt. God showed himself as victorious.

Sections of Exodus	Themes	Events
Israel in Egypt: God Frees His People (1:1–15:21)	■ God is redeemer and rescuer. ■ God is the supreme King. ■ God has control over his creation.	■ Egypt oppressed Israel and became God's enemy. ■ God heard Israel's cries and remembered his commitment to Abraham. ■ Moses, a child of slaves, was threatened to be killed along with many other children. However, God rescued him. ■ God called and sent Moses to free his people from Egypt. ■ The exodus: God, through Moses, confronted Pharaoh in a struggle for the future of Israel. After ten terrible plagues, Pharaoh relented and freed Israel. ■ The day of redemption was celebrated and commemorated in the Feast of Passover. ■ God saved Israel from Pharaoh's army through one more spectacular miracle—the parting of the Red Sea.
Israel on the Way toward Sinai: God Travels with His People (15:22–18:27)	■ God is provider.	■ God led Israel through the wilderness of Zin toward his holy mountain at Sinai. ■ God provided for the people's needs during the journey in the wilderness. ■ Israel grumbled against Moses and God. ■ God brought Israel to the meet with him at Sinai.
Israel at Sinai: God Instructs and Organizes His People (19:1–40:38)	■ God is king. ■ God is just and merciful. ■ God is with his people. ■ God wants to relate personally to his people.	■ On Mount Sinai, God instructed Moses on God's law for Israel. These laws would teach Israel how to become God's holy nation. ■ The people grew restless at Moses' delay on the mountain. They built for themselves a golden calf to worship. God punished them. However, because Moses interceded for them, God did not destroy them. ■ God ordered Moses to build a special dwelling, the tabernacle. God's presence would travel with the people to the place he promised Abraham, Isaac, and Jacob. ■ God equipped the Israelites to carry on the building of the tabernacle. ■ Once the tabernacle was completed, God's presence descended to dwell in it.

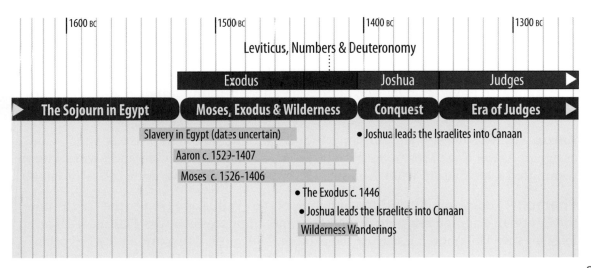

| 1600 BC | 1500 BC | 1400 BC | 1300 BC |

Leviticus, Numbers & Deuteronomy

| Exodus | Joshua | Judges ▶ |

▶ The Sojourn in Egypt | Moses, Exodus & Wilderness | Conquest | Era of Judges ▶

Slavery in Egypt (dates uncertain) • Joshua leads the Israelites into Canaan

Aaron c. 1529-1407

Moses c. 1526-1406

• The Exodus c. 1446

• Joshua leads the Israelites into Canaan

Wilderness Wanderings

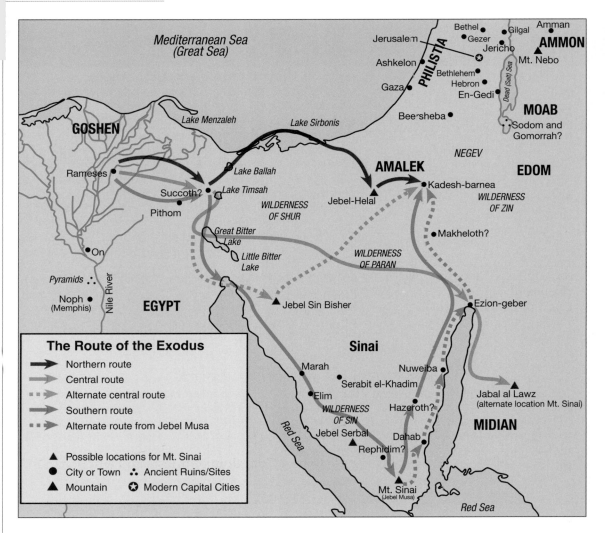

The Route of the Exodus

→ Northern route
→ Central route
▸ Alternate central route
→ Southern route
▸ Alternate route from Jebel Musa

▲ Possible locations for Mt. Sinai
● City or Town   ∴ Ancient Ruins/Sites
▲ Mountain   ✪ Modern Capital Cities

Key People

Moses – He was born to a Hebrew slave family but rescued by Pharaoh's daughter. Having grown up in the Egyptian royal court, Moses had inside knowledge of the royal court and the political subtleties of the time. As an educated Egyptian, Moses knew the religion, traditions, and political practices in Egypt. But when he fled Egypt after killing an Egyptian overseer, he became a shepherd in Midian. He was 80 years old when God called him to face an imposing Pharaoh.

Aaron – He was Moses' and Miriam's brother and the first high priest of Israel. God assigned Aaron to be Moses' assistant. Despite his closeness to God and Moses, Aaron committed a terrible sin when he agreed to build an idol—the golden calf—for Israel.

Pharaoh – Following the traditional dating of the exodus as 1446 BC (the "high" date), the Egyptian Pharaoh reigning during the times of oppression was Thutmose III and later his son Amenhotep II during the exodus. Thutmose III expanded the Egyptian empire as never before to the north, east, and south (possibly as far as Kenya today), then Amenhotep II consolidated the empire through massive building projects in Egypt. Some Bible scholars date the exodus much later, around 1290 BC (the "low" date), putting it during the reign of Pharaoh Ramesses II, one of the most powerful pharaohs of Egypt's New Kingdom period.

Miriam – She was Moses' and Aaron's sister and also a prophetess. She interceded on behalf of her infant brother Moses when Pharaoh's daughter found him in the Nile River. She also led the Israelite women in a song of praise after crossing the Red Sea.

Key Verses

God said to Moses, *"I AM WHO I AM. This is what you are to say to the Israelites: 'I AM has sent me to you.'"*—Ex. 3:14

"'You yourselves have seen what I did to Egypt, and how I carried you on eagles' wings and brought you to myself. Now if you obey me fully and keep my covenant, then out of all nations you will be my treasured possession. Although the whole earth is mine, you will be for me a kingdom of priests and a holy nation.' These are the words you are to speak to the Israelites." —Ex. 19:4–6

"I am the LORD your God, who brought you out of Egypt, out of the land of slavery. You shall have no other gods before me."—Ex. 20:2–3

Being God's People

Then: In Exodus, God called his people to be a "kingdom of priests and a holy nation" (Ex. 19:6). But he did not leave them to do this on their own. Instead he was with them, equipping and instructing them how to achieve this. God's presence dwelled in the tabernacle in the midst of the camp. The tabernacle was a visual reminder that God was among them. For Israel, being God's people was more than just following rules. It was about learning to live as a holy nation with a holy God in their midst.

Now: Jesus promises his followers, "And surely I am with you always, to the very end of the age" (Matt. 28:20). Being followers of Jesus today means learning how to live with the presence of God within us.

Jesus in Exodus

Moses' ministry as judge, priest, and prophet anticipated Jesus' own ministry (Heb. 3:1–6). The Passover celebration and sacrifice (Ex. 12) help us understand Christ's own sacrifice on the cross on our behalf. In the exodus, God liberated Israel from the bondage of Pharaoh with great acts of power. Through it, God gave birth to a new people (Deut. 32:18). Now, God has freed us from the bondage of sin and death with the greatest act of grace and power: Jesus' death and resurrection. In Christ, God has recreated us as a new people (2 Cor. 5:17; 1 Pet. 2:10).

LEVITICUS

SHAPING A WORSHIPING PEOPLE

Priests in the Courtyard of the Tabernacle by Jerry Allison

Torah

Often translated as "law," the Hebrew word *torah* is better translated as "instruction." In the Bible, the Torah can refer to the Ten Commandments, the Law of Moses (Exodus and Leviticus), or to the whole Pentateuch—the first five books of the Bible.

Purpose

Leviticus is the heart of the Pentateuch! One of the main functions of the first five books of the Bible is to give an identity to God's people. At the core of this identity lies Leviticus; at the center of the book lies holiness. It is not a mere dry and boring rule book. Rather, the wellspring of holiness is the living God, the God of Abraham, Isaac, and Jacob; the God who defeated Egypt and divided the waters; the God whose presence dwells in the tabernacle. Leviticus teaches God's people how to safely live in the presence of a holy God.

Outline

1. Instructions about Sacrifices (1–7)
   a. Various offerings: the burnt, grain, fellowship, sin, and guilt offerings

2. Instructions about Priests (8–10)
   a. Aaron and his sons (8)
   b. The priests present offerings (9–10)

3. Instructions about Ritual Purity (11–15)
   a. Clean and unclean foods (11)
   b. Purity laws (12–15)

4. Instructions about the Day of Atonement (16)

5. Instructions for Holy Living (17–27)
   a. Animal sacrifices (17)
   b. Sexual relations (18)
   c. Punishment for sins (19–20)
   d. Priestly requirements (21–22)
   e. Sabbath, feasts, and the Year of Jubilee (23–25)
   f. God's favor and the consequences of disobedience (26–27)

Background

Author: Although the book of Leviticus does not name its author, Jewish and Christian tradition has accepted the author of Leviticus (and the other four books of the Pentateuch) to be Moses.

Date: Moses would have written Leviticus (and the rest of the Pentateuch) between 1446 BC (a possible date of the exodus) and 1406 BC (the date of Moses' death).

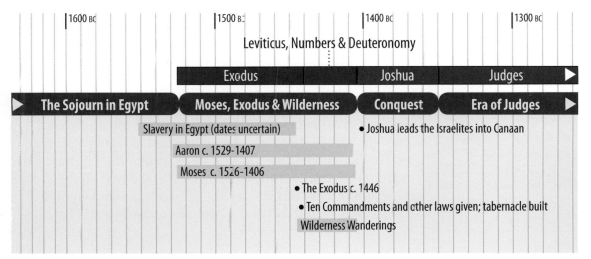

Setting: Leviticus takes place within the two years that Israel spent camped at the foot of Mount Sinai. In Hebrew, the first word in Leviticus (which is translated "and he called") connects the narrative of Leviticus with the narrative of Exodus. That is, Leviticus continues the story of Israel receiving God's instructions at Sinai. The main difference between the instructions in Exodus and Leviticus is that in Exodus, God speaks from the mountain, whereas in Leviticus God speaks from the tabernacle.

Themes

Reading the book of Leviticus can be intimidating. It may seem to be a barren list of rules that couldn't possibly be useful for people nowadays. Yet the book of Leviticus can be a wonderful spiritual adventure. By looking at the themes in the book, we can gain insight into the value of Leviticus for us today.

Sacrifices and God's Grace. Sacrifices were God's merciful provision for Israel so the people could dwell with a holy God. Sacrifices today are not necessary because Jesus' sacrifice was perfect and sufficient. However, the truths about our need for sacrifices remains. Leviticus helps us understand the meaning and importance of Jesus' sacrifice. In the Old Testament, the shedding and use of animal blood for the purifying and atoning rituals was a reminder for the worshiper that a life had been taken: the cost of sin is high indeed. The sacrifice of an animal allowed the Israelites to dwell alongside God as his presence dwelt in the tabernacle.

Leviticus

The English name of the book is derived from the name in the Greek Old Testament, *leyiticon*, meaning "things concerning the Levites." The name is somewhat misleading because Leviticus was not meant to be only for Levites. Rather, it is a book of great importance to all of God's people. The Hebrew name *vayyiqra'* meaning "and he called..." follows the tradition of naming books by the first word in them.

Priests. Priests were intermediaries. At different moments and in different ways during their ministries, priests stood in the gap that separates God and humans. Their holiness did not come from their actions or position; rather, their holiness depended on their nearness to the tabernacle, to God's presence. As representatives of the people, the priests were held to rigorous moral, ritual, and purity standards.

Purity. Purity was necessary as people lived around the tabernacle. God's presence rejected the ritually impure. Purification rites were God's provision for the people to be able to approach his presence. Today, the blood that Christ shed on the cross purifies us and makes us fit to approach God's presence. Instead of ritual purity, today we are called to godliness (2 Peter 1:3–8).

The Day of Atonement. This feast was the climax of the liturgical calendar. In it, the high priest made atonement for sin in the tabernacle. Atonement is God's way to bring reconciliation and restoration to the problem of human sin and its effects. The high priest would take two animals. He would pray on one, lay the guilt of the whole nation on it, and send it out of the camp into the desert. Then, he would sacrifice the second animal and bring its blood into the most holy place in the tabernacle to offer it to God. Christ's sacrifice on the cross bore our guilt and fully paid the price for human sin. No other sacrifice is necessary.

Holy Living. A holy life is not one filled with dread and mired in guilt. Rather, it is a hopeful, joyful, and satisfied way of living; a life lived according to God's original plans. The many rules (laws and ordinances) are boundaries that guide us during our lives. Although many of these regulations depended on the sacrificial and purity rituals, which have become redundant after Christ, the principles on which they operate continue to be relevant for us today. Whereas the Israelites could see the presence of God in the tabernacle, we experience it in a more direct way because God's presence, the Holy Spirit, dwells in us.

Key Verses

"I am the LORD, who brought you up out of Egypt to be your God; therefore be holy, because I am holy. —Lev. 11:45

"Keep my decrees and laws, for the person who obeys them will live by them. I am the LORD." —Lev. 18:5

Atonement

The invention of the English word *atonement* has been attributed to William Tyndale, the sixteenth-century English Bible translator, to express what Jesus accomplished on the cross: the cancellation of sins and reconciliation of God with humanity. The word has two parts: "at" and "onement." Atonement, then, is God's way to bring reconciliation and restoration to the problem of human sin and its effects.

The Torah (Pentateuch)

Book	Focus
Genesis	■ Origins of the world ■ Origins of the nations ■ Origins of God's people
Exodus	■ Focus on God's people and their origin as a nation ■ Focus on organizing the Israelites to become God's people
Leviticus	■ Equipping the people to become God's holy nation ■ The heart of Torah (the Pentateuch) is holiness
Numbers	■ Organization of God's people as God's army ■ On the way to reclaim the Promised Land ■ Death of the old generation ■ Birth of the new generation
Deuteronomy	■ God's instructions for a new generation ■ God's instructions for a generation at the entrance of the Promised Land ■ Basing the identity of God's people on the covenant

Being God's People

Then: The many regulations in Leviticus were a reminder of God's grace. They demonstrated God's grace by giving an unholy people a way to approach their holy God. These rules existed for the benefit and blessing of the people. God challenged his people: "Be holy because I am holy" (Lev. 11:44).

Now: Though the purification rites and sacrifices are no longer necessary because of the perfect cleansing in Jesus' blood and sacrifice on the cross, holiness is still something believers today should pursue. In the New Testament, Peter quotes Leviticus when he instructs believers, "... just as he who called you is holy, so be holy in all you do; for it is written: 'Be holy, because I am holy'" (1 Peter 1:14–16). Being holy is not a legalistic activity. It's one full of humility, love, and surrender to the work of the Holy Spirit in our lives. (See also Matt. 5:48; Rom. 8:1–14.)

Jesus in Leviticus

God instructed his people from the tabernacle. The tabernacle, where God's presence dwelt, was the place of revelation. In it, God revealed his glory and his will for his people. Christ is God's perfect revelation (Heb. 1:1; Col. 1:15). Jesus himself came to the world as a human to "tabernacle" (dwell) among us (John 1:14) because he is God. Jesus fulfilled all the requirements of the law (Matt. 5:17), and he was the perfect sacrifice that makes all other sacrifices unnecessary (Heb. 9:11–28).

The Ark of the Covenant
The ark rested in the Most Holy Place of the tabernacle. It was the place where God met and talked with Moses. It contained the stone tablets with the Ten Commandments, a jar of manna, and Aaron's rod (Deut. 10:5; Ex. 16:32–34; Num. 17:10).

NUMBERS

THE DEATH OF THE OLD, THE BIRTH OF THE NEW

Sinai Wilderness

Numbers

The English name of the book comes from the Greek translation, *arithmoi*, which means "numbers." It is a reference to the two censuses in the book (chapters 1 and 26). These were military censuses, rather than just population censuses. In Numbers, Israel is organized as a marching army, God's army.

Purpose

Numbers is a story of rebellion and disobedience. Yet it is also a story of grace and mercy. Numbers narrates the years God's people spent traveling in the wilderness, depicting them as God's army advancing toward the Promised Land. Even when the people grumbled and rebelled, God's grace prevailed. The people were still punished for their rebellion, but God did not destroy them. Rather, he extended his grace to the coming generation.

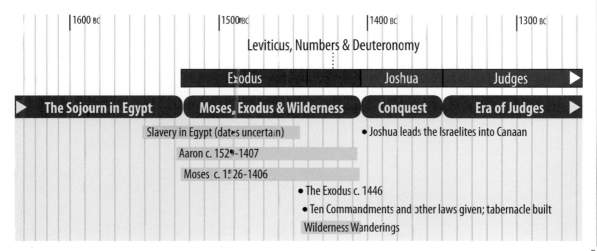

1600 BC	1500 BC	1400 BC	1300 BC

Leviticus, Numbers & Deuteronomy

Exodus	Joshua	Judges ▶

▶ The Sojourn in Egypt	Moses, Exodus & Wilderness	Conquest	Era of Judges ▶

Slavery in Egypt (dates uncertain)

• Joshua leads the Israelites into Canaan

Aaron c. 1529-1407

Moses c. 1526-1406

• The Exodus c. 1446

• Ten Commandments and other laws given; tabernacle built

Wilderness Wanderings

Outline

1. The End of the Old Generation (1–25)
   a. First census (1–4)
   b. Regulations for purity and offerings (5:1–10:10)
   c. Israelites leave Sinai and grumble (10:11–12:26)
   d. Twelve spies explore Canaan; the people rebel (13–16)
   e. God instructs Moses and Aaron (17–19)
   f. Israelites face challenges: thirst, venomous snakes, hostile nations (20–25)

2. The Birth of the New Generation (26–36)
   a. Second census (26)
   b. Joshua commissioned to succeed Moses (27)
   c. Laws for offerings, feasts, and vows (28–30)
   d. Israelites defeat their enemies (31–32)
   e. Instructions for when the new generation enters the Promised Land (33–36)

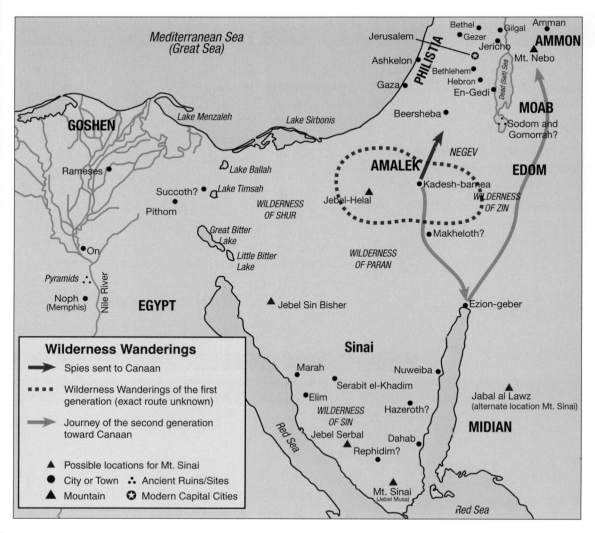

Background

Author: Although the book of Numbers does not name its author, Jewish and Christian tradition has accepted the author of Numbers (and the other four books of the Pentateuch) to be Moses.

Date: Moses would have written Numbers (and the rest of the Pentateuch) between 1446 BC (a possible date of the exodus) and 1406 BC (the date of Moses' death).

Setting: After the people take the first census of military age men, they leave Mount Sinai and travel toward the Promised Land. They camp in the desert of Paran, south of Judah in the northern part of the Sinai Peninsula, around Kadesh-barnea. But because they chose not to trust in God's promise and enter the land, the Israelites spent the next forty years wandering in the wilderness.

Key People

Moses – He continued to lead Israel from Sinai to the Promised Land. Along with the rest of the first generation, Moses was not allowed to enter the Promised Land.

Aaron – He was Moses' brother. Despite his own failures in leadership and sin, God allowed Aaron to continue acting as Israel's high priest. During the journey, Aaron died and was greatly mourned.

Miriam – She was Moses' sister. Despite Miriam's personal rebellion, God forgave her and restored her to the community. She also died during the wilderness wanderings.

Joshua – He was one of the twelve spies that Moses sent into the land. After Moses' death, Joshua took over Moses' leadership role and led Israel into the Promised Land.

Caleb – Along with Joshua, Caleb was the other spy who believed God and encouraged the Israelites to conquer the land, despite the odds. Caleb and Joshua were the only two people of the old generation who entered the Promised Land.

Eleazar – He was a son of Aaron who became the next high priest after Aaron died.

Korah – He led a rebellion against Moses and Aaron. God severely punished him along with his family.

Balaam – He was a pagan prophet-for-hire who was under contract to curse Israel. Having been warned by God, Balaam could only bless Israel.

The Wilderness

In Numbers, the word *wilderness* is very important. In addition to the literal meaning (the Israelites had to cross the wilderness to get to the Promised Land), the concept of *wilderness* had a symbolic meaning as well. The wilderness was a place of danger, of death and barrenness, of chaos and darkness. It represented a life-negating reality that opposes God's life-giving will. The wilderness became a symbol of God's absence, of evil itself. On the other hand, the wilderness came to represent a place of transition, a place for meeting God. The tabernacle, and its surroundings, with God's presence, was a place of life, hope, order, and light.

Key Verses

The LORD bless you and keep you; the LORD make his face shine on you and be gracious to you; the LORD turn his face toward you and give you peace.—Num. 6:24–26

The LORD is slow to anger, abounding in love and forgiving sin and rebellion. Yet he does not leave the guilty unpunished; he punishes the children for the sin of the parents to the third and fourth generation.—Num. 14:18

I see him, but not now; I behold him, but not near. A star will come out of Jacob; a scepter will rise out of Israel.—Num. 24:17

Census

The census numbers report a fighting force of 600,000, which would suggest a general population of over 2 million. Such a large population, wandering in the desert for forty years, would require a miracle to be supported. And that's precisely what happened. God miraculously provided for the Israelites through their journey.

Being God's People

Then: In Exodus, God had promised the Israelites that he would be with them on their way to the Promised Land (Ex. 33:14). In Numbers, we see that despite Israel's unfaithfulness and hardness of heart, God remained faithful to that promise. His presence remained with Israel, and his protection and provision followed them through the wilderness (for example, Num. 11:21–23, 31–32). Even in the middle of the wilderness, when everything seemed chaotic, dark, and hopeless, God's grace continued to offer new possibilities for the future.

Now: Traveling through the wilderness of life can often be a grueling test to our faith, and it's all too natural to respond with anger. But journeying through these difficulties remind us that we must depend on God and trust that he will be faithful to his promises to us.

Jesus in Numbers

God's grace extending to a new generation—an important theme in Numbers—is echoed in the New Testament. Just as Moses had characterized the generation of Israelites that died in the wilderness as "wicked and adulterous" (Deut. 1:35), Jesus later characterized his generation using the same words (Matt. 12:39; 16:4). And just as in Numbers, God's grace reached out to the following generation. Today, all believers are the next generation that has been reached by God's grace in Jesus. As the Israelites did at the end of the book of Numbers, we stand at the edge of the Promised Land (Paradise) and await the glorious and triumphant moment when we will dwell in God's presence (Rev. 21:3).

DEUTERONOMY

ALREADY, BUT NOT YET

Fragment of the oldest mosaic floor map of the Jordan River and Dead Sea

Purpose

Deuteronomy is a fascinating book that describes God's people in a time in between. After forty years of wandering in the wilderness, they arrived at the Promised Land but hadn't entered yet. Deuteronomy mostly consists of the speeches Moses gave to the second generation on the plains of Moab before they entered the Promised Land. The first generation, those who had left Egypt and witnessed God's mighty acts of salvation, had died—all except Joshua, Caleb, and Moses. The second generation had not witnessed first hand God's powerful acts against Egypt, nor his awesome glory revealed on Mount Sinai. Moses took a long pause to instruct this new generation about what makes them God's people and to challenge them to find their identity and purpose in the covenant with God. As the people waited at the edge of the Promised Land, God's promises were already there to the reaching hand, but they had not yet been fulfilled.

Deuteronomy

The name derives from the Greek name of the book, *deuteronomion*, meaning "second law." However, the book is not really a second law, but rather a repetition of the Torah. Moses repeated God's instructions for the second generation of God's people. The Hebrew name of the book is *'eleh haddebarim*, "these are the words (or discourses)," which are the first two words of the book.

Outline

1. A Look Backward (1–3)
   a. Summary of the wilderness wanderings

2. The Great Discourse (4–11)
   a. Fear, Love, and Obey God
   b. The Ten Commandments

3. Covenant Stipulations (12–26)
   a. Worship one true God in one place
   b. Various laws for Israel

4. Covenant Ceremony (27–30)
   a. Blessings and curses of the covenant

5. A Look Forward (31–34)
   a. Joshua confirmed as Moses' successor
   b. The song and blessings of Moses
   c. Moses' death on Mount Nebo

Ancient Covenants

Many scholars consider that Deuteronomy was written according to the structure of ancient covenant documents. Thus Deuteronomy's outline would be as follows:
1. Preamble (1:1–5)
2. Historical Prologue (1:6–4:43)
3. Stipulations of the Covenant (4:44–26:19)
4. Ratification: Curses and Blessings (27–30)
5. Leadership Succession under the Covenant (31–34)

Background

Author: Although the book of Deuteronomy does not name its author, Jewish and Christian tradition has accepted the author of Deuteronomy (and the other four books of the Pentateuch) to be Moses.

Shema

The famous quote from Deuteronomy known as *shema*—from the Hebrew word that means "hear!"—is the basis for Israel's monotheistic ("one God") faith. "Hear, O Israel: The LORD, our God, the LORD is one" (Deut. 6:4). Deuteronomy instructs the Israelites to bind God's commandment to their hands and foreheads, as well as write them on the doorposts of their homes. Many Jews today tie small boxes with Scripture quotations (usually the *shema*) to their foreheads and hands, and also attach them to their doorpost.

Date: Moses would have written Deuteronomy (and the rest of the Pentateuch) between 1446 BC (a possible date of the exodus) and 1406 BC (the date of Moses' death).

Setting: The entire book of Deuteronomy takes place while Israel is encamped at the border of the Promised Land, east of the Jordan River, in the plains of Moab. Moab became one of Israel's most adamant enemies. As Israel approached the land, Moab formed an alliance with several Medianite kingdoms to stop the advance of the wandering tribes—the Moabite King Barak sent the prophet Balaam to curse Israel, with surprising results (see Num. 22:2–24:25). To the east of the Jordan River, the majestic Mount Nebo was a silent witness of Israel's preparations to enter the land. On Mount Nebo, Moses saw the land for the last time.

Old Testament Covenants

Covenant	Reference	Type	Description
Noah	Gen. 9:8–17	Unconditional	God promised not to destroy again his creation.
Abraham	Gen. 15:9–21	Unconditional	God promised to give Abraham's descendants the land. The covenant was sealed with an animal sacrifice.
Abraham	Gen. 17	Conditional	God confirmed his covenant with Abraham and made a commitment to Abraham. He specified Abraham's commitment and reaffirmed his promise of land and Abraham agreed to keep the sign of the covenant: circumcision.
Covenant at Sinai	Ex. 19–24	Conditional	God promised to make Israel his people and also expressed what he expected of Israel.
Phinehas	Num. 25:10–31	Unconditional	God granted Phinehas, a priest, a descendant of Aaron and his descendants a "covenant of lasting priesthood" (25:13).
David	2 Sam. 7:5–16	Unconditional	God promised to preserve David's descendants on the throne of Israel.
The New Covenant	Jer. 31:31–34	Unconditional	God declared that he "will make a new covenant with the people of Israel and with the people of Judah" (31:31). It establishes a new relationship with his people by writing his law on their hearts.

1600 BC	1500 BC	1400 BC	1300 BC

Leviticus, Numbers & Deuteronomy

Exodus	Joshua	Judges ▶

▶ The Sojourn in Egypt	Moses, Exodus & Wilderness	Conquest	Era of Judges ▶

Slavery in Egypt (dates uncertain)

• Joshua leads the Israelites into Canaan

Aaron c. 1529-1407

Moses c. 1526-1406

• The Exodus c. 1446

• Ten Commandments and other laws given; tabernacle built

Wilderness Wanderings

Key Verses

But if from there you seek the LORD your God, you will find him if you seek him with all your heart and with all your soul.—Deut. 4:29

The LORD your God will raise up for you a prophet like me from among you, from your fellow Israelites. You must listen to him.—Deut.18:15

The LORD your God will circumcise your hearts and the hearts of your descendants, so that you may love him with all your heart and with all your soul, and live.—Deut. 30:6

Themes

Torah. In the retelling of God's instructions, Deuteronomy offers anew his law—*Torah* more properly means "instruction"—for each generation of believers.

Covenant. The entire book can be read as a covenant renewal between the second generation and God. The blessings and curses of the covenant play a prominent role in Israel's history.

The Land. God's promises to Abraham were concretely represented by the land. The land was a visual reminder of God's faithfulness to his promises.

Being God's People

Then: The book of Deuteronomy is a reminder to God's people that God is faithful to his covenant. He's the holy God, full of mercy and grace, who led his people to the Promised Land. The next generation is challenged to remember and learn from the mistakes of the previous generation (1 Cor. 10:1–13). In Deuteronomy, the second generation must not forget the source of their blessings, take the land for granted, become indistinguishable from the people living in the land, make idols for themselves, rely on their economic or political power to survive, or abandon the covenant.

Now: God's people in Deuteronomy are in the already-but-not-yet state that still describes Christians today. In a symbolic sense, all believers are the second generation. We all stand at the borders of the Promised Land—the New Jerusalem—already enjoying some of God's wonderful promises, but knowing that the fullness of his promise is yet to come. As the Israelites required instruction to live in the land God had promised them, we are learning also to live in God's presence. In many ways, life today is the training ground for life in a new heavens and new earth in the presence of God.

Jesus in Deuteronomy

The glory to which we look forward will be revealed when Jesus returns. In the meantime, we continue to train and "press toward the goal to win the prize for which God has called me heavenward in Christ Jesus" (Phil. 3:14).

Quotable Deuteronomy

Deuteronomy is the third most quoted Old Testament book in the New Testament—only after Psalms and Isaiah. Jesus quotes from Deuteronomy during his confrontation with Satan in the desert (Matt. 4:1–11). Some scholars suggest that Jesus is doing what Israel was incapable of: fulfilling all obedience. In this view, Jesus embodies the new Israel.

HISTORICAL BOOKS

LIVING WITH GOD IN THE LAND

What Are the Historical Books?

The Historical Books are the second section of the Bible. This section continues where the Pentateuch ended. At the end of the Pentateuch, the Israelites are poised at the edge of the Promised Land after hearing instructions, advice, and commands from Moses. Moses, the great leader, has died on Mount Nebo (Deut. 34:1–12). God has chosen Joshua, Moses' longtime assistant, to lead the Israelites into the land.

What Are They About?

The books in this section deal with Israel's historical experience with the land and God. The books range from conquering, settling, and experiencing the many joys, temptations, failures, and challenges of living in the land as the Israelites learned how to live as God's people. The books cover the history of Israel from the time of the conquest (around the 1400s BC) to the time of Ezra and Nehemiah (around the 400s BC). In between, we find a dramatic history of a people, their kings, many painful disappointments and some remarkable accomplishments. Israel changed from a loosely organized group of 12 tribes to a united kingdom under David and Solomon, and then to a divided kingdom: Israel in the north with 19 kings who did evil in God's eyes, and Judah in the south with 19 kings also, although eight kings did right in God's eyes.

The dominant figure in the Historical Books is King David. God chose David and his descendants. God would rule and bless his people through the house of David. From this promise, in time, the Messianic hope would arise. This hope refers to God's people longing to be restored and redeemed. God's people were punished for breaking the covenant with God. The historical books give us a theological account of Israel's failure to keep the covenant and God's compassionate and just dealings with them.

Why Are They Important?

The many stories in these books illustrate for us how God relates in history to his people and the whole world. These stories show how God's will works out in history.

- God works in direct ways, as in the stories of Joshua entering the Promised Land.

- God works in indirect ways, through prophets like Samuel and Elijah, or through other nations, like Assyria or Babylon.

- God works behind the scenes, as in the story of Esther.

Historical Books

Joshua
Judges
Ruth
1 & 2 Samuel
1 & 2 Kings
1 & 2 Chronicles
Ezra & Nehemiah
Esther

The apostle Paul wrote, "Now these things occurred as examples to keep us from setting our hearts on evil things as they did…. These things happened to them as examples and were written down as warnings for us, on whom the culmination of the ages has come" (1 Cor. 10:6, 11).

The Scriptures teach us a new way of thinking and seeing the world. Becoming God's people means that we progressively grow more sensitive to God's actions in the world. To understand what God is doing around us and in us, we must understand how God has been acting throughout history. Learning to read the Historical Books equips us to be perceptive to the Spirit's promptings in our lives. They also remind us in powerful ways that punishment is never God's final word.

The Exile

There are important, decisive moments in the Old Testament: The calling of Abraham, the exodus, entering the Promised Land, God's covenant with David, the building of the temple in Jerusalem. Two other decisive moments were the Assyrian exile of the northern kingdom of Israel in 722 BC and the Babylonian exile of the southern kingdom of Judah (including Jerusalem) in 586 BC.

Assyria and Babylon deported people from newly conquered territories. The idea was to remove the possibility of rebellion, making it easier to control the territory. They did not relocate the entire population. Rather, they took into exile the nobles—kings, princes and princesses, priests and royal officers. They would also move other people from city to city. And, finally, they would destroy the capital cities of the kingdoms they conquered.

Samaria in the northern kingdom and Jerusalem in the south were destroyed and made almost uninhabitable places. It is not possible to exaggerate the spiritual, emotional, and social trauma of these type of events. The historical books, along with the prophetic books, show that these two events were punishments for Israel and Judah's disloyalty to God. However, punishment is never God's final word. God restored a remnant of his people from Babylon. Ezra the priest and Nehemiah the governor returned with them. They reorganized the religious and political life of the people in Jerusalem. God's grace was paving the way for the coming of the promised Messiah, the only one who could rescue humans from sin and death.

JOSHUA

CLAIMING THE PROMISE

View of Galilee

Purpose

Deuteronomy prepared God's people for the task ahead in the Promised Land and the book of Joshua shows how God brought his people into the land and gave them rest. The book of Joshua functions as a bridge between the wilderness experience and the time in the Promised Land. The book is named after Joshua whom God chose to be Moses' assistant since their journey from Egypt to Sinai (Ex. 17) and to become the leader of Israel after Moses' death (Deut. 31:7–8). The book of Joshua shows how and why Israel would eventually end in exile. The book is a reminder that the sin and rebellion that would result in Israel's exile began long before God executed his judgment against Israel and Judah.

1500 BC		1400 BC		1300 BC	
Leviticus, Numbers & Deuteronomy		Book of Joshua		Book of Judges	▶
Exodus					
▶ **Moses, Exodus & Wilderness**		**Conquest**		**Era of Judges**	▶
Aaron c. 1529-1407		● Joshua leads the Israelites into Canaan			
Moses c. 1526-1406			● Era of the Judges begins c. 1350		
	● The Exodus c. 1446				
	● Ten Commandments and other laws given; tabernacle built				
	Wilderness Wanderings				

Outline

Although the conquest of the land is an important first step in the book, the crucial section is, in fact, the distribution of the land—that's why it's the longest section in the book. Just as the organization of the camp and the march were so important in their wilderness journey, the arrangement of the tribes in the land occupies the central interest of the book. Settling in the land showed the fulfillment of God's promises.

1. The Entrance (1:1–5:12)
   a. Joshua succeeds Moses (1)
   b. Rahab hides the spies (2)
   c. Israelites cross the Jordan River (3:1–5:12)

2. The Conquest (5:13–12:24)
   a. Fall of Jericho (5:13–6:27)
   b. Achan's sin in the camp (7)
   c. Battles against kings and inhabitants (8–12)

3. The Distribution (13–21)

4. The Future (22–24)
   a. Joshua's farewell and death

ROUTE OF THE CONQUEST

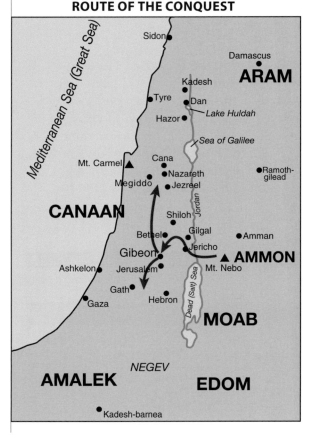

Background

Author: The book does not indicate who its author was. An ancient tradition offers two possibilities. First, it suggests that Joshua wrote the book. Second, it suggests that Samuel, the prophet, was either one of the main authors or worked as editor of the book.

Date: The book was likely composed early in Israel's history, perhaps late in the second millennium (1300s BC). There is some linguistic evidence that the book was edited later in the era of the kings and, perhaps, even in during the time of exile.

Setting: When the Israelites came to the borders of the Promised Land, the political and military powerhouses of the area—Egypt and Mesopotamia—were in a time of transition. The Canaanite kingdoms were independent and small, without an internal organization.

Themes

- God's faithfulness to his promises
- Conquest, settlement, and life in the land
- The covenant between God and Israel
- God's holiness and judgment
- The unity of God's people
- The role of Joshua as leader of Israel

Key People

Joshua – God chose him to be Israel's leader after Moses' death. He organized, led, and settled Israel in the land God had promised them.

Rahab – A pagan prostitute who showed hospitality to Israel's spies, demonstrated amazing faith in God, and became part of God's covenant people. She is listed as one of Jesus' ancestors in his genealogy (Matt. 1:5).

Achan – His disobedience—he took plunder from the battlefield when Israel had been instructed to not take anything—caused Israel to lose an important battle against Ai. He was stoned to death as punishment (Josh. 7).

Eleazar – Son of Aaron, he took over the high priest's duties after Aaron had passed away (see Ex. 6:23; Num. 20:28). He helped Joshua leading Israel into the Promised Land.

Phinehas – Son of Eleazar, the high priest, and priest of Israel. His intervention to prevent the Israelites from polluting themselves and his zeal for God's covenant granted him a special covenant with God. He and his descendants would be priests of Israel forever (Josh. 22:13, 32–34; 24:33).

The Conquest

A common worry regarding the book, and a shocking realization for those who read it for the first time, are the commands to Israel to kill all inhabitants of the land, including women and children. God is serious about sin and its consequences. In this case, the Israelites were God's tool for punishing sin in the land. This war was no more cruel than any other at the time. As we find in the book of Judges, not all Canaanites were killed, since we find many of them living in the land. Most likely, women and children had fled to the woods to safety, something they were likely used to doing, since the region experienced much war.

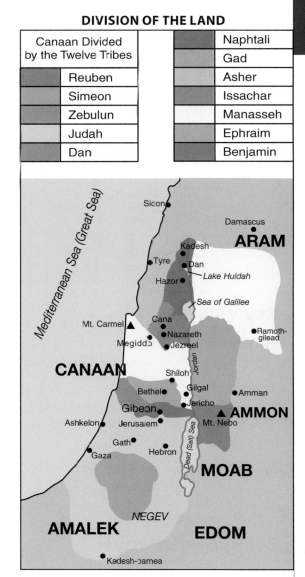

DIVISION OF THE LAND

Canaan Divided by the Twelve Tribes		
		Naphtali
		Gad
Reuben		Asher
Simeon		Issachar
Zebulun		Manasseh
Judah		Ephraim
Dan		Benjamin

Moses and Joshua

Joshua's leadership mirrored in some important ways Moses' leadership.

Moses	Joshua
The people recognized Moses' leadership.	The people acknowledged Joshua as their new leader (Josh. 1:17; 4:14).
Moses led Israel out of Egypt by the crossing of the Red Sea (Ex. 14).	Joshua led Israel into the Promised Land by the crossing of the Jordan River (Josh. 3–4).
Moses was Israel's military leader during the exodus and the wilderness wanderings.	Joshua was Israel's military leader in the conquest of the land (Josh. 1:8–9).
Moses removed his sandals when God spoke to him through the burning bush (Ex. 3:5).	Joshua removed his sandals before God's presence (Josh. 5:10–11).

Key Verses

[Rahab to the spies:] *"When we heard of it, our hearts melted in fear and everyone's courage failed because of you, for the LORD your God is God in heaven above and on the earth below."*—Josh. 2:11

So the LORD gave Israel all the land he had sworn to give their ancestors, and they took possession of it and settled there. The LORD gave them rest on every side, just as he had sworn to their ancestors.... Not one of all the LORD's good promises to Israel failed; every one was fulfilled.—Josh. 21:43–45

Now fear the LORD and serve him with all faithfulness. Throw away the gods your ancestors worshiped beyond the Euphrates River and in Egypt, and serve the LORD... But as for me and my household, we will serve the LORD.—Josh. 24:14–15

Being God's People

Then: God was faithful to his promises by giving his people victory and rest in the land. He will prevail against his enemies because the whole universe belongs to him. Yet, God expects his people to be courageous, obedient, and trusting.

Now: God has made wonderful promises to us as well, and we can be assured that he will carry them through to their fulfillment: "being confident of this, that he who began a good work in you will carry it on to completion until the day of Christ Jesus" (Phil. 1:6).

Jesus in Joshua

The name Joshua is connected to the Hebrew word *yehoshua* which means "The Lord [Yahweh] is salvation," or "The Lord [Yahweh] gives victory." His initial name was Hoshea (Num. 13:8, 16), which means "salvation." Moses changed his name to Joshua. The Greek form of the name Joshua is Jesus. Jesus is God's victory over sin and death. In Jesus, Christians are more than conquerors (Rom. 8:37).

JUDGES

THE STRUGGLE OF SIN AND GRACE

Purpose

The book of Judges is a long narrative warning to all of God's children against forgetting God's instruction and acting like the nations of the land. After the tribes of Israel settled in the Promised Land, they began a fast moral and spiritual decline. There were still Canaanites left to fight. The conquest wasn't complete. The Israelites were disobedient despite their claims to be faithful to God (Josh. 24:16–18). But even in those times when the Israelites turned their back to God, he was filled with compassion and mercy. He raised leaders (judges) to deliver his people from oppression.

The book of Judges offers a theological (or prophetic) look at the history of God's people. Like the book of Joshua, Judges contrasts God's faithfulness to humanity's unfaithfulness and fickleness. One of its main purposes is to demonstrate the need for kings who would care for Israel's safety, lead the people to obedience of the law, and promote the pure worship of the Lord.

THE CYCLE PATTERN IN JUDGES

Israel Disobeys

Israel is at Peace

Israel is Oppressed

Israel is Delivered

Israel Cries Out

God Raises up a Deliverer

What Was a "Judge"?

The English word *judges* makes us think of people presiding in the court. Although the judges in the Old Testament made judicial decisions (Deut. 16:18–20), their main function was that of liberators. The Hebrew word for judge, *shofet*, can be translated as "judge or deliverer." Moses was a judge of the people, both in the sense of deliverer and legal judge (Ex. 12 and 18). The judges were God's response to specific crises. In time, the role of judge, in both senses, was taken over by the kings and, sometimes, the high priests.

Outline

1. Introduction: An Incomplete Conquest and a Failing Faith (1:1–3:6)

2. A Cycle of Sin, Punishment, and Grace (3:7–16:31)
   a. Judges Othniel, Ehud, Shamgar (3)
   b. Judge Deborah (4–5)
   c. Judge Gideon (6–9)
   d. Judges Tola, Jair, Jephthah, Ibzan, Elon, Abdon (10–12)
   e. Judge Samson (13–16)

3. Spiritual and Moral Decay (17–21)

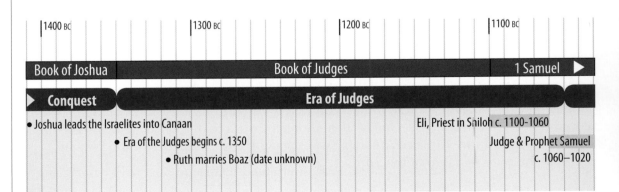

1400 BC   1300 BC   1200 BC   1100 BC

Book of Joshua	Book of Judges	1 Samuel ▶
▶ Conquest	Era of Judges	

• Joshua leads the Israelites into Canaan

     • Era of the Judges begins c. 1350

       • Ruth marries Boaz (date unknown)

Eli, Priest in Shiloh c. 1100-1060

Judge & Prophet Samuel c. 1060–1020

The Judges

Judge	Reference	Tribe	Oppressors	Period of Oppression	Period of Rest
Othniel	3:7–11	Judah	Mesopotamians	8 years	40 years
Ehud	3:12–30	Benjamin	Mesopotamians	18 years	80 years
Shamgar	3:31	unknown	Philistines	unknown	unknown
Deborah	chs. 4–5	Ephraim	Canaanites	20 years	40 years
Gideon	chs. 6–8	Manasseh	Midianites	7 years	40 years
Tola	10:1–2	Issachar	unknown	unknown	23 years
Jair	10:3–5	Gilead-Manasseh	unknown	unknown	22 years
Jephthah	10:6–12:7	Gilead-Manasseh	Ammonites	unknown	24 years
Ibzan	12:8–10	Possibly Judah or Zebulun	unknown	unknown	7 years
Elon	12:11–12	Zebulun	unknown	unknown	10 years
Abdon	12:13–15	Ephraim	unknown	unknown	8 years
Samson	chs. 13–16	Dan	Philistines	40 years	20 years

Background

Author: There is no indication in the book as to who its author was. Ancient Jewish tradition credits the prophet Samuel with having written the book, though this is far from certain.

Date and Setting: Like its author, the date that the book of Judges was written also remains uncertain. The events the book describes occurred between the time of Joshua (around 1400 BC) and Samuel (around 1000 BC) in the Promised Land where the tribes of Israel had settled.

Themes

- Sin and punishment
- God's justice and mercy
- Covenant loyalty and disloyalty
- God's holiness and judgment
- The unity of God's people

Being God's People

Then: Throughout Judges, God challenges the Israelites to be faithful to his covenant. Their rejection of God's instructions (Moses' teachings) resulted in oppression and sharp moral and spiritual decline. Yet God still had mercy on his people and raised up judges to deliver them.

Judge Deborah by Charles Landelle

Flawed People

The epistle to the Hebrews lists five of the judges as "heroes of the faith": Barak, Gideon, Jephthah, Samson, and Samuel (Heb. 11:32). Contrary to the common understanding of "hero," the judges were not super-humans. Rather, they were ordinary, flawed people, chosen by God to carry on his purposes. Just as Israel, they were not chosen because they were stronger, holier, or more spiritual (see Deut. 7). They were chosen because in their flaws and weaknesses, God's power, grace, authority, and love shone through all the more powerfully (see 2 Cor. 12:7–10).

Now: Although God challenges us to be faithful to him, the book of Judges shows that God accepts us just the way we are and that he extends his mercy to us just when we need it the most. Evil increases sometimes rapidly, sometimes in sneaky ways. For this reason, the apostle Paul reminds us to remain cautious, even if we feel secure, lest we fall (1 Cor. 10:12).

Key Verses

Then the Israelites did evil in the eyes of the LORD and served the Baals... In his anger against Israel the LORD gave them into the hands of raiders who plundered them... Then the LORD raised up judges, who saved them out of the hands of these raiders.
—Judg. 2:11–16

In those days Israel had no king; everyone did as they saw fit.
—Judg. 21:25

Jesus in Judges

The judges were deliverers God raised when they were needed. Jesus is God's final solution to the problem of sin, oppression, suffering, and evil. His work is definite and final, though we are still waiting for the final fulfillment of God's promises.

RUTH

BEING GOD'S PEOPLE

Ruth in Boaz's Field by Julius Schnorr von Carolsfeld

Purpose

The book of Ruth is a beautiful story that happens in a difficult time. It was the time of the judges (Ruth 1:1), when "In those days Israel had no king; everyone did as they saw fit" (Judg. 21:25). Besides this lawlessness, the land was experiencing a severe famine. In these dire circumstances, it was difficult to be God's people. The book, then, has two main purposes:

■ It presents a wonderful, concise, yet deep story of emptiness that turns into fullness, of despair into hope, of bitter sadness into joy and celebration. It shows how God turns around his people's fortunes.

■ It presents the origins of King David's royal house.

Outline

1. Naomi's Emptiness: Famine, Migration, and Tragedy in Naomi's Family (1:1–5)

2. Naomi Back Home with a Moabite Daughter-in-Law (1:6–22)

3. Ruth Meets Boaz: Kindness and Generosity Meet Need (2:1–23)

4. Ruth and Boaz: Hope and Grace in Action (3:1–18)

5. Ruth and Boaz Married: Naomi's Fullness (4:1–22)

In this book, the Hebrew names of the main characters are part of the story.

Name	Meaning	Significance
Naomi	"pleasant"	Early in the story, her life is quite unpleasant. So, Naomi changes her name to Mara, which means "bitter."
Elimelek	"God is my King"	Kings in the ancient world were supposed to provide for the needs of their people, including food and security. Yet, a great famine forces a family into exile.
Bethlehem	"house of bread"	Elimelek and his family leave Bethlehem during a famine to find bread in Moab, Israel's hated enemy.
Mahlon and Kilion	Something like, "weakly" and "sickly"	Their names suggest that the two brothers will have a tragic end.
Ruth	Related to the idea of "refreshment" or maybe "friendship"	Although a Moabitess, Ruth became a "friend" of God's people, and a "refreshment" to her mother-in-law, Naomi.
Boaz	Though difficult to determine, the most accepted meaning is "by strength, with strength."	Boaz surely demonstrated great strength of character and convictions to carry on another person's—Naomi's closer relative's—responsibility toward Naomi.

Background

Author: The author of this book is unknown. Jewish tradition attributes it to the prophet Samuel, though nothing in the text indicates this.

Date: The events in the book took place during the time of the judges (Ruth 1:1), sometime between the death of Joshua (around 1350 BC) and David's ascension to the throne of Israel (around 1000 BC).

Setting: The story happened when a severe famine struck the land of Israel. Naomi and her family left Bethlehem and traveled to Moab to escape the famine. Moab was one of Israel's fiercest enemies.

Themes

- God's care and providence in the life of his people is evident in the life of Naomi and Ruth.
- Loyalty, obedience, and trust in God is not limited to Israel. Ruth is an example of this point.
- Redemption. The story shows the ancient practice of "levirate marriage"—a word that refers to the "husband's brother"—and the redemption of property by a near relative. Boaz, although not Naomi's brother-in-law, redeemed Ruth and, indirectly, Naomi herself. Through the famine, the death of Naomi's husband and children, the loyalty of a Moabite woman, and Boaz's kindness, God brought about an unexpected redemption. Through it all, God gives as a gift David, the future king of Israel.

Key People

Naomi – Wife of Elimelek, she went to Moab escaping the famine in Bethlehem. After the death of her husband and sons, Naomi returned to Bethlehem with her daughter-in-law Ruth. Naomi's sadness was such that she changed her name to Mara, which means "bitterness"(1:20).

Ruth – A Moabitess, she married one of Naomi's sons. After the death of her husband, she remained faithful to her mother-in-law and showed great faith in God. She married Boaz and gave birth to sons. King David was her descendant and, eventually, Jesus as well.

Boaz – A compassionate and wealthy relative of Naomi, he fulfilled the levirate marriage and became Ruth's kinsman redeemer.

Key Verses

"Where you go I will go, and where you stay I will stay. Your people will be my people and your God my God."—Ruth 1:16

"May the LORD repay you for what you have done. May you be richly rewarded by the LORD, the God of Israel, under whose wing you have come to take refuge."—Ruth 2:12

Ruth in the Fields
by Hughes Merle

Being God's People

Then: In the dark times of the judges, even in dire conditions of famine and suffering, God showed his presence in powerful and providential ways. God promised to give Israel the land as a sign of his fulfillment of the covenant. Through the story of Ruth, God arranged things so David would be born and become the seed of a new hope for his people. Through him, God's ultimate solution to the problem of sin and evil was born: Jesus, son of David, Son of God, and redeemer of humanity.

Now: The story of Ruth warns against placing people in definite boxes. In ancient Israel, the Moabites were pagans and enemies of God and God's people. Surely, God wouldn't use a Moabitess as an ancestor of the great King David. Yet, God reminds us that "my thoughts are not your thoughts, neither are your ways my ways" (Isa. 55:8). Today we must be careful to not place people in boxes—making assumptions about what people believe and how dedicated they are to God. Neither must we place God in a box, thinking that God only acts in one way.

Jesus in Ruth

The idea of redeemer is important when we think of Jesus. Jesus redeems us from our fallen, low state. However, more directly, the genealogy that connects Ruth with King David, also connects her with Jesus (Matt. 1:5).

1 & 2 SAMUEL

GOD IS KING, BUT WE WANT A KING

David and Saul by Ernst Josephson

One or Two Books?

The Hebrew Bible has only one book of Samuel. When the book was translated into Greek—the Septuagint—the translated text was significantly longer. To make it fit better in the scrolls, the translators of the Septuagint decided to break the book of Samuel into two parts. Originally, Samuel was called 1 and 2 books of Kings, and Kings was divided into 3 and 4 books of Kings.

Purpose

■ When the Israelites entered the Promised Land, they were a collection of tribes, the tribes of the children of Israel. They hardly were the nation God had promised Abraham (Gen. 12:2). The time of the judges was a time of lawlessness and disorder, where "everyone did as they saw fit" (Judges 21:25). Israel's moral and spiritual decline is well represented by the high priest Eli and his children. The book of Samuel explains how and why the monarchy started after the era of the Judges.

■ The book of Samuel is a prophetic book. It gives a prophetic assessment to a crucial time of Israel's history: the early era of the kings. It is meant to expose sin, warn people against rebellion, and instruct people about how God works in history.

■ The book also shows the beginning of the monarchy with Saul, the rise, importance, and limits of David's reign, and the spiritual state of the nation during David's reign.

Outline

1. Samuel: A Prophet in Times of Transition (1 Sam. 1–7)
   a. Birth of Samuel and early ministry (1 Sam. 1–3)
   b. Samuel's ministry as judge and prophet (1 Sam. 4–7)

2. Samuel and Saul: Establishment of the Monarchy in Israel (1 Sam. 8–15)
   a. Transition to Saul's reign (1 Sam. 8)
   b. Saul's leadership in Israel (1 Sam. 9–15)

3. Saul and David: Transition from Saul's Failed Kingdom to David (1 Sam. 16:1–2 Sam. 5:5)
   a. Anointing of David (1 Sam. 16:1–13)
   b. David and Goliath (1 Sam. 16:14–17:58)
   c. Saul, Jonathan, and David (1 Sam. 18–23:6)
   d. David flees Saul (1 Sam. 23:7–26:25)
   e. David in Philistia (1 Sam. 27–30)
   f. Death of Saul and Jonathan (1 Sam. 31–2 Sam. 1)
   g. David becomes king (2 Sam. 2:1–5:5)

4. David's Victorious Reign over Judah and Israel (2 Sam. 5:6–8:18)
   a. David conquers Jerusalem (2 Sam. 5:6–5:16)
   b. David defeats the Philistines (2 Sam. 5:17–25)
   c. David brings the ark to Jerusalem (2 Sam. 6:1–8:18)

5. David's Weakness and Failures as King (2 Sam. 9–20)
   a. David and Saul's descendants
   b. The Ammonite-Syrian threat
   c. David and Bathsheba
   d. Absalom's rebellion

6. Afterword on David's Reign (2 Sam. 21–24)
   a. God's wrath: Famine and Saul's descendants
   b. David's mighty men
   c. Song of David
   d. David's last song
   e. David's mighty men
   f. God's wrath: The census of Israel

The Child Samuel Dedicated by Hannah by Frank W. W. Topham

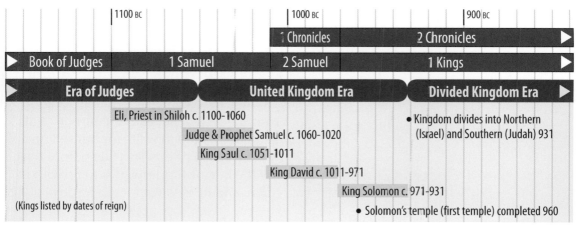

	1100 BC		1000 BC		900 BC	
			1 Chronicles		2 Chronicles	▶
▶ Book of Judges		1 Samuel	2 Samuel		1 Kings	▶
▶ Era of Judges			United Kingdom Era		Divided Kingdom Era	▶

Eli, Priest in Shiloh c. 1100-1060

Judge & Prophet Samuel c. 1060-1020

King Saul c. 1051-1011

King David c. 1011-971

King Solomon c. 971-931

• Kingdom divides into Northern (Israel) and Southern (Judah) 931

(Kings listed by dates of reign)

• Solomon's temple (first temple) completed 960

THE UNITED KINGDOM

Canaan Divided by the Twelve Tribes	
	Reuben
	Simeon
	Zebulun
	Judah
	Dan

	Naphtali
	Gad
	Asher
	Issachar
	Manasseh
	Ephraim
	Benjamin

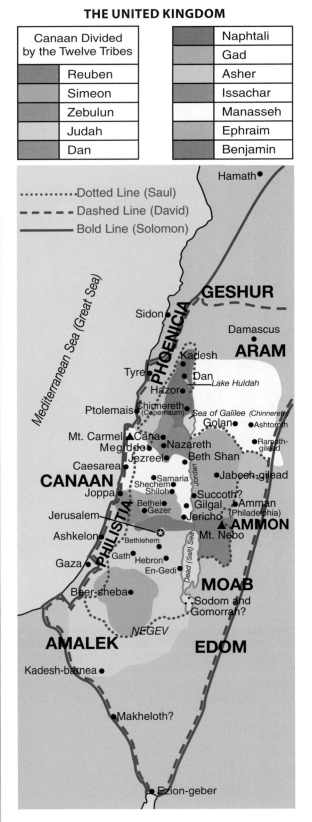

············ Dotted Line (Saul)

‒ ‒ ‒ ‒ Dashed Line (David)

——— Bold Line (Solomon)

Background

Author: The author of the book of Samuel is unknown. We know that Samuel, Nathan, and Gad wrote some of the story the book narrates (1 Chron. 29:29–30), but the extent of those writing remains unknown. Many scholars agree that some later editor collected written and oral traditions and, guided by the Holy Spirit, put together the book of Samuel as we know it.

Date: The events the book presents occurred at the end of the period of the judges (around 1350–1100 BC). The prophet Samuel was the last judge. His ministry transitioned the time of the judges to the monarchy. As for the time of writing, it appears that different people, in different times, contributed to the writing of the book. It is possible that the book was completed, or nearly so, around the time of Solomon, though it is far from certain.

Themes

God's Kingship. One of the central teachings of the Old Testament is that God is King. This is, perhaps, the main metaphor used for God. Israel's relationship with God through the covenant uses this important metaphor. It is the central proclamation of God's people: "The LORD reigns for ever and ever" (Ex. 15:18).

Human Kingship. The book of Samuel does not reject human kingship entirely. Rather, it expects that a human king would "When he takes the throne of his kingdom, he is to write for himself on a scroll a copy of this law, taken from that of the Levitical priests. It is to be with him, and he is to read it all the days of his life so that he may learn to revere the LORD his God and follow carefully all the words of this law and these decrees" (Deut. 17:18–19). In Saul and David, we get to see both sides of the coin. They began their reign well but ended up in disaster and failure. Yet, despite its limitations, God chose to use human kingship, David's royal line, to bring the Messiah, Jesus of Nazareth.

Covenant. God chose to relate to humans using covenants, as ancient kings would with their subjects. A covenant implies a relationship with commitments, promises, and conditions. The book of Samuel assumes the validity and importance of the Mosaic covenant. To it, the book adds God's covenant with David. It is a covenant that shows God's commitment to solve the problem of human sin.

Key People

Eli – High Priest of God at the town of Shiloh. Under his watch, Samuel was born and trained. His own decline as a priest exemplifies Israel's moral and spiritual decline.

Hannah – Samuel's mother. Despite her inability to bear children, she showed an amazing, humble faith in God. God rewarded her with a child, Samuel. Hannah dedicated the child to God. Her song of gratitude is echoed by Jesus' mother, Mary, in the Gospel of Luke (1:46–55).

Samuel – God's servant who acted as prophet, priest, and judge for Israel. He led the transitional period from the time of the judges to the time of the monarchy. He anointed Saul, Israel's first king, and David, the great king who united the tribes of Israel into a nation.

Saul – First king of Israel, he is described as one "without equal among the Israelites…" (1 Sam. 9:2). Saul rebelled against God's instructions and made serious mistakes. In time, God removed his Spirit from upon him. He grew jealous of David and tried to kill him.

Jonathan – As Saul's first son, he was in charge of Saul's armies. He became David's closest friend and interceded on David's behalf before Saul. He died with Saul in the field of battle (1 Sam. 31).

David — God chose him to become Saul's successor as king of Israel. He unified the tribes of Israel into a kingdom, brought peace to Israel, and found favor with God. God made a covenant with him to have David's descendants on the throne of Israel forever.

Bathsheba – David lusted after her when he saw her. Although she was married to Uriah, one of David's loyal army officers, David had an affair with her. After David had her husband killed in the field of battle, David married her. Bathsheba became pregnant. However, the baby died because of David's sin. She later gave birth to another son Solomon.

Nathan – God's prophet, he came to David with a clever parable that denounced David's sin. David recognized his sin, repented, and accepted God's punishment.

Absalom – Son of David, he led a rebellion against his father. Although at first he succeeded, eventually David's faithful generals chased him out of Jerusalem and killed him.

Solomon – He was the son of David and Bathsheba. "The LORD loved him; and because the LORD loved him, he sent word through Nathan the prophet to name him Jedidiah" (2 Sam. 12:24–25). This lesser known name means, "loved by the Lord."

Names in the book of Samuel

Name	Meaning	Significance
Samuel	"God has heard"	Not only did God hear Hannah's prayer, he also heard Israel's requests for a king. Samuel, the prophet, represented God's willingness to hear his people's requests.
Saul	"the one who has been requested"	Saul was the answer to what Israel had requested: "appoint a king to lead us, such as all the other nations have" (1 Sam. 8:5).
Absalom	"father of peace"	He produced strife against his father.

Key Verses

It is not by strength that one prevails; those who oppose the LORD will be broken. The Most High will thunder from heaven; the LORD will judge the ends of the earth.—1 Sam. 2:9–10

The LORD does not look at the things people look at. People look at the outward appearance, but the LORD looks at the heart.—1 Sam. 16:7

The LORD declares to you that the LORD himself will establish a house for you: When your days are over and you rest with your ancestors, I will raise up your offspring to succeed you, your own flesh and blood, and I will establish his kingdom. He is the one who will build a house for my Name, and I will establish the throne of his kingdom forever. I will be his father, and he will be my son. When he does wrong, I will punish him with a rod wielded by men, with floggings inflicted by human hands. But my love will never be taken away from him, as I took it away from Saul, whom I removed from before you. Your house and your kingdom will endure forever before me; your throne will be established forever.—2 Sam. 7:11–16

Being God's People

Then: Despite Samuel's warnings, the Israelites wanted to have a king like the nations around them. God granted their request. However, the monarchy turned out to be a great failure, beginning with the first king, Saul. Even though David accomplished great things, and God chose him to be the father of the future Messiah, his failures illustrate that the way of redemption and restoration is God's own plan. Nevertheless, God turned David's weakness into a future blessing for Israel and all peoples (see

Rom. 8:28). Through David's royal descendants, God sent the Messiah who is the way, the truth, and the life (John 14:6).

Now: God is King. Although he appoints humans to lead his people—Moses, Samuel, Paul, Peter, and others—he doesn't surrender his authority. Only he is King, to him alone belongs all glory and honor. For that reason, we must not allow other humans, or things, to take the place of God. In the book of Samuel, the kings forgot their place and acted as having ultimate authority. God does not share his glory.

Jesus in Samuel

Jesus is present in the book of Samuel in many different ways:

- **Samuel.** His roles as prophet, judge, and priest anticipated Jesus' work during his earthly ministry. Jesus is the best example that God hears the pleas of his people and knows the needs of all human beings.

- **Saul.** Saul was God's answer to the people's request for a king. Saul's failure contrasts sharply with Jesus' victory: Jesus is God's answer to humanity's greatest need for a redeemer.

- **David.** He was God's chosen king. David unified Israel into a nation, brought political peace to the land, and expanded its boundaries. God's covenant with David anticipated the coming of a Messiah. This Messiah would unify God's people, not just in Israel but in the whole world, bring true peace to the world, and bring about God's kingdom to the whole earth.

©Kim Walton/Walton Image Supply

"House of David" Inscription. Discovered in Tel Dan in 1993, the inscribed stone contains the expression "the house of David," referring to David's descendants. The stone was quite possibly part of a victory pillar of a neighboring king of Damascus. The stone has been dated to two or three centuries after David's time. This is a very important archaeological finding since it is the first reference to King David found outside of the Bible and establishes the existence of David's dynasty.

1 & 2 KINGS

THE LIMITS OF HUMAN RULE

King Solomon

Purpose

The book of Kings is a prophetic view of Israel's history. The book answers the question, "Why did God allow Israel to be taken into exile?" To understand this question, a quick overview of the history in the book of Kings is important.

■ After David died, he named Solomon as his successor. Solomon's kingdom experienced peace and prosperity, but showed signs of rebellion against God. After Solomon's death in about 931 BC, the Kingdom of Israel became divided

1100 BC		1000 BC		900 BC		800 BC
		1 Chronicles		2 Chronicles		
1 Samuel		2 Samuel	1 Kings			2 Kings
▶ Judges	United Kingdom Era			Divided Kingdom Era		

King Saul c. 1051-1011

King David c. 1011-971

King Solomon c. 971-931

● Kingdom divides into Northern (Israel) and Southern (Judah) 931

● Solomon's temple (first temple) completed 960

Prophet Elijah c. 870-845

Prophet Elisha c. 845-800

(Kings listed by dates of reign)

between Rehoboam and Jeroboam. The Kingdom of Israel in the North followed Jeroboam and established its capital in Samaria. The Kingdom of Judah in the South remained with Rehoboam, son of Solomon, in the capital of Jerusalem, City of David.

- The history of both kingdoms is filled with rebellion, internal struggles, abuse, greed, and idolatry. Even the good kings—like Hezekiah and Josiah—showed very human limitations. The ministries of Elijah and Elisha show the spiritual state of the kingdoms, as represented by their kings.

- Israel, the northern kingdom, and its capital Samaria fell to the Assyrian armies in 722 BC. The ten northern tribes of Israel were scattered throughout the Assyrian Empire.

- Although God protected Jerusalem, the southern kingdom of Judah became a weak kingdom. After a few generations, in 586 BC the powerful Babylonian Empire conquered and destroyed the southern kingdom, including Jerusalem and the temple.

One or Two Books?

Although in our English Bibles there are two books of Kings, the Hebrew text has only one book. The reason to divide it was purely practical. When the book was translated into Greek—the Septuagint—the translated text was significantly longer. To make the book fit better in the scrolls, the translators decided to break Samuel and Kings. Originally, Samuel was called 1 and 2 books of Kings, and Kings was divided into 3 and 4 books of Kings.

Israel had been warned about the consequences of unfaithfulness. In the writing prophets—such as Isaiah or Jeremiah—we see God's warnings and judgments, as well as hopeful promises, in very direct ways. In the book of Kings, we see a different kind of prophecy. It is a prophecy that shows rather than tells of God's warnings and judgments.

It also is prophetic history because it is designed to instruct God's people about God's ways in the world. As an instruction book, the message of the book of Kings is based on the Torah—God's instructions to his people.

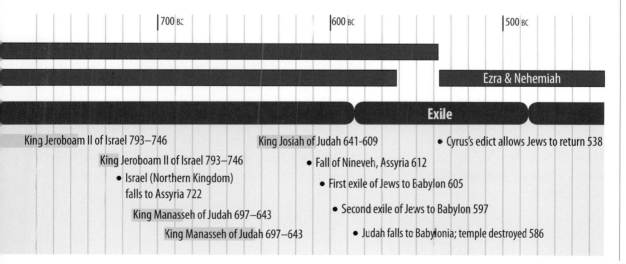

700 BC   600 BC   500 BC

Ezra & Nehemiah

Exile

King Jeroboam II of Israel 793–746

King Jeroboam II of Israel 793–746

- Israel (Northern Kingdom) falls to Assyria 722

King Manasseh of Judah 697–643

King Manasseh of Judah 697–643

King Josiah of Judah 641-609

- Fall of Nineveh, Assyria 612
- First exile of Jews to Babylon 605
- Second exile of Jews to Babylon 597
- Judah falls to Babylonia; temple destroyed 586

- Cyrus's edict allows Jews to return 538

Outline

1. David-Solomon Succession (1 Kings 1:1–2:12)

2. Solomon's Reign (1 Kings 2:13–11:43)
   a. His wisdom (3–4)
   b. His building projects (5–10)
   c. His folly (11)

3. A Kingdom Divided (1 Kings 12–2 Kings 17)
   a. Rehoboam, Jeroboam (12–14)
   b. The kings of Judah and Israel (15–16)
   c. The ministry of Elijah and Elisha (1 Kings 17–2 Kings 13)
   d. Destruction of Samaria and exile of Israel (14–17)

4. The Kingdom of Judah (2 Kings 18–25)
   a. Hezekiah (18–20)
   b. Manasseh, Amon (21)
   c. Josiah (22–23)
   d. On the road to exile (24)
   e. Fall of Jerusalem and exile of Judah (25)

Sources

The book of Kings mentions several sources from which some of the content was taken: (1) the book of the acts of Solomon (1 Kings 11:41); (2) the book of the chronicles of the kings of Judah (1 Kings 14:29; 15:7, 23, etc.); (3) the book of the chronicles of the kings of Israel (1 Kings 14:19; 15:31; 16:14, 20, 27, etc.).

Background

Author: The book does not specify an author. An ancient Jewish tradition attributes the book to the prophet Jeremiah. It is possible and reasonable that Jeremiah was the author. However, there is no way to prove or disprove that he was. We must be content with the author's own intention to remain anonymous. Having an anonymous author does not change the fact that the book is God's Word for his people then and today.

Date: The date the book was composed is equally difficult to determine. All we can say is that the book was written after the last event recorded in the book (2 Kings 25:27–30), which occurred around 561 BC. Since the book does not mention Cyrus's decree to allow the Jews to return to their land (in 539 BC), it is possible that the book was written before that date.

Setting: To understand the history and writings of Israel, we must keep in mind some important facts of geography and history. The kingdom of Israel was located in the crossroads of crucial trading routes that connected Egypt, the superpower to the south, and Assyria or Babylon in the north. Although a small kingdom, Israel's strategic location made it a prize area for the great powers at different times. The time of Solomon's prosperity in the United Kingdom was possible in part due to the many internal struggles and external pressures that Egypt and Assyria experienced at the time.

The history of Israel, united and divided, was deeply marked by the changes and interventions of the Empires that surrounded her. Egypt, Assyria, and Babylon exerted great pressure on the internal and external life of Israel. When those Empires were occupied with their own struggles, Israel and the kingdoms that surrounded her were free to fight against each other for control of the all-important trading routes.

The challenges to Israel's faith are better appreciated in her history. It might be easier trusting God and being obedient when things around us are under control and going well. However, when we must make moral or spiritual choices in the face of serious physical, political, economic, or social threats, the state of our faith becomes clearer. Israel's wealth, political influence in the region, and military power became the testing ground for the people's faith, reliance on God, and faithfulness to the covenant.

King Solomon in His Old Age Led Astray into Idolatry by His Wives by Giovanni Venanzi di Pesaro

Themes

There are two main themes in the book of Kings: Kingship and Covenant.

Kingship

- *Human Kingship.* Although the book of Kings doesn't regard the monarchy as evil, it shows that when human kings take their authority and leadership out from under the umbrella of God's own authority and leadership, they are condemned to failure. Kings, like all other members of God's people, must remain subjects of God's covenant. Their reign must be based on their knowledge and submission to the Torah—God's instructions (Deut. 17:14–20). The book shows the kings' failures to guide Israel to live as God's people. The failures of the Israelite kings resulted in a divided people, a corrupted land, a polluted worship, abuse of weak people, and reliance on military power. These were symptoms of a deep spiritual disease that left the prophet Elijah wondering if he was the last faithful follower of the Lord (1 Kings 19:14).

- *Divine Kingship.* God is the Great King. Above all earthly kings and all supposedly divine kings, the Lord, the God of the covenant with Abraham and Moses, whose presence dwelled in the Jerusalem temple, is the King, the Creator, Owner, and Ruler of the whole creation. As the Owner of the universe, God gave Israel a land. In this land, God provided for the needs of his people, as kings were supposed to do. He ruled and guided his people through his Torah. Also, as the Great King, God rendered judgment upon the nations, including Israel itself. So God ruled against Israel and Judah's unfaithfulness. As instruments of his judgment, Assyria and Babylon conquered and exiled the northern kingdom of Israel and the kingdom of Judah.

■ *The King in the Land*. As God's presence accompanied his people in their wilderness journeys, his presence remained in the land. God's presence was the visible demonstration of God's faithfulness to his covenant. The temple that King Solomon built in Jerusalem was this visible presence of God with Israel. The temple was also a reminder to Israel that God demanded exclusive worship.

■ *The Messiah*. In the prophetic message of the Old Testament, judgment was never the last word. God always provided words of hope for the future of his people. Although the book of Kings ultimately explains God's judgment against his unfaithful people, the book's words of hope are decisive for God's plans of redemption. God promised David that his descendants would reign over Israel forever (2 Sam. 7:16). The exile of Judah would appear to thwart this promise. However, the book ends with hope and reveals God's faithfulness to his promise to David: "In the thirty-seventh year of the exile of Jehoiachin king of Judah, in the year Awel-Marduk became king of Babylon, he released Jehoiachin king of Judah from prison.… Day by day the king gave Jehoiachin a regular allowance as long as he lived" (2 Kings 25:27, 30). Jehoiachim, David's descendant, was no longer a prisoner. David's royal line was poised to continue and, eventually, return to Jerusalem as God had promised in the past. The promise and the hope remained alight.

Covenant

Israel, a collection of tribes that came out of Egypt freed by a powerful God who wanted to relate to them and had chosen them as his special treasure, had to learn what it meant to be God's people. So God gave them his Torah—instructions—that allowed them to learn how to be God's people. The book of Deuteronomy records God's wisdom for a people about to enter the Promised Land.

Throughout the book of Kings, we read about God's faithfulness to the covenant in action. For Israel, faithfulness to the covenant was demonstrated through obedience and proper worship of the Lord. Their faithfulness assured for them the blessings of the covenant (Deut. 7:12–24; 8:1, 4, 7–9; 11:9, 11, 14–15; 28:2–13; 33:6–25). Unfaithfulness to the covenant brought about curses against Israel (Deut. 3:16–19; 4:26–28; 11:17; 27:15–26; 28:16–45, 48–68).

Among those curses were, "The LORD will drive you and the king you set over you to a nation unknown to you or your ancestors. There you will worship other gods, gods of wood and stone.… You will be uprooted from the land you are entering to possess. Then the LORD will scatter you among all nations, from one end of the earth to the other. There you will worship other gods—gods of wood and stone, which neither you nor your ancestors have known" (Deut. 28:36, 63–64). The exiles of Israel in 722 BC and of Judah in 586 BC, then, were God's judgments against his unfaithful people.

Key People

David – King of Israel, he unified the tribes and the kingdoms. God made a covenant with him to have one of his descendants on the throne of Israel forever (2 Sam. 7).

Solomon – David's son, he inherited the throne and built the temple of Jerusalem for the Lord. Under him, Israel experienced peace and prosperity.

Rehoboam – Solomon's son, his lack of wisdom caused the kingdom to divide into the northern kingdom of Israel and the southern kingdom of Judah (1 Kings 11:43–12:24; 14:21–31).

Jeroboam – Officer of Solomon's administration, he rejected Rehoboam's leadership and contributed to the division of the kingdom. He became the king of the northern Israel and led them astray by worshiping other gods (1 Kings 11:24–14:20).

Elijah – Mighty servant of God, Elijah's prophetic ministry opposed Israel's unfaithfulness and King Ahab's evil reign. He faced Baal's prophets on Mt. Carmel and demonstrated that only the Lord is God (17:1–19:1; 20:1–22:40).

Elisha – Elijah's disciple, he continued with Elijah's powerful prophetic ministry in the kingdom of Israel (2 Kings 2:1–9:3; 13:14–21).

Ahab – Eighth king of Israel, the Bible describes his reign as evil. He allowed the cult of Baal to take root in Israel. He actively opposed Elijah (2 Kings 16:28–17:1; 18:1–19:1; 20:1–22:40).

Naaman – A Syrian army officer, he suffered of leprosy and sought help from the prophet Elisha. Naaman showed the kind of faith that the Israelites should have had (2 Kings 5).

Jezebel – Evil queen of Israel, she promoted the worship of Baal and attempted to kill Elijah (2 Kings 9:7–37).

Hezekiah – Thirteenth king of Judah, he listened to the advice of the prophet Isaiah, remained faithful to God, and was granted peace and safety for the kingdom (2 Kings 16:20–20:21).

Manasseh – Son of Hezekiah, his rule became synonymous with disloyalty and evil (2 Kings 20:21–21:18).

Josiah – Sixteenth king of Judah and Hezekiah's great-grandson, he remained faithful to God and brought about a spiritual revival in the kingdom (2 Kings 21:24–23:30).

Sennacherib – Assyrian king, in 722 BC he conquered and destroyed Samaria, and threatened Jerusalem itself (2 Kings 18:13–19:36).

Nebuchadnezzar – Babylonian king, he became God's instrument to punish Judah. In the 580s BC, he conquered Judah and, eventually, destroyed the temple in Jerusalem (2 Kings 24:1–25:22).

Key Verses

So give your servant a discerning heart to govern your people and to distinguish between right and wrong. For who is able to govern this great people of yours?—1 Kings 3:9

As for you, if you walk before me faithfully with integrity of heart and uprightness, as David your father did, and do all I command and observe my decrees and laws, I will establish your royal throne over Israel forever, as I promised David your father when I said, 'You shall never fail to have a successor on the throne of Israel.—1 Kings 9:4–5

The LORD warned Israel and Judah through all his prophets and seers: "Turn from your evil ways. Observe my commands and decrees, in accordance with the entire Law that I commanded your ancestors to obey and that I delivered to you through my servants the prophets."—2 Kings 17:13

And Hezekiah prayed to the LORD: "LORD, the God of Israel, enthroned between the cherubim, you alone are God over all the kingdoms of the earth. You have made heaven and earth."—2 Kings 19:15

Being God's People

Then: The book of Kings shows God's faithfulness to his promises. God's faithfulness has two sides: A positive side in which God blesses his people's own faithfulness, and a negative side in which God punishes his people's unfaithfulness. Amazingly, even in punishing Israel for her own rebellion, God offers hope and makes promises that assure us that his plans to redeem humanity will happen.

Now: The book of Kings challenges believers to be obedient and faithful. However, its greater challenge to God's people is to trust God. Trusting God must happen at all times and in all circumstances. Trust happens over time, it requires work, and it must be exercised daily. Learning to trust Jesus as the Great King means that the values of the kingdom of God affect every area of our lives.

Jesus in Kings

God's promise to David, of a continuous descendant on the throne of Israel, is the historical and theological basis for the coming of a Messiah, one who would unify God's people, redeem them, and reconcile them with God. This promise was fulfilled in Jesus, the Messiah, who saves Israel and the world.

Mesha Stele
(Moabite Stone)

The Book of Kings and Archaeology

The following archaeological discoveries help us understand the history in the book of Kings in the larger context of world history. They show not only that events in the Bible occurred in history, but that they had a significant effect in other nations as well.

1. The Mesha Stele, also known as the Moabite Stone, records the rebellion of Mesha, King of Moab, against Israel just after King Omri (876–869 BC).

2. The Black Obelisk of Assyrian King Shalmaneser III (859–824 BC) shows Israel's next king, Jehu (842–815 BC), paying tribute and allegiance to Assyria. This event is not recorded in the Old Testament.

3. A jasper seal found at Megiddo from the time of Jeroboam II (786–746 BC) names King Jeroboam.

4. The Khorsabad Annals describe the reign and fall of Samaria to Assyria's Sargon II (722–705 BC) in 722 BC (2 Kings 17).

5. Sennacherib's Prism gives an account of the siege of Jerusalem in 701 BC during Hezekiah's reign (715–687 BC; see 2 Kings 18:13–19:37; Isa. 36–39).

Scene on the Black Obelisk; Jehu before Shalmaneser III

1 & 2 CHRONICLES

STILL THE PEOPLE OF GOD

Solomon's Dedication of the Temple (2 Chron. 2) by William Brassey Hole

Pre, Post, and Exilic Time

For convenience, scholars often use the words *pre-exilic, exilic,* and *post-exilic* to describe three important periods in Israel's history. *Pre-exilic* refers to the time before the 586 BC exile to Babylon. *Exilic* refers to the time the Israelites were in Babylon (586–539 or 515 BC). *Post-exilic* refers to the time after the Israelites had returned to Jerusalem (after 539–515 BC because they returned in three separate waves).

Purpose

The Pentateuch—the first five books of the Bible—provides an identity to the Israelites as God's people as they were about to enter the Promised Land. Similarly, the book of Chronicles provides an identity to the Israelites who returned from the Babylonian exile to Jerusalem. The book reviews the historical and theological continuity that exists between the pre-exilic community and the post-exilic one.

Unlike Samuel and Kings that try to explain the reasons that led to the terrible exile, Chronicles wants to connect the recently arrived Jews to their history. The promise and hope for a restored Israel is found in the ancient history of the people, a history that the Jews must remember, understand, and make their own.

Through genealogies, remembered history, connection with the Davidic kingdom and covenant, and God's activities in Israel, especially in Judah, the book identifies what it means to be God's people once again in the land. Although a hopeful time, it is still a time of uncertainty. Israel is not a kingdom, a nation, because it is a vassal region of the Persian Empire. The land where the returning Jews dwell is a city, Jerusalem, a destroyed city without walls or a temple. The returned Jews were direct historical and spiritual descendants of ancient Israel, especially of the Davidic line.

However, the history the Chronicler has narrated must be a warning against complacency, rebellion, and idolatry. The monarchy cannot be successful without God as the true King. The words of the prophets are God's warning system to his people; they must be carefully heard. The instructions of the Torah are more than empty rituals; they teach God's people how to approach and please the King. God's warnings to Israel's unfaithfulness are not empty threats. God punishes rebellion.

Outline

1. Genealogies from Adam to Saul (1 Chron. 1–9)

2. David's Kingship (1 Chron. 10–29)
   a. Death of Saul (10)
   b. Rise of David (11–12)
   c. David and the ark (13–17)
   d. David's wars (18–20)
   e. David's census (21–27)
   f. David's speeches (28:1–29:20)
   g. Solomon's rise to the kingship (29:21–30)

3. Solomon's Kingship (2 Chron. 1–9)
   a. Solomon's wisdom (1)
   b. Solomon and the temple (2–7)
   c. Reign of Solomon (8–9)

4. The Kings of Judah (2 Chron. 10–36)
   a. Division of the kingdom (10:1–11:4)
   b. Reign of Rehoboam (11:5–12:16)
   c. Reign of the kings of Judah (13:1–36:14)
   d. Babylonian exile and Cyrus's decree (36:15–23)

Background

Author and Date: A Jewish tradition attributes the book to Ezra the scribe. Although it is plausible, it is almost impossible to know who wrote the book. The author may have been an educated priest. The book shows great interest in and familiarity with the temple and the worship of the Lord. Since the genealogy list goes at least two generations after Zerubbabel, and the name of the money received for the temple is mentioned (*darics*, the official coin name of the Persian empire, see 1 Chron. 29:7),

Naming Chronicles

In the Hebrew Bible, this book doesn't follow the traditional way to get a name: using the first few words of the book (in the case of this book, the first words are the names of Adam, Seth, and Enoch). Rather, the name of the book is *dibre hayyamim*, "the annals (events, happenings) of the days." The Greek translation of the Hebrew Old Testament—the Septuagint—used the term *paraleipomena*, which means "things omitted" or "supplements." For the Greek translators, the book of Chronicles repeated the information of Samuel and Kings and supplemented them with new information. In the fourth century AD Jerome, who made the Latin translation of the Bible—the "Vulgate"—described the book as a chronicle, a summary of divine history. From that description, the German Reformer and translator Martin Luther in the sixteenth century AD used the title of *Chronicles*. As with Samuel and Kings, Chronicles was originally one book. When the Jewish translators made the Greek translation of the Hebrew Bible—the Septuagint—the book was too long to fit into one book. For practical reasons, they divided the book into 1 and 2 Chronicles.

these would suggest that the book might have been written in the middle or the end of the fifth century (450–400 BC). However, many scholars have proposed a later date in the 300's and the 200's BC.

Another consideration for dating the text of Chronicles is the historical background:

1. Babylon exiled the southern kingdom of Judah in 586 BC.

2. Babylon fell to the Persian Empire in 539 BC.

3. The Persian king, Cyrus the Great, allowed all exiled peoples of the empire to return to their homelands in 538 BC. A group of Jews returned to Jerusalem.

4. In 536 BC, the returned Jews began the rebuilding of the temple.

5. The second temple, also called Zerubbabel's temple, was completed in 516 BC.

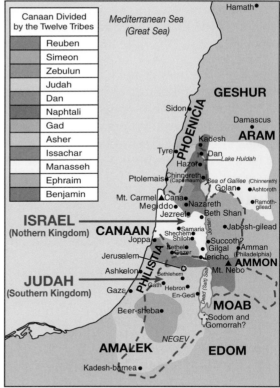

THE DIVIDED KINGDOM

Canaan Divided by the Twelve Tribes
Reuben
Simeon
Zebulun
Judah
Dan
Naphtali
Gad
Asher
Issachar
Manasseh
Ephraim
Benjamin

6. Another group of Jews returned to Jerusalem from Mesopotamia in 558–557 BC. The priest and scribe Ezra returned to Jerusalem with them.

7. A third wave of Jewish exiles returned to Jerusalem around 445 BC. The Persian king Artaxerxes I named Nehemiah governor of the Yudit Province. He arrived with the other Jews to Jerusalem and began the construction of the walls around Jerusalem.

Many scholars believe that Chronicles was written before Ezra and Nehemiah and by a different author.

1100 BC	1000 BC	900 BC	800 BC
	1 Chronicles	2 Chronicles	
1 Samuel	2 Samuel	1 Kings	2 Kings
Judges	United Kingdom Era	Divided Kingdom Era	

King Saul c. 1051-1011

King David c. 1011-971

• Kingdom divides into Northern (Israel) and Southern (Judah) 931

King Solomon c. 971-931

Prophet Elijah c. 870-845

Prophet Elisha c. 845-800

• Solomon's temple (first temple) completed 960

(Kings listed by dates of reign)

Themes

Faithfulness of God. God was faithful to Israel in the past and he would be again in their time. The Israelites had returned with the protection and permission of the Persian king, but they knew that God brought them back to Jerusalem.

Kingship. The kings were central in the life of Israel until the exile. The Israelites were no longer a nation, so they did not have a king. Yet, their history told them that God was their King, and he had promised that one day a human king would sit on the throne of David, restore Israel, defeat its enemies, and bring Israel into God's peace. That promise, the coming of the Messiah, is a central hope in the book of Chronicles.

David. Two crucial themes related to David are showcased in the book of Chronicles: (1) David's kingship and (2) God's covenant with him. His kingship is looked to as a source of hope and continuity. The covenant between God and David is the basis for creating a new community of restored Jews in Jerusalem.

Temple. The temple was important because it was the visible representation of God's presence. It dominated the view on Mt. Zion, and reminded Israel that God's presence with them was a sign of his faithfulness to the covenant and the fulfillment of his promises.

Unity of Israel. As a group of Jews returned to Jerusalem, there were no longer two nations in opposition to each other (Israel and Judah). They were just one people in one city struggling to survive, rebuild, and find an identity as God's people. The unity of the people and the promises of restoration of all of Israel were central to that community.

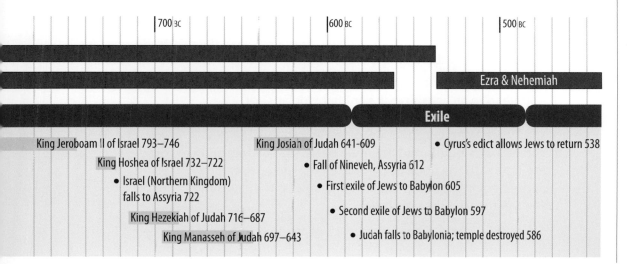

| 700 BC | 600 BC | 500 BC |

Ezra & Nehemiah

Exile

King Jeroboam II of Israel 793–746

King Hoshea of Israel 732–722

• Israel (Northern Kingdom) falls to Assyria 722

King Hezekiah of Judah 716–687

King Manasseh of Judah 697–643

King Josiah of Judah 641-609

• Fall of Nineveh, Assyria 612

• First exile of Jews to Babylon 605

• Second exile of Jews to Babylon 597

• Judah falls to Babylonia; temple destroyed 586

• Cyrus's edict allows Jews to return 538

Key People

David – King of Israel, he unified the tribes and the kingdoms. God made a covenant with him to have one of his descendants on the throne of Israel forever.

Nathan – Prophet who ministered during the reign of David. He faced David about his sin, brought word from God regarding the temple and God's covenant with David, and was part of the choosing of Solomon.

Solomon – David's son, he inherited the throne and built the temple of Jerusalem for the Lord. Under him, Israel experienced peace and prosperity.

Rehoboam – Solomon's son, his lack of wisdom caused the kingdom to divide into the northern kingdom of Israel and the southern kingdom of Judah.

Hezekiah – Thirteenth king of Judah, he listened to the advice of the prophet Isaiah, remained faithful to God, and was granted peace and safety for the kingdom.

Josiah – Sixteenth king of Judah and Hezekiah's great-grandson, he remained faithful to God and brought about a spiritual revival in the kingdom.

Cyrus – Persian King who conquered Babylon and extended the Persian Empire. He pronounced a decree that allowed the Jews to return to Jerusalem. He also provided funds to rebuild the temple in Jerusalem.

Genealogies

We find genealogies all over the Bible, especially in the Old Testament. These often long and tedious lists of names have two important purposes:

1. Genealogies establish a sense of continuity between generations. It is an essential source of identity for a person or a group. In the Old Testament, a link to Abraham connected individuals to the covenant and its promises. For the Israelites, their connection to the ancestors of the faith connected them also to God.

2. Another central role of genealogies was to connect people to royal lines. The ancient Babylonians, for example, wrote long lists of kings that connected later kings with the early, founders of the empire. Such connections legitimized their rule before the people and their gods. In the book of Chronicles, the long genealogy at the beginning of the book (1–9) connects the returning Jews to the royal line of David.

Key Verses

And you, my son Solomon, acknowledge the God of your father, and serve him with wholehearted devotion and with a willing mind, for the LORD searches every heart and understands every desire and every thought. If you seek him, he will be found by you; but if you forsake him, he will reject you forever.—1 Chron. 28:9

If my people, who are called by my name, will humble themselves and pray and seek my face and turn from their wicked ways, then I will hear from heaven, and I will forgive their sin and will heal their land.—2 Chron. 7:14

Being God's People

Then: God had promised to restore his people to the land. His promise was partially fulfilled in the return of the Jews during the Persian rule. In this, God's faithfulness assured the people that his presence and his promises were still valid for them. However, as the other prophets understood and Chronicles implies, the complete fulfillment of God's promises hadn't arrived yet. The promised Messiah would one day come to finish the work that began in 538 BC.

Now: God continues to expect obedience and loyalty from his people. It is not an obedience born out of fear or obligation. The obedience God expects from his people is born from our faith in Christ. Our obedience does not earn us "brownie points" with God. Our obedience—good works, proper worship, love of our neighbors including our enemies, our help and love for the needy and the weak—reflects our faith in God, our trust that God provides, protects, and cares.

Jesus in Chronicles

In Chronicles, God began to fulfill his promise to restore Israel by bringing them back from exile. The hopeful ending anticipates a time that goes back to David's kingdom, with Israel once again a united people in the Promised Land. In Jesus, God showed his intention to restore humanity as a whole through David's descendant, the Messiah, God's own Son. Jesus is the fulfillment of that ancient promise to save humanity from the bondage of sin, restore them to a relationship with God, and renew their hearts and minds.

EZRA & NEHEMIAH

A FAITH UNDER SIEGE

One Book or Two?

In the Hebrew Bible these two books are one work. The Jewish scholars who were dedicated to copying the Hebrew text developed a system to count syllables and words to ensure the accuracy of the copy. In their counting of words, Nehemiah 3:32 is the center of the books. Origen in the third century AD was the first Christian scholar who divided the books into two.

Purpose

Unlike the Israelites who entered the Promised Land many centuries before under Joshua's leadership, the Jews who came back from exile to Jerusalem were not a conquering army. Rather, they were a religious community of builders who built first the temple, then the city walls, and in the process the community itself. It was a community in constant danger: from outside, they faced opposition to building the temple of the Lord and rebuilding the walls of the city; from inside, they faced the threats of rebellion and apathy.

The books of Ezra and Nehemiah follow a similar pattern. The royal court of Persia authorizes them to rebuild the temple; then there is a journey, opposition, and success. Ezra and Nehemiah look at that history with the eyes of faith and discern God's actions in their time. The actions of the Persian kings are, in fact, God's own actions.

More specifically, the books of Ezra and Nehemiah relate the life-and-death struggle the community experienced to fulfill its calling to build. The restored community of Jerusalem experienced a social and spiritual siege. At stake was not land or political power, but rather spiritual faithfulness to God.

Outline

1. Rebuilding the Temple (Ezra 1–6)
   a. Cyrus' decree to rebuild the temple in Jerusalem (1)
   b. Restored exiles rebuild the temple (2–3)
   c. Opposition of the enemies (4)
   d. Temple rebuilt and dedicated (5–6)

2. The Restored Community and the Law of Moses (Ezra 7–10)
   a. With royal authorization, Ezra returns to Jerusalem (7–8)
   b. Internal opposition: intermarriage that leads to idolatry (9–10)

3. Rebuilding the Walls of Jerusalem (Neh. 1–6)
   a. Nehemiah obtains royal authorization to rebuild the walls of Jerusalem (1)
   b. Nehemiah returns to Jerusalem as governor of the province (2–3)
   c. Opposition of the enemies (4:1–6:14)
   d. The wall is rebuilt (6:15–19)

4. The Restored Community and Nehemiah's Reforms (Neh. 7–13)
   a. Administration of Jerusalem (7:1–3)
   b. Genealogical registry of the Israelites in Jerusalem (7:4–73)
   c. Reading of the law (8)
   d. The communities repentance and covenant renewal (9:1–12:26)
   e. Dedication of the walls (12:27–47)
   f. Nehemiah's reforms (13)

	600 BC		500 BC		400 BC

2 Chronicles | Ezra & Nehemiah

2 Kings | Esther

Divided Kingdom Era | **Exile** | **Restoration of Jerusalem**

- Cyrus's edict allows Jews to return 538
- Rebuilding of temple 536–516   • Ezra sent to Judah 457
- Fall of Nineveh 612
- Zerubbabel and Joshua 520–516
- First exile of Jews to Babylon 605   Haggai c. 520
- Zechariah c. 520–518
- Nehemiah governs Judah 444–432
- Second exile of Jews to Babylon 597
- Malachi (date unknown)
- Judah (Southern Kingdom) falls to Babylonia; temple destroyed 586   Joel (date unknown)

☐ = Minor Prophet (listed by dates of ministry)

Background

Author: Based on an ancient Jewish and Christian tradition, the books of Ezra and Nehemiah are attributed to one author, usually Ezra, the scribe. Ezra's training as a court scribe would have prepared him to compile different sources, such as his own memoirs, Nehemiah's memoirs, and other official documents from before his time in Jerusalem.

Date: The books of Ezra and Nehemiah cover almost a century of history. Ezra 1–6 covers 537–515 BC and Ezra 7–Nehemiah 13 covers 458–433 BC. It is not clear when the books were written and finalized. It is quite possible that the books were finished as late as 400 BC, though some scholars argue that the final form of the books might have been finished as late as 300 BC.

Setting: Because of Israel's unfaithfulness, God punished Israel. In 722 BC, the Assyrians conquered and exiled the northern kingdom of Israel. In 586 BC, the Babylonians destroyed and exiled the southern kingdom of Judah. Babylon itself was taken over by the Persian king Cyrus in 539 BC. Ezra and Nehemiah mention four Persian kings: Cyrus (who reigned between 559–530 BC), Darius I (521–486 BC), Xerxes I or Ahasuerus (485–465 BC), and Artaxerxes I (465–424 BC). These kings expanded the Persian empire westward, including into Egypt and parts of Greece. The power and influence of the Persian empire lasted until 330 BC, when the Macedonian Alexander the Great defeated the Persian armies and entered the cities of Susa and Persepolis.

Cyrus the Great reorganized the empire into administrative provinces or districts. Jerusalem was part of the Arabian province. After praying to God, Nehemiah, a cupbearer of the Persian King Artxerxes I, requested permission and support from the king to return and rebuild the walls of Jerusalem. The king granted Nehemiah's request and named him governor of Judea and Jerusalem the administrative center of the region. The story of Ezra and Nehemiah allows us to see the precarious life the Jews in Jerusalem had. The dangers were more than just physical: the very existence of the community as the remnant of God's people was in danger. Ezra and Nehemiah responded to these very concrete and immediate physical, social, political, and spiritual needs.

Themes

Faithfulness of God. Isaiah 40–50 anticipated the restoration of Israel to the land after the exile as a second exodus. The first section of Ezra suggests that the restoration of Jews under the leadership of Zerubbabel and Joshua was another exodus. God showed his faithfulness to his promises through his prophets and restored Israel to the Promised Land.

Cupbearer

This official court position was a great responsibility in the ancient world. The cupbearer ensured that the king's wine was safe—not poisoned. It was a position of great trust and closeness. Nehemiah's official position as cupbearer granted him direct interaction with King Artaxerxes I and an amount of intimacy—note that the king perceived that Nehemiah was sad (Neh. 2:2).

Divine Providence. Although the main actions in the books (returning to Jerusalem to build the temple, sending Ezra to teach God's law to the restored Jews, sending Nehemiah to rebuild the walls of Jerusalem) appear on the surface to be the Persian king's initiative, the books show that God is acting behind the scenes to fulfill his promises.

Consecration. In a way, Ezra and Nehemiah are the stories of two walls. The wall of stone built by Nehemiah physically separated the Israelites from their enemies. This wall provided safety to the community to be consecrated to God. The second "wall" provided a spiritual and moral boundary that kept the community safe to be God's covenant people and to avoid the sins of the past. This "wall" consisted of God's law, which Ezra was entrusted to teach. God's law provided a separation from other people and allowed the Jews to consecrate themselves to God.

God's People. As a community of builders, they learned to survive in their unstable situation, while also hoping for a more complete restoration of Israel's good fortunes.

Key People

The Cyrus Cylinder. A nine-inch long clay cylinder found at ancient Babylon, dating to around 539 BC. The cylinder narrates Cyrus's conquest of Babylon in 539 BC. It also includes the king's edict to allow exiled peoples to return to their homelands and restore their religious and social lives.

Ezra — Scribe and teacher of God's law. He returned to Jerusalem with the second wave of Jews from Babylon.

Nehemiah — Cupbearer of the Persian King Artaxerxes. He led more exiles back to Jerusalem, became governor, and led the rebuilding of the walls of the city.

Cyrus — Persian king who allowed the Jews to return to Jerusalem to rebuild the temple.

Zerubbabel — Descendant of David, he led the Jews back to Jerusalem to rebuild the temple.

Darius I — Persian king who supported the rebuilding of the temple in Jerusalem.

Artaxerxes I — Persian king who commissioned Ezra to go to Jerusalem to teach God's law to the returned exiles.

Sanballat — Governor of Samaria, he attempted to hinder the rebuilding of the walls of Jerusalem (Neh. 2–6).

Tobiah — An Ammonite official who tried to thwart the rebuilding of the walls of Jerusalem (Neh. 2–6).

Key Verses

Praise be to the LORD, the God of our ancestors, who has put it into the king's heart to bring honor to the house of the LORD in Jerusalem in this way.—Ezra 7:27

They stood where they were and read from the Book of the Law of the LORD their God for a quarter of the day, and spent another quarter in confession and in worshiping the LORD their God.—Neh. 9:3

Being God's People

Then: The returned exiles faced a hostile environment in Jerusalem. The peoples of the land, most likely people's from many places of the ancient Near East that were brought in from their homelands, represented a physical and spiritual danger for the community. Ezra and Nehemiah erected walls to protect the people and allow them to settle once again in the land. The walls of Jerusalem represented God's protective care for his people. The walls of the Torah—Moses' Law—represented God's desire to consecrate his people and make them holy.

Now: Jesus' prayer expresses a view similar to Ezra and Nehemiah: "My prayer is not that you take them out of the world but that you protect them from the evil one. They are not of the world, even as I am not of it. Sanctify them by the truth; your word is truth" (John 17:15–17). Jesus' prayer "builds a wall" of protection around his disciples as they remain in the world. Just like Ezra's wall—Torah—Jesus' wall is also God's Word.

Jesus in Ezra and Nehemiah

The books of Ezra and Nehemiah show the fulfillment of God's promises to restore Israel. However, the promise was only partially fulfilled. The complete fulfillment of God's promise occurs in Jesus.

Temple Time Line

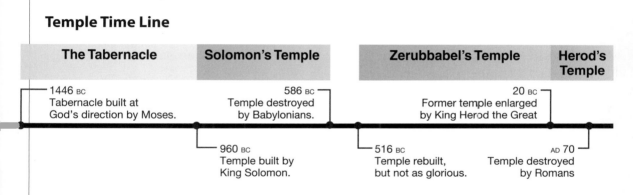

The Tabernacle	Solomon's Temple	Zerubbabel's Temple	Herod's Temple
1446 BC Tabernacle built at God's direction by Moses.	586 BC Temple destroyed by Babylonians.	20 BC Former temple enlarged by King Herod the Great	
	960 BC Temple built by King Solomon.	516 BC Temple rebuilt, but not as glorious.	AD 70 Temple destroyed by Romans

ESTHER

COURAGE IN DIFFICULT TIMES

Esther Denouncing Haman by Ernest Normand

Purpose

The book of Esther is the story of an orphan, Jewish girl thrown into a world of political intrigue and power plays in the Persian court in Susa. Although the book does not mention God, his hand is seen throughout the story. Esther became a queen and had to make choices that required much courage and faith. The book offers reassurance that even when God seems to be absent from our world or suffering, he is ever present, interested, and ready to act. The book affirms in narrative form what the apostle Paul affirms in his letter to the Romans: "And we know that in all things God works for the good of those who love him, who have been called according to his purpose" (Rom. 8:28). Another important purpose of the book is establishing the celebration of Purim. This feast celebrates God's deliverance of his people from the Haman's evil plans.

600 BC		500 BC		400 BC
2 Chronicles		Ezra & Nehemiah		
2 Kings			Esther	
Divided Kingdom	Exile		Restoration of Jerusalem	

- Fall of Nineveh 612
- First exile of Jews to Babylon 605
- Second exile of Jews to Babylon 597
- Judah falls to Babylonia 586

- Cyrus's edict allows Jews to return 538
- Rebuilding of temple 536–516
- Haggai c. 520
- Zechariah c. 520–518

- Ezra sent to Judah 457
- Nehemiah governs Judah 444–432
- Malachi (date unknown)

Outline

1. Introductions: The Setting and the Characters (1–2)
   a. King Xerxes and Queen Vashti (1:1–2:4)
   b. Mordecai and Esther (2:5–2:23)

2. Of Banquets, Plots, and Survival (3:1–9:19)
   a. Haman's plot to destroy the Jews (3)
   b. Mordecai and Esther take action; Esther's banquet (4:1–5:8)
   c. Haman tries to destroy Mordecai; the king honors Mordecai
      and Haman is humiliated (5:9–6:14)
   d. Esther's second banquet; Haman's plot is revealed (7)
   e. Haman is destroyed and the safety of the Jews is assured (8:1–9:19)

3. Time to Celebrate: Purim (9:20–10:3)
   a. The Feast of Purim is established (9:20–9:32)
   b. Mordecai becomes the second in rank in the kingdom (10)

The Book of Esther

In the Hebrew Bible, the book of Esther is part of the *Megillot*, which means "scrolls." Esther is read during the Feast of Purim, which happens on the 14th or 15th of Adar—in February or March. The Dead Sea Scrolls, an ancient library of biblical books and other ancient writings discovered in 1947, contain copies of all books of the Old Testament except for Esther.

Background

Author: Although unknown, the author demonstrates firsthand knowledge of the Persian court. This knowledge suggests that the author could have been a Jew in exile around the time the events happened.

Date: It is not possible to know with precision when the book was written. However, we can narrow down the time of writing to the period between when Xerxes I (also known as Ahasuerus) reigned over Persia (486–465 BC) and the fall of the Persian empire to the Macedonian conqueror Alexander the Great (331 BC).

Setting: The events in the book of Esther occurred while the Jews were in exile. Around the middle of the fifth century BC, some Jews had returned to the Promised Land (see the books of Ezra and Nehemiah). However, many Jews remained in Babylon and Persia, as the stories of Daniel and Esther show.

The book of Esther is notable for its lack of references to God. The lack of references to God is especially noticeable when considering that the events in the book happened while the Jews were in exile in Persia. God's people had been for decades in a hostile environment, away from the Promised Land, and without a temple. If they had spent many years learning how to be God's people with God dwelling in their midst, now they needed to learn how to be God's people away from the land, without a temple, and surrounded by people with different beliefs.

THE PERSIAN EMPIRE

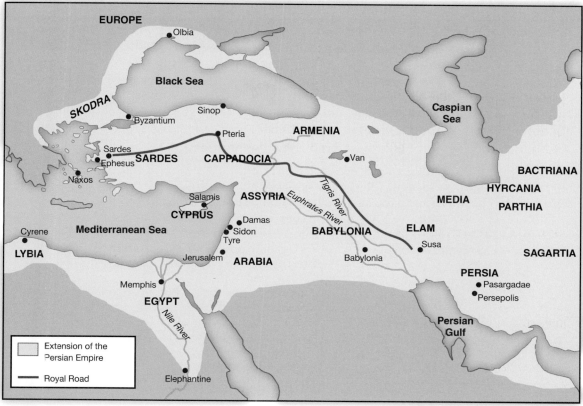

Themes

- God's protects his people even when he appears absent.
- God blesses courage and faithfulness in his people.
- God is faithful to his promises.
- Human wickedness is foolish and will not go unpunished.

Key Verses

"For if you remain silent at this time, relief and deliverance for the Jews will arise from another place, but you and your father's family will perish. And who knows but that you have come to your royal position for such a time as this?" Then Esther sent this reply to Mordecai: "Go, gather together all the Jews who are in Susa, and fast for me. Do not eat or drink for three days, night or day. I and my attendants will fast as you do. When this is done, I will go to the king, even though it is against the law. And if I perish, I perish."—Est. 4:14–16

Purim

The word *pur* is Akkadian—the language of ancient Babylon and Assyria. The biblical writer explains that the word *pur* means "lot" (Est. 9:24). Haman cast lots to choose a day to destroy the Jews. However, God's plans were different. Instead of destroying the Jews, God chose that day to deliver them and grant them victory. The feast of Purim derives its name from this word.

Key People

Character	Genealogy	Actions in History
King Ahasuerus (Xerxes)	■ Persian king ■ Son of Darius I of the royal Persian line	■ The king in the book of Esther ■ Invaded Greece, but later defeated by Greece ■ Assassinated by courtiers
Queen Vashti	■ Queen of King Xerxes ■ May be Amestris, daughter of Otanes	■ Loses her position as queen for disobeying the king's orders
Mordecai	■ Son of Jair (Esther 2:5) of the first royal line of Israel (Kish/Saul 1 Sam. 9:1)	■ Raised his cousin Esther ■ Prevented the assassination of the king ■ Became the king's main advisor
Esther	■ Mordecai's cousin	■ Lost both of her parents; raised by her cousin. ■ Wins over the king to become queen in a dangerous time ■ Saves the Jewish people from extermination
Haman	■ Born of the royal line of the Amalekites (line of King Agag).	■ King's main advisor ■ Plots the destruction of all the Jews in the Persian empire ■ Is hung on the gallows

Being God's People

Then: God promises to be with his people (Gen. 28:15; Ex. 33:14; Isa. 43:2; Matt. 28:20). The book of Esther shows that, although God is apparently absent in the story, his protection is ever present with his people.

Now: Faith is active. God expects us to exercise our faith, as Esther did, especially in times of danger, uncertainty, or suffering. The activity is not moved by "blind faith." Rather, by a faith that knows God to be present, powerful, and willing to act on our behalf.

Jesus in Esther

Although God is not explicitly named in the book, his presence is unmistakable throughout the story. In our busy lives, we often go on living as if Jesus were not present in our lives. Yet, as in Esther, he is ever present and interested in our lives.

Queen Esther by Andrea Castagno

WISDOM AND SONGS FOR LIFE

What Are the Poetry and Wisdom Books?

This section is composed of five books, four of them are written in poetry: Job (most of it), Psalms, Proverbs, and Song of Songs. Ecclesiastes is written mostly in prose, with a long poem at the end of the book. These books are different from the rest of the Old Testament because they do not deal directly with Israel's life at a specific time in history. Rather, they reflect on the life of God's people and their relationship with God in a more general way.

Hebrew poetry is not always easy to distinguish from prose. Prose is writing that reproduces the way we normally speak. Besides being the Word of God, the Old Testament is also beautiful, carefully written literature. So prose can be as beautiful as poetry. Poetry exists in other books of the Old Testament: the song of Moses in Exodus, the song of Deborah in Judges, and many passages in the prophets.

Wisdom books deal with questions that affect humans everywhere and at any time: Questions about human suffering, death, what makes for a good life, knowledge for living. Poetry has a unique ability to express deep feelings and thoughts in affective and beautiful ways. For that reason, poetry is the perfect instrument for wisdom.

Poetry & Wisdom

Job
Psalms
Proverbs
Ecclesiastes
Song of Songs

Poetry and Wisdom Books Today

These books continue to be important for Christians today. Their main themes— praise and prayer, guidance for holy lives, our inner relationship with God and others around us—and their powerful, evocative language continue to shape the hearts and minds of God's people. As we read Psalms, meditate on Proverbs, are moved by the beauty of Songs of Songs, and wrestle with the difficult topics of Job and Ecclesiastes, the Holy Spirit transforms and renews our hearts and minds.

How to Read Poetry and Wisdom

In English, poetry is characterized primarily by meter and rhyme. Old Testament poetry is characterized primarily by terseness, parallelism, and imagery. Hebrew poetry is composed with short lines that say much with a few words. It is, perhaps, because of this characteristic that poetry is able to express concepts that are almost impossible to express otherwise.

Parallel lines are an important feature of biblical poetry. For example, English-language proverbs normally have one line—"a penny saved is a penny earned."

Hebrew poetry normally has two or three lines—"A fool finds pleasure in evil conduct, but a man of understanding delights in wisdom" (Prov. 10:23). The sense of the poem is found in the interplay of these lines. Parallelism means that the second line of the verse advances the thought of the first line in some way. Determining how this movement occurs allows us to understand the sense and meaning of the poem.

There are different kinds of parallelism; the following examples from the book of Proverbs are the most common types of parallelism in the Wisdom and Poetry Books.

Kings take pleasure in honest lips; they value a man who speaks the truth (16:13).	In this example, we find these parallels: ■ *Kings* is the main subject of the whole verse. ■ *Taking pleasure* is parallel to *value*. However, valuing something is a step beyond merely taking pleasure. ■ *Honest lips* is parallel to *a man who speaks the truth*. Although both expressions mean the same, the second one further specifies what honest lips are. ■ Some call this type of parallelism *synonymous parallelism*.
A fool finds pleasure in evil conduct, but a man of understanding delights in wisdom (10:23).	This verse presents a contrast which provides the parallelism. ■ *A fool* is contrasted with *a man of understanding*. ■ Another parallel is the action of each person: one *finds pleasure* whereas the other *delights*. The two concepts are closely related, though the first one seems more impulsive. ■ The true contrast is on what each one finds delight in: the fool finds pleasure in *evil conduct*, while the man of understanding delights in *wisdom*. ■ The final contrast is the key to the verse. Like the rest of Proverbs, the book invites its readers to delight in wisdom. ■ Some call this contrasting parallel *antithetical parallelism*.

In addition to terseness and parallel lines, Hebrew poetry also contains heightened imagery. Powerful images—metaphors—have a way of dwelling in and sparking our imaginations so we understand God's revelation to us in exceptional ways. These are images such as God is king—of course he is more than a king; in fact, he is the King of kings, the image can only go so far—shepherd, rock, and so on. In Proverbs, wisdom is personalized as a woman. And, of course, the wonderful, though often difficult to understand, images in the book of Song of Songs: eyes are compared to doves, hair to a flock of goats, teeth to newly shorn ewes, neck to the tower of David, and so on. Today, one could hardly use those images to describe a beloved. This shows we must be careful when understanding the images of poetical texts, which draw from the cultural world of ancient Israel.

JOB

WISDOM, SUFFERING, AND GOD'S PEOPLE

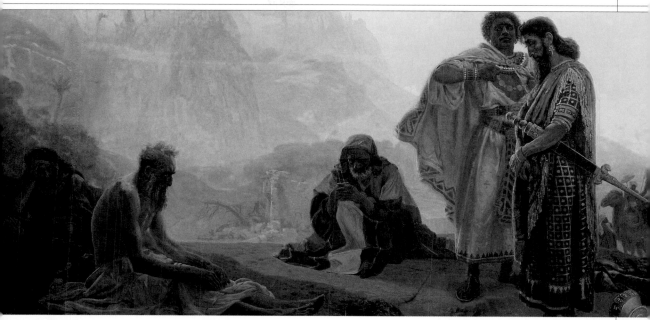

Job and His Friends by Ilya Repin

Purpose

The book of Job looks at the problem of human suffering. The book concludes that to deal with suffering, believers do not need knowledge but trust. It is the story of a just man who, unaware of the conversations happening in the celestial court between God and Satan, finds his life overthrown. His painful experience and intense conversations invite us to reflect about suffering and justice.

The conversations between Job and his friends—Eliphaz, Bildad, Zophar, and Elihu—show the limits of human wisdom. What the book of Job establishes is that God is sovereign over all created beings and nature. God is far beyond our experience and understanding. Our wisdom can never fully fathom his ways and plans.

God created all things. He is in control of the universe. Most often, we cannot see or understand his rule behind the scenes. However, God wants us to trust in his wisdom, his goodness, and his plans. At the end of the book, Job comes to know that there is a good, holy, just, and compassionate God who loves him and cares for him.

Outline

1. Introduction in Prose (1:1–2:13)
   a. Job, a righteous person (1:1–5)
   b. First test (1:6–22)
   c. Second test (2:1–13)

2. Cycle of Dialogues as Poetry (3:1–27:23)
   a. Job's lament (3:1–26)
   b. First cycle (4:1–14:22)
   c. Second cycle (15:1–21:34)
   d. Third cycle (22:1–27:23)

3. Poem about Wisdom (28:1–28)

4. Monologues as Poetry (29:1–42:6)
   a. Job's final speech (29:1–31:40)
   b. Elihu's monologue (32:1–37:24)
   c. Divine monologue (38:1–42:6)

5. Conclusion in Prose (42:7–17)
   a. God rebukes Job's friends (42:7–9)
   b. God restores Job (42:10–17)

Job Rebuked by His Friends by William Blake

Background

Author and Date: The book of Job is an anonymous work. Although we can read in between the lines to find out some characteristics about the author, we do not know enough to decide who the author might have been or when the book was written. The story seems to take place around the time when Abraham, Isaac, and Jacob were alive. Some scholars believe that Moses was the author of the book.

Other scholars believe that, based on oral traditions, a wisdom teacher during the time of the kings (possibly around the time of King Solomon) wrote the book of Job. Others suggest that the book was written during or after the Babylonian exile (around 586 BC).

However, the themes of the book are relevant for all people in all places and at all times regardless of who wrote the book or when it was written.

The Story: Think of the book of Job as a sandwich. The book has two frames, the bread in the sandwich, written in prose. In a sandwich, the slices hold and give structure to the most important part of the meal, the center: the meat with the vegetables and cheese. Without the center, the sandwich would be only two slices of bread. Without the bread, the center would be a very different meal. To enjoy it as a sandwich, the meal must be eaten together. So, with the book of Job, the prose bookends give structure to the poetical sections in the middle.

In the first prose section (the bread) we learn about God's conversation with Satan. Satan appears to question Job's integrity, arguing that he worships and trusts God only because God provides for him and protects him. In reality, Satan is questioning God's integrity. Job's refusal to sin shuts Satan's argument down.

The theological problem about God's integrity has been solved, but Job is still left with his suffering. And the series of dialogues and monologues (the meat) begin with Job expressing his terrible grief. Three of his friends come to console him: Eliphaz, Bildad, and Zophar. Their speeches move from words of encouragement and empathy to accusations against

Job's integrity. Throughout the dialogues, Job reaffirms his integrity and innocence. Job's friends are wisdom teachers, so they are using traditional wisdom to persuade Job.

The speeches of Job's friends grow progressively shorter—the order of the speeches is always Eliphaz, Bildad, and Zophar. Eventually, Job's arguments make them remain quiet. Job defends his integrity with great passion. Job appeals to the covenant. He complains that although he had been faithful to the covenant, God refuses to play by the rules! (Job 9:1–35).

After Job's friends run out of arguments, a new friend shows up, Elihu. Elihu says in his speech that although he is young, his wisdom should not be brushed off. He makes similar arguments as the other friends, and concludes that Job is suffering because he has sinned. Although Elihu does not really add anything new to the discussion, the repetition of the arguments emphasizes the inability of human wisdom to fully understand suffering.

Throughout his speeches, Job requests a personal interview with God to have a chance to defend his innocence (23:2–7). Unexpectedly, he gets his chance when God speaks to him from a storm. However, rather than answering Job's many questions and challenges, God raises questions of his own. God's questions relate to the creation and operation of the universe, as well as the wisdom and power necessary to care for the creation.

The divine speeches do not answer Job's questions. Rather, they move the focus from Job's suffering to God. When it comes to suffering, the answers are not found in human wisdom. The answers to the human predicament, whether it is suffering, or sin, or grief, or anything else, are found in God, in focusing and trusting the God who created and sustains creation.

Job is left speechless. He acknowledges God's power, confesses his own ignorance and limitations, and sees God in a new light. He knows God. And that knowledge, not the reasons for his suffering, leaves him satisfied. Job finds comfort in God's presence and power.

In the story, in his speech, God replies to those questioning his honor. His ways are not our ways, and his thoughts are not our thoughts. He also replies in the last prose section (the other slice of bread) to Job's friends, who misrepresent God and try to place him in a box, acting as if they fully understand his ways and plans. God defends Job and rebukes Job's friends. To confirm God's words about Job—God had called Job blameless and upright (1:8)—he instructs Job's friends, "So now take seven bulls and seven rams and go to my servant Job and sacrifice a burnt offering for yourselves. My servant Job will pray for you, and I will accept his prayer and not deal with you according to your folly. You have not spoken the truth about me, as my servant Job has" (42:8).

Themes

Divine Wisdom. Although God has revealed to us his wisdom, especially in relation to Jesus and his work of salvation, divine wisdom is far beyond human ability or imagination. God's wisdom can be seen in his works of creation.

Divine Power. God's creative power did not stop when he finished the universe. God is engaged with the world, ruling it, caring for it, and keeping the powers of evil in check.

Human Suffering. The book of Job does not answer the question of why suffering exists. Instead, the book shows that trusting in God's wisdom, power, and goodness is a better comfort to those who suffer than having an answer.

Retribution. The story provides a correction for the basic idea of retribution. In the books of Deuteronomy, Proverbs, many Psalms, and many other sections of the Old Testament, the teaching of retribution correctly teaches that if you sin, then you will suffer. However, Job's friends turn the teaching on its head. They argued, if you are suffering, then you must have sinned. The book of Job shows that to be a wrong teaching.

Key Verses

Naked I came from my mother's womb, and naked I will depart. The LORD gave and the LORD has taken away; may the name of the LORD be praised.—Job 1:21

I know that my redeemer lives, and that in the end he will stand on the earth. And after my skin has been destroyed, yet in my flesh I will see God.—Job 19:25–26

My ears had heard of you but now my eyes have seen you. Therefore I despise myself and repent in dust and ashes.—Job 42:5–6

Being God's People

Then: Job is not identified as an Israelite in the story. However, God refers to him as "my servant Job" (1:8). Job represents all of God's people, all those who are God's servants. Human suffering is universal, and people suffering often want answers. Job realized that he was not asking the most relevant question. It was not just a question of suffering or justice. Rather, it was a question of trust.

Now: We cannot fully explain the existence of evil. However, God wants our trust. To trust God we must know him, just like Job knew him. We need a personal encounter with that wise, powerful, and good God who met Job from the storm. But we do not need a storm to meet this God. We now can meet him in the person of Jesus Christ, through the Holy Spirit.

Jesus in Job

Jesus experienced suffering and can empathize with our own suffering (Heb. 4:15). Jesus, the innocent and righteous servant, suffered in our place and paid the price of our sin. This same Jesus invites us to meet him, have a personal relationship with him, and rest in him: "Come to me, all you who are weary and burdened, and I will give you rest" (Matt. 11:28). Trusting in Jesus does not give us all the answers to our many doubts and questions. However, trusting in him gives abundant life, true and deep peace, and comfort in times of suffering.

PSALMS

Purpose

The book of Psalms is a compilation of many songs, by many authors, over a long span of time. The book of Psalms is a book of songs and prayers for God's people. The psalms provide us with the vocabulary of God's people for worship. How do we approach this holy, awesome, and terrifying God? What words can we use to express our love, joy, praise, sadness, anger, frustration, doubts, need for forgiveness, and loneliness to God?

Because the psalms are poems, they have a wonderful way to express the deepest emotions of our hearts. Whether in times of suffering and sadness or joy and celebration, the psalms have been close to God's people at all times and places. Poetry relies on heightened language and powerful images. The psalms are terse and beautiful. They say much with a few words and can express deep feelings that are not easily spoken.

Psalms

The ancient Greek translation of the Hebrew Bible, the Septuagint, calls this book *psalmos*, which refers to stringed instruments that accompany songs. The word *psalmos* is also used to translate the Hebrew word *mizmor* meaning "songs." The Hebrew name for the book of Psalms is *tehillim* which means "praises."

Psalms is also a book of instruction. It might not be coincidence that the psalms are divided into five books, just like the Pentateuch, a book that instructs us what it means to be God's people. However, unlike the Pentateuch, the psalms do not give instructions about how to pray and praise God. Rather, like Jesus did when his disciples asked him to teach them how to pray, the psalms show us how to do it. As the fourth-century theologian Athanasius famously wrote, "Most of Scripture speaks *to* us; the Psalms speak *for* us."

Finally, the psalms express God's people's longing for the coming of the Messiah. God had promised through his prophets that a descendant of King David would always sit on the throne of Israel. The promise of this anointed King, the Messiah, became one with God's other promises to restore and redeem his people and the world. Although the psalms are not prophecies in the same sense as the prophetic books, they do anticipate, so they speak prophetically about the coming of the Messiah. The New Testament quotes or alludes to many psalms in connection to Jesus.

Outline

1. Book 1 (Psalms 1–41)

2. Book 2 (Psalms 42–72)

3. Book 3 (Psalms 73–89)

4. Book 4 (Psalms 90–106)

5. Book 5 (Psalms 107–150)

David Playing the Harp by Jan de Bray

Background

Author: The book of Psalms is a collection of collections. These collections were put together at different times and for purposes we might never know. However, when the songs and prayers were put together, along with an introduction (Ps. 1) and a conclusion (146–150), the book of Psalms became a learning tool for God's people.

One hundred and sixteen psalms have a title. It is not certain if the titles were part of the original writing or were added at later dates. However, they do provide important and helpful information. In general, the titles give information about the psalm's author, historical background, melody, use during worship, and a few other items. According to the titles, some of the named authors of psalms were: David (73 times), Asaph (12 times), the sons of Korah (11 times), Solomon (2 times), Jeduthun (4 times), and Heman, Etan, and Moses (1 time each).

Date: Dating of individual psalms is difficult. The poems were collected over a long period. Most were composed between the time of David (around 1000 BC) and the time of Ezra (450 BC).

Psalms 1–150

Five Books	I	II	III	IV	V
	(1–41) Prayers of lament and expressions of confidence in God dominate this book.	(42–72) Communal laments dominate the prayers in this book. The book ends with a royal psalm.	(73–89) In this book, the prayers of lament and distress are more intense and bleak.	(90–106) This book presents the answers to the bleakness of book III. The theme of "The Lord Reigns" dominates this book.	(107–150) This book declares that God is in control, will redeem his people, and praises God's faithfulness and goodness.
Two Main Collections	**First Collection** (2–89)			**Second Collection** (90–145)	
	Collections within the Collections: 1. Introduction: Torah Psalms (Ps. 1) 2. Two Davidic Collections (3–41 and 51–72) 3. Two Collections of Temple Musicians Korah (42–49; 84–85; 87–88) Asaphat (50; 73–83)			Collections within the Collections: 1. "The Lord Reigns" (93–100) 2. Hallelujah Psalms (111–118) 3. Songs of Ascent (120–134) 4. Davidic Collection (138–145) 5. Conclusion: Hallelujah Psalms (146–150)	

Genres in the Psalms

Genres are different kinds of writings—or paintings, for example—that share specific elements of content and form. Most of the time we read the psalms in a devotional way. This kind of reading is refreshing for our spirits and leads us closer to God and other fellow believers. However, other times we may want to explore a psalm deeper. In those times, knowing about their genres will help us in our spiritual exploration. Each genre lists a sample of representative psalms for each of the following main genres in the book of Psalms.

The Hymn. The beautiful and glorious songs of praise to God characterize the psalms. These hymns highlight God's character and deeds like his goodness, majesty, and virtue (Ps. 8, 19, 29, 33, 65, 100, 145), or his righteous Kingship over all of creation (47, 93–99).

The Lament. Curiously, the psalms of lament outnumber any other type of psalm. This fact might reflect the messiness of life, the many reasons for suffering and sadness. However, the psalms do not typically end in lament. They move from lament to praise, from grief to joy. The conclusion of the psalms, the magnificent hallelujah songs 146–150, reflect that with God, all tears will be dried, all sufferings will turn to joy, and all injustices will receive the proper and righteous response. There are individual prayers of lament (13, 22, 31, 42–43, 57, 139, etc.) and community laments (12, 44, 80, 85, 90, 94). These prayers provide us with the language to ask God to intervene in our favor. They might include a plea to God for help, the specific cause of the suffering, a confession of faith or innocence, a curse of the enemies, confidence in God's response, and a song of thanksgiving for God's intervention. Prayers of lament may include one or more of these elements.

Songs of Thanksgiving. These songs focus on thanking God for his answer to a specific request. The request is not always explicit in the song, though it seems that they are connected to laments. Songs of thanksgiving can also be individual (32, 34, 92, 116, 118, 138) or communal (107, 124).

Songs Related to the Temple. Some songs were to remind the community of their covenant with God (50, 81). Other songs, royal psalms, make mention of King David or his descendants (2, 18, 110). Songs of Zion celebrate God's presence with his people (46, 84, 122). It appears that the singing of these psalms took place during the worship at the temple in Jerusalem.

Teaching Psalms. Songs have a unique way of teaching the people who hear and sing them. The wisdom psalms use traditional wisdom themes to guide and shape the view of those singing them (37, 49, 73). Closely related to them, other psalms praise the wonders of God's law and encourage God's people to obey it and delight in it (1, 19, 119).

Themes

The Lord Reigns. This is the main claim of the book of Psalms—and the whole Bible. No matter who or what claims control over creation, God is the rightful and just ruler of all. Psalms 47, 93, and 95–99 offer a splendid and beautiful account of the claim that the Lord reigns.

Creation. One of the best examples of God's rule over all is creation. God created everything and sustains it with his power, wisdom, and justice (93, 104, 29).

Salvation. The Lord reigns because he has already defeated evil and has redeemed his people (47, 68, 98, 114).

Judgment. The Lord reigns because his judgment is worthy, righteous, wise, and universal (50, 82, 94, 96, 97, 105).

God's People. God's people are "the people of his pasture, the flock under his care" (95:7; 100:3). God redeemed them (74) and has intervened in their history with power and grace (44, 74, 77, 80).

The King. Unlike other cultures surrounding ancient Israel, the kings were not worshiped or held in higher esteem than other Israelites (see, for example, the story of Naboth's vineyard in 1 Kings 21). The importance of the kings, however, was that God chose them to work through them to carry on his divine purposes. Toward the end of Psalms, the focus is more on the future king who is to come, who will restore and redeem Israel. This promised King, the Messiah, became the emphasis of Israel's hope and longing.

Key Verses

O Lord, our Lord, how majestic is your name in all the earth! You have set your glory above the heavens.—Ps. 8:1

The Lord is my shepherd, I lack nothing.—Ps. 23:1

Have mercy on me, O God, according to your unfailing love; according to your great compassion blot out my transgressions. Wash away all my iniquity and cleanse me from my sin.—Ps. 51:1–2

Shout for joy to the Lord, all the earth. Worship the Lord with gladness, come before him with joyful songs.—Ps. 100:1–2

I lift up my eyes to the mountains—where does my help come from? My help comes from the Lord, the Maker of heaven and earth.—Ps. 121:1–2

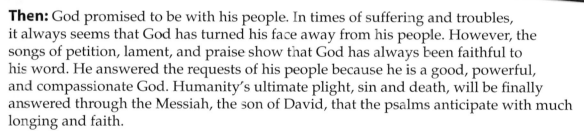

Being God's People

Then: God promised to be with his people. In times of suffering and troubles, it always seems that God has turned his face away from his people. However, the songs of petition, lament, and praise show that God has always been faithful to his word. He answered the requests of his people because he is a good, powerful, and compassionate God. Humanity's ultimate plight, sin and death, will be finally answered through the Messiah, the son of David, that the psalms anticipate with much longing and faith.

Now: The Messiah has come and has defeated sin and death! But we still live in a world filled with trials, temptations, and suffering. However, the songs of petition, lament, and praise in Psalms invite us to trust that God is always present, that he reigns over all, and he will intervene in the perfect time and with the perfect answers to our needs.

Jesus in Psalms

When Jesus said that all of the Scriptures spoke of him he specifically mentioned the psalms (Luke 24:44). The New Testament writers quote many of the psalm texts in connection to Jesus being the promised Messiah. In Acts 4:11, the apostle Peter cites Psalm 118:22, "the stone you builders rejected, which has become the cornerstone," as he explained the identity of Jesus. Psalms 2, 16, 22, 69, and 110 are the most quoted psalms in the New Testament. All of them anticipate and explain the identity of the promised King.

PROVERBS

A GUIDE TO GODLY LIVING

Purpose

The purpose of the book of Proverbs is to persuade and instruct God's people to gain wisdom. The book invites readers to make a decision. The choice is not only a rational one; it involves desires and emotions, as well as intelligence and discernment. The writer attempts to capture the reader's will by appealing to the imagination.

Proverbs invites its readers to make a life-changing choice. Choosing wisdom over folly changes people's lives in a powerful way. The readers "hear" from both Lady Wisdom and Lady Folly. Their invitations become alternatives between life and death. When reading the book of Proverbs, we must allow it to touch our emotions and our wills. We must allow ourselves not just to choose Lady Wisdom but also to love and pursue her.

The introduction to the book states its own purpose: "for gaining wisdom and instruction; for understanding words of insight; for receiving instruction in prudent behavior, doing what is right and just and fair" (Prov. 1:2–3).

We must remember that biblical proverbs are not promises, nor are they universal or always applicable. Proverbs are not adequate for every occasion. The wisdom of the proverbs is limited by their genre and good timing for their use (26:9; 15:23).

Outline

Background

Author: The book of Proverbs is an anthology of different authors who wrote at different times. Proverbs 1:1, 10:1, and 25:1 affirm that King Solomon, King David's son, was the main author. Proverbs 25:1 also affirms that "the men of Hezekiah king of Judah" copied them. The book also recognizes other contributors: Wise men (22:17; 24:23), Agur (30:1), and Lemuel (31:1). However, nothing is known about these writers. Although 1 Kings 4:32 affirms that Solomon wrote 3,000 proverbs, we should not assume that Solomon wrote all or most of the book of Proverbs.

Date: As a collection, the book was written in a span from the 900s BC to the 700s BC. The book may have been put together in its final form at a later time, perhaps even after the Jews returned from the exile in Babylon after 539 BC.

Setting: Proverbs do not occur exclusively in the Bible. The book of Proverbs is an example of a wider category of wisdom literature. In ancient Egypt and Mesopotamia, wisdom writings played an important role. In those societies, wisdom writings belonged to the royal court. Wise teachers instructed their royal students for important positions within the kingdom. From scribes to nobles, wisdom taught the proper—wise—behavior in the court, correct speech, and an understanding of society and the world that allowed them to serve the ruler effectively.

Themes

Wisdom. The whole book presents an appeal to choose wisdom over all other things:

■ God created wisdom (8:22–23).

■ God used wisdom to create the universe (8:24–31).

■ God reveals and is the source of wisdom (2:6–7; 30:5–6).

■ The beginning of wisdom is "the fear of the Lord" (1:7; 2:5; 9:10; 10:27; 14:27).

■ Wisdom is desirable over all things (4:7–9; 8:10–11).

Humanity. Proverbs is an invitation to accurately identify the source of all wisdom and the limits of human wisdom:

- Humans are God's creation (29:13).

- Humans delude themselves (12:15; 14:12; 16:2; 25; 28:26).

- The heart is central and reveals humanity's true character (27:19).

- Humans are inherently foolish (22:15).

Description of a Wise Person. Wisdom is not something easily taught. As with many important things, it is easier to *show* what a wise person looks like than describe wisdom. Wise people are recognized by their:

- *Character*—they are righteous (13:5–6), loyal (16:6), humble (2:5, 9), teachable (12:1, 15), self-controlled and not rash (17:27), forgiving (10:12), thoughtful (13:16), honest (12:22), do not boast (27:2), do not reveal secrets (17:9), do not slander (6:12), and are peaceful (12:16).

- *Speech*—they understand that words have power (10:11) and limit their words (14:23).

- *Relationship with Spouse*—they recognize that their spouse is from God (18:22), acknowledge their spouse as their crowning glory (12:4), and are faithful to their spouse (5:15–20).

- *Relationships with Children*—they acknowledge the need for wisdom in their children's lives (1–9), recognize their children's natural condition (22:15), understand children can be guided (19:18), and they love and discipline them (13:24).

- *Relationships with Other People*—they choose kind friends (22:24–25), value and are loyal to their friends (27:10), behave fairly and justly with all (3:27–28), are considerate (25:17), and live in peace with all (3:29).

- *Possessions*—they recognize the proper value of money (30:7–9), honor God with possessions and recognize that blessings come from God (3:9–10), recognize that foolish behavior leads to poverty (6:6–11; 10:4–5; 21:17), as do injustice and oppression (13:23; 16:8; 22:16); they are generous with possessions (3:27–28), and are kind to animals (12:10).

Kingship. In the world of ancient Israel, the king represented the people. Kings were meant to model attitudes, behaviors, and character that all people should display in their lives. Jesus, the King of kings, plays this role when he shows us what it means to be God's children. Thus, the king should: Know his place (21:1), be wise (8:15–16), be righteous (25:5), be just (28:8; 29:4, 14), have self-control (31:1–7), be compassionate (31:8–9), and be surrounded by godly people (16:13; 22:11).

Key Verses

Let love and faithfulness never leave you; bind them around your neck, write them on the tablet of your heart. Then you will win favor and a good name in the sight of God and man. Trust in the LORD with all your heart and lean not on your own understanding; in all your ways submit to him, and he will make your paths straight.—Prov. 3:3–5

The fear of the LORD is the beginning of wisdom, and knowledge of the Holy One is understanding. —Prov. 9:10

King Solomon

In their hearts humans plan their course, but the LORD establishes their steps.—Prov. 16:9

Being God's People

Then: God promised Abraham to give them a land flowing with milk and honey (Gen. 15:2–7). God was faithful to his promises and gave Abraham's children the Promised Land. However, God also gave the people the tools they needed to live in the land. God gave them the Torah (the law of Moses) and revealed to them his wisdom. Wisdom is a tool that helps people to live godly lives. Throughout the Old Testament, wisdom appears guiding God's people: Joseph was a wise man; through his wisdom, God saved Jacob's family and the world (Gen. 45:7–8). With wisdom, the Israelites built the tabernacle (Ex. 35:30–35). The prophet Hosea ends his prophecy saying: "Who is wise? Let them realize these things. Who is discerning? Let them understand. The ways of the LORD are right; the righteous walk in them, but the rebellious stumble in them" (Hos. 14:9). Luke tells us that Jesus "grew in wisdom and stature" (Luke 2:52).

Now: Today we must answer the call of wisdom: will we choose to be with Lady Wisdom or Lady Folly? Jesus' use of wisdom in his teachings shows the continued importance of wisdom for our lives (Mark 1:22; Luke 2:41–50). Even now, we still must recognize the path that takes us to life itself (Jesus Christ) from the one that leads to death and destruction (Rom. 1:22–23).

Jesus in Proverbs

Jesus embodies God's wisdom (1 Cor. 1:30). In him "are hidden all the treasures of wisdom and knowledge" (Col. 2:3). We must be careful to not confuse Jesus embodying God's wisdom with Jesus being wisdom. Lady Wisdom in Proverbs 8 is the personification of wisdom. Personification is a literary tool to make an inanimate object or concept, like wisdom, come to life as if it were a person. In Proverbs 8:22, Lady Wisdom is God's first creation (8:22), but Jesus is the eternal and uncreated Son of God.

ECCLESIASTES

SEARCHING FOR TRUTH AND MEANING

Ecclesiastes

The name of Ecclesiastes in Hebrew is *Qoheleth*, often translated as "The Preacher" or "The Teacher." The name comes from a Hebrew word, *qohelet*, which means "the one who assembles or gathers." The Greek translation of the Hebrew text uses the word *ekklesia*, from which we get the name *ekklesiastes*. It refers to the one who speaks in an assembly or gathers people into an assembly. From that idea, we derive the translation "the Teacher."

Purpose

The author of Ecclesiastes, known as the Teacher or the Preacher (1:1), wants to make sense out of life, wisdom, and truth. At first, he proposes that everything is "meaningless." After careful observation, the pursuit of all worldly pleasures, an assessment of wisdom, and an analysis of the meaning of life, he concludes that truth and meaning is found in remembering, fearing, and obeying the Creator of all.

The book's conclusion: A meaningful, fulfilling, and joyous life is not found in the frivolous pursuit of wealth, success, and pleasure. Instead, meaning and fulfillment is found when we pursue God as our number one priority—trusting and obeying God in all circumstances.

Outline

1. Introduction (1:1–11)
   Bookend: "Meaningless! Meaningless!" says the
   Teacher. "Everything is meaningless!" (1:2)

2. First Part: A Time for Everything (1:12–6:9)

3. Second Part: Death Comes to All (6:10–11:6)

4. Third Part: Remember the Creator (11:7–12:7)
   Bookend: "Meaningless! Meaningless!" says the
   Teacher. "Everything is meaningless!" (12:8)

5. In Conclusion—Trust in and Obey God
   (12:9–12:14)

Background

Author: The book is anonymous. However, the traditional view is that King Solomon authored the book of Ecclesiastes late in his life. Yet, many scholars do not believe Solomon was the author. They believe that a later, unknown person wrote the book.

Date: King Solomon reigned in Israel from 971 BC to 931 BC. If Solomon wrote Ecclesiastes, he did it late in his life. If it was a later author, most scholars believe it was written after God brought the Jews back from exile (after 539 BC).

Setting: If Solomon wrote the book, then his famous wisdom and lifestyle would give the context to the book (1 Kings 10:23). Everyone came to Israel in order to hear Solomon's wisdom. Solomon pursued worldly wealth and pleasures (1 Kings 10:22–26; 11:3). Still, his great wisdom led him to conclude that true joy and meaning is found only in the Lord.

If it was a writer after the Babylonian exile, the author was reflecting on the past history of luxury and excess. That past history led to the breaking of the covenant with God. The prophets Amos and Micah, among others, reflect the prophetic critique of these times.

Themes

Meaninglessness. It is meaningless to pursue truth and joy apart from God.

The Inevitability of Death. Wealth, power, fame, success, and frivolous pleasures are worthless pursuits because death is unavoidable.

The Certainty of God. God, and one's ambition to please God, are the only things worth pursuing.

Key Verses

"Meaningless! Meaningless!" says the Teacher. "Utterly meaningless! Everything is meaningless."—Eccl. 1:2

There is a time for everything, and a season for every activity under the heavens. —Eccl. 3:1

Remember your Creator in the days of your youth, before the days of trouble come and the years approach when you will say, "I find no pleasure in them"—before the sun and the light and the moon and the stars grow dark, and the clouds return after the rain.—Eccl. 12:1–2

Now all has been heard; here is the conclusion of the matter: Fear God and keep his commandments, for this is the duty of all mankind. For God will bring every deed into judgment, including every hidden thing, whether it is good or evil.—Eccl. 12:13–14

Being God's People

Then: The world "under the sun" is meaningless apart from God. The pursuit of joy, worth, and truth through worldly things such as success, wealth, power, and pleasure is pointless because death is inevitable. The ultimate purpose and meaning of life is seeking God and pleasing him through obedience and worship.

Prose and Poetry

Unlike the other wisdom books (Job and Proverbs) that are written in poetry, the book of Ecclesiastes is written in prose.

Now: The apostle Paul wrote, "If Christ has not been raised, your faith is futile; you are still in your sins.… If the dead are not raised, 'Let us eat and drink, for tomorrow we die'" (1 Cor. 15:17, 32). Paul's perspective on the resurrection of Christ is similar to Solomon's perspective on seeking the Creator and obeying him. Without Christ and the resurrection, all of our pursuits are meaningless. But because Jesus rose from the dead, our work, suffering, joys, and life in general are filled with meaning and purpose.

Jesus in Ecclesiastes

The end of the search for truth and meaning is Jesus Christ. Seeking worldly pleasures, wealth, or power will not lead to righteousness or salvation—only by seeking Christ and believing in his death and resurrection will we find righteousness, salvation, and true meaning: "Now this is eternal life: that they know you, the only true God, and Jesus Christ, whom you have sent" (John 17:3).

SONG OF SONGS

THE LOVE SONG

Purpose

Song of Songs begins as a courting song. Woven throughout the first three chapters is a poetic declaration of mutual love and affection between both the lover and his beloved.

Moving from courtship to wedding ceremony and banquet, Song of Songs emphasizes the beauty, passion, and intimacy found within marriage. The book illustrates the love that should exist between husband and wife.

Outline

1. The Courtship of the Lover and His Beloved (1:1–3:5)

2. The Marriage of the Groom and His Bride (3:6–5:1)

3. The Passion and Intimacy within a Loving Relationship (5:2–8:14)

Song of Songs

"Song of Songs" means the best of all songs, like "King of kings" or "Lord of lords." The book is also known as the Song of Solomon.

Background

Author: Although the title identifies King Solomon as the author (1:1), the different poems within the book seem to have been written by different authors, similar to the book of Psalms. It is possible that many of the poems were written at the time of Solomon, while a later compiler completed the book with other similar poems.

Date: King Solomon reigned for 40 years, in Israel from 971 BC to 931 BC. Because of the reflective nature of the songs, it seems that Solomon would have written toward the end of his life. Many scholars also suggest that other authors wrote some poems after the Babylonian exile in 586 BC.

Setting: The setting of the book could not have been Solomon's own marital experience, since he had 700 wives and 300 concubines (1 Kings 11:3), hardly an example of marital faithfulness! However, assuming that he was the main author of the book, Solomon did not write from his own personal experience. Rather, the book presents the way things should be within a loving, covenant relationship. More than Solomon's own life, the background to the book is the garden of Eden because the book describes what love should be, according to God's original intention for his creation.

Interpreting the Book

A long tradition has interpreted the book as an allegory that expresses love between God and his people. Most interpreters have moved away from this kind of interpretation. However, seen this way, the book can illustrate how the people of God long for intimacy with God is the same way that a lover longs for intimacy with his or her beloved.

Themes

■ **Love and Marriage.** Joy, passion, intimacy, and authentic love can exist within the gift of marriage.

■ **Love of God.** We can experience joy, passion, and intimacy within a loving relationship with God.

Key Verses

I am my beloved's and my beloved is mine.—Song of Songs 6:3

Place me like a seal over your heart, like a seal on your arm; for love is as strong as death, its jealousy unyielding as the grave. It burns like blazing fire, like a mighty flame. Many waters cannot quench love; rivers cannot sweep it away. If one were to give all the wealth of one's house for love, it would be utterly scorned.—Song of Songs 8:6–7

Being God's People

Love, intimacy, and marriage are gifts from God. Being in the presence of your beloved is intoxicating and his or her absence is awful. The love, passion, and intimacy found within the context of marriage are part of God's design.

Jesus in Song of Songs

The apostle Paul wrote, "Husbands, love your wives, just as Christ loved the church and gave himself up for her" (Eph. 5:25). The church is the bride of Christ. As Christ's bride, we are his beloved and participate in a loving, passionate, and intimate relationship with him. Although Song of Songs is not primarily an allegory of our relationship with Jesus, it is a superb example of a loving relationship with our Lord and Savior.

PROPHETIC BOOKS

REPENT, BELIEVE, AND BE RESTORED

What Are the Prophetic Books?

The Prophetic Books are records of the prophetic ministry of individuals whom God chose and sent to encourage, warn, exhort, and guide his people. They are divided into two sections: the Major and the Minor Prophets. The distinction is very old. Since biblical books were written in scrolls, they had a size limit. It appears that all twelve Minor Prophets fit well into one scroll, so they became one unit. Apart from being shorter, the Minor Prophets are the same type of prophetic literature as the Major Prophets.

What Is Prophecy?

Biblical prophets were God's servants especially called to be his witnesses. In the Old Testament, prophecy was a tool that God used to communicate his will to his people. Prophets were not simply teachers of the law, which was the main job of the priests (Deut. 33:10). God sent prophets to his people during times of crisis, such as: (1) during times of military threats against God's people (Isa. 36–37); (2) when the people rebelled against God's will (Gen. 3:11–19; Ezek. 2:3–5); (3) when hope seemed all but lost (Jer. 29:11); and (4) when the people needed comfort in difficult times (Isa. 40:1–5).

Old Testament prophets were intermediaries between God and his people. They stood in the gap that separates God from humans. They brought the word of God to the people, and they interceded on behalf of the people before God. As the Scriptures say, "Surely the Sovereign Lord does nothing without revealing his plan to his servants the prophets" (Amos 3:7).

Most often prophecy dealt with issues current to the prophet's time. However, in the Old Testament, God also revealed the future to his prophets. An important characteristic of Old Testament prophecy is called prophetic telescoping or prophetic perspective. It means that one prophecy could be fulfilled more than one time even though the prophet saw it and spoke about it as single event. An excellent example of this characteristic is the "day of the Lord." Whereas Joel (Joel 2:28–32) and Amos (Amos 5:18–19) present the day of the Lord as a onetime event, we know that in fact the day of the Lord refers to two separate events: when God brought punishment on Judah in the Babylonian destruction of Jerusalem (586 BC), and the second coming of Christ (2 Peter 3:10–13; 1 Thess. 5:2).

Major Prophets

Isaiah
Jeremiah
Lamentations
Ezekiel
Daniel

Minor Prophets

Hosea
Joel
Amos
Obadiah
Jonah
Micah
Nahum
Habakkuk
Zephaniah
Haggai
Zechariah
Malachi

Main Themes of the Prophetic Books

1. *One true God.* Only the Lord, the God of Abraham, is the true God, creator of the universe. All other claims to divinity are false.

2. *God is Holy.* Holiness is in God's very being. God's holiness means that he is not part of nature but is its Creator. God is beyond his creation. For this reason, any attempt to represent God—make an image of him—becomes idolatry. God cannot be manipulated with offerings or sacrifices. Because of his holiness, God does not tolerate sin. Sin offends God because it is the opposite of what he desires for his creation.

3. *God is Sovereign.* As the creator of all, God rules and owns it all. The best image to express this truth is that God is King. Yet, because he is beyond the created world and our own experience, God is much more than just a king. He is the King of kings. Nature is under God's rule, as are the nations and his people.

4. *God is Merciful and Full of Grace.* Although God is holy and sovereign, he is interested in humanity and his creation. God is deeply involved in what humans do and do not do. His willingness to send prophets to correct, warn, comfort, and guide his people shows this interest. Mercy and grace are also part of God's nature.

5. *God is Just and Good.* Because of his great mercy, God has shown amazing patience with his people and faithfulness to his covenant. The prophets make it clear that God wishes his people to be obedient and repentant, he wishes to forgive and transform them. Yet, he will punish and discipline in love when necessary.

6. *The Torah.* The prophets alluded, quoted, enforced, and applied the law of Moses to specific events, persons, or circumstances.

7. *The Covenant.* God's activities, both his promises of restoration and his acts of judgment, spring from his faithfulness to his covenant.

8. *The Exile and Restoration.* The exiles to Assyria in 722 BC and to Babylon around 586 BC became a central theme. The prophets warned, called to repent, announced God's judgment upon Israel, and explained the reasons for exile. However, they also comforted the people with assurances that God would save and restore them.

9. *The Messiah.* The central component of the prophets' announcement of salvation was the coming of a special person who would represent, save, and restore Israel.

The Minor Prophets

Name & Meaning	Approx. Date BC	Location from	Audience	Subject
Hosea "salvation"	752–722	Northern Kingdom of Israel	Northern Kingdom of Israel (Ephraim)	Israel's unfaithfulness to their covenant with God
Joel "Yahweh is God"	Unknown	Unknown	Possibly Judah and surrounding nations	The great and dreadful day of the Lord
Amos "burden bearer"	760–753	Town of Tekoa in Judah	Northern Kingdom of Israel	God's judgment upon Israel for their injustice and lack of mercy
Obadiah "servant or worshiper of Yahweh"	586	Unknown	Edom (neighbor to Judah) and the people of Judah	God's judgment upon Edom
Jonah "dove"	783–753	Town of Gath Hepher in Zebulun	Nineveh (capital of Assyrian empire)	God's judgment upon Nineveh; yet God's mercy extends to all
Micah "who is like Yahweh"	738–698	Town of Moresheth southwest of Jerusalem	Samaria (capital of Israel) and Jerusalem (capital of Judah)	God's judgment upon Israel and Judah for their wickedness
Nahum "the Lord comforts"	663–612	Town of Elkosh (possibly Capernaum)	Nineveh (capital of Assyrian empire)	God's judgment upon Nineveh for their cruelty against God's people
Habakkuk "embrace"	609–598	Unknown	All God's people	God's judgment, justice, love, and mercy
Zephaniah "the Lord hides"	641–628	Jerusalem	Southern Kingdom of Judah and surrounding nations	A call to repentance before the coming judgment on the day of the Lord
Haggai "festival"	520	Unknown	Judah and Jerusalem	A call to rebuild the temple and a message of hope
Zechariah "Yahweh remembers"	520–518	Unknown	Judah and Jerusalem	A call to rebuild the temple and a message of future glory
Malachi "my messenger"	Mid to late 400s	Unknown	Jerusalem	A call to spiritual renewal

The Genres in the Prophetic Books

The Prophetic Books contain many different kinds of writings, some of it in poetry and others in prose. These are some of the most important genres—types of literature that share similar characteristics—in the Prophetic Books:

1. **The Judgment Speech:** This is one of the basic forms of the prophetic messages. These speeches usually start with an introduction of the prophet (Amos 7:15), a detailed list of the accusations or the reasons for the judgment, and the prediction of the punishment (Amos 7:17).

2. **Prophecy of Blessing or Deliverance:** Similar to the judgment speech, these speeches of blessing or deliverance elaborate the life situation that produces a difficulty that requires deliverance. The blessing follows it (Isa. 41:8–20; Jer. 33:1–9).

3. **The Woe Oracle:** The word "woe" is an expression of sorrow. The prophets used this interjection "woe" to express the imminence of God's judgment against rebellion and sin (Amos 5:18–20; Isa. 5:8–24; Hab. 2:6–8).

4. **The Lawsuit:** It uses the language of legal courts to present God as the plaintiff, prosecuting attorney, and judge. In a sense, the prophets sue God's people for breaking the covenant. The indictment or accusations are either directly stated or implied, and the judgment sentence is announced (Isa. 2:13–26; Hos. 3:3–17; 4:1–19).

ISAIAH

JUDGMENT AND SALVATION

Purpose

Called to prophesy to the kingdom of Judah, the prophet Isaiah preached a message of judgment and salvation. With powerful enemies on all sides and war looming, Judah formed many political and military alliances in hopes of protecting itself. Isaiah opposed these alliances because they showed Judah's reliance upon human power over divine power. Isaiah knew that any alliance with a world power would place Judah in submission as a vassal to the powerful nation. This would lead Judah to serve the gods of those states. Vassal states during Isaiah's time usually adopted the religions of their overlords.

The prophet Isaiah exhorted Judah and her kings to seek God and maintain their faith in God's providence and faithfulness rather than trusting the military and political strength of other nations. God would save and deliver Judah if they trusted God to do so. If Judah continued to doubt God, then Judah would meet the same end as the northern kingdom of Israel, which Assyria conquered and sent into exile. Just as God used Assyria to judge the nations, he would use Babylonia to destroy Assyria and, eventually, Judah.

Isaiah is outraged by the idolatry, injustice, unrighteousness, rebellion, disdain, arrogance, and scandalous behavior of God's people. The main purpose of the book of Isaiah is to communicate God's anger, disappointment, and sorrow with his people's behavior and to warn them of impending judgment. Judah could continue to turn to political treaties, other gods, and military strength to save them, but their efforts to do so would prove worthless. Unless the people of Judah repented and fully relied on God as their Savior, they would never be safe from destruction.

However, Isaiah is more than a prophecy of doom. Isaiah, whose name means "Yahweh saves," wrote beautiful and memorable prophecies of hope and salvation. Isaiah's prophecy anticipates the coming of a king, a Messiah, who will fulfill all of God's promises to Israel. A remnant of God's people will find their full redemption in the coming of this Messiah—a suffering servant—who will die to save them.

Outline

The Prophet Isaiah

1. Oracles of Judgment and Promise for Judah (1–5)

2. Isaiah's Commission (6)

3. Judgment against Aram, Israel, and Assyria (7–10)

4. The Branch from Jesse (11–12)

5. Prophecies against the Nations—Babylon, Philistia, Moab, Damascus, Cush, Egypt, Arabia, Jerusalem, and Tyre (13–23)

6. The Lord's Destruction of the Earth (24–27)

7. Woe to Ephraim, Judah, and Jerusalem (28–32)

8. Judgment against Israel's Enemies and Joy to Israel (33–35)

9. Judah Escapes the Assyrian Threat and Isaiah Predicts the Babylonian Exile (36–39)

10. The Fall of Babylon and the Restoration of Israel (40–48)

11. The Suffering Servant and the Salvation He Brings (49–57)

12. Judgment, Worship and the Everlasting Kingdom of God (58–66)

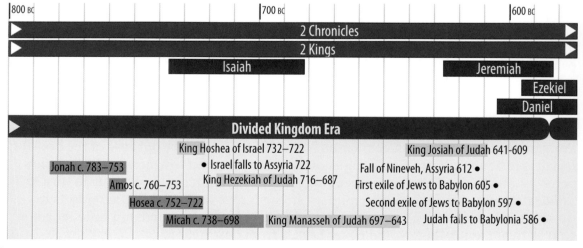

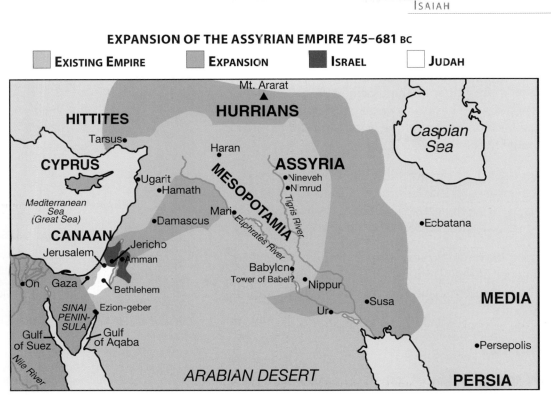

EXPANSION OF THE ASSYRIAN EMPIRE 745–681 BC

EXISTING EMPIRE   **EXPANSION**   **ISRAEL**   **JUDAH**

Kings: Tiglath-Pileser III (745–727 BC); Shalmaneser V (727–722 BC); Sargon II (722–705 BC); Sennacherib (705–681 BC)

Background

Author: The author is the prophet Isaiah, the son of Amoz (Isa. 1:1). Isaiah was married and had at least two children—Shear-Jashub (7:3) and Maher-Shalal-Hash-Baz (8:3). Isaiah lived at the time of Amos, Hosea and Micah. According to Jewish tradition, Isaiah died by being sawed in half during the reign of King Manasseh (Heb. 11:37).

Some scholars argue that there were at least three different authors of the book of Isaiah. Many agree that Isaiah wrote chapters 1–39 in the eighth century BC. However, some believe that a second author (or group of authors) wrote chapters 40–55 in the mid-sixth century BC and a third author (or group of authors) wrote chapters 56–66 in the late sixth century BC. However, based on literary analysis, many scholars today argue for a single author for the book.

Date: Isaiah wrote during the reigns of Uzziah, Jotham, Ahaz and Hezekiah, kings of Judah (1:1). Some sections of the book are dated: The events in chapter 7 occurred around 735 BC (7:1) and chapters 36–38 around 701 BC (36:1). However, the remaining sections are not dated. It is very possible that Isaiah wrote the book in sections throughout his life, starting around 701 BC and ending as late as 681 BC, the date that Assyrian King Sennacherib died (37:38).

Setting: In 745 BC, Tiglath-Pileser III, king of Assyria, began to expand the Assyrian empire westward. As he threatened the borders of many small kingdoms, they frequently formed coalitions to fight the advancing armies. In 733 BC, Syrian King

Rezin and King Pekah of Israel formed a coalition. When King Ahaz of Judah refused to join them, Syria and Israel attacked Judah. Instead of trusting in God's providence, Ahaz formed an alliance with Assyria. Judah became a vassal kingdom of Assyria. Ahaz had to appear before Tiglath-Pileser to pay homage to the Assyrian god.

After the fall of the northern kingdom of Israel in 722 BC, the southern kingdom of Judah continued to struggle with the consequences of their alliance with Assyria and later alliances with Babylonia and Egypt.

During his long ministry, Isaiah warned the kings of Judah about their political and military deals as well as their unrighteousness, complacency, injustices, and arrogance.

Taylor Prism. Made around 689 BC and found in 1830 in Nineveh (modern Iraq), this copy of the Prism is known as the Taylor Prism and is housed in the British Museum. The Assyrian inscription details Sennacherib's military campaign in the Middle East. In it, Sennacherib boasts that he had Hezekiah "like a bird in a cage." Two copies of the prism were found later and are housed in Chicago and Jerusalem. These copies are nearly identical, with minor text differences.

Themes

God the Holy One of Israel. God is a holy God, and he will not tolerate sin. Sin will be punished.

God as Savior and Redeemer. God is a merciful, loving, and forgiving God. Israel and Judah deserved to be completely destroyed, but God promised salvation and restoration to a remnant.

God's Suffering Servant—The Promised Messiah. Only through the suffering of the promised Messiah, God's Servant, will God's people be healed and forgiven of their iniquities. The promised Messiah, through his suffering, will inaugurate the kingdom of God—the new heaven and the new earth.

Key Verses

Come now, let us settle the matter,' says the LORD. 'Though your sins are like scarlet, they shall be as white as snow; though they are red as crimson, they shall be like wool.—Isa. 1:18

Therefore the LORD himself will give you a sign: The virgin will conceive and give birth to a son, and will call him Immanuel.—Isa. 7:14

For to us a child is born, to us a son is given, and the government will be on his shoulders. And he will be called Wonderful Counselor, Mighty God, Everlasting Father, Prince of Peace. Of the greatness of his government and peace there will be no end. He will reign on David's throne and over his kingdom, establishing and upholding it with justice and righteousness from that time on and forever. The zeal of the LORD Almighty will accomplish this.—Isa. 9:6–7

The wolf will live with the lamb, the leopard will lie down with the goat, the calf and the lion and the yearling together; and a little child will lead them.—Isa. 11:6

Surely he took up our pain and bore our suffering, yet we considered him punished by God, stricken by him, and afflicted. But he was pierced for our transgressions, he was crushed for our iniquities; the punishment that brought us peace was on him, and by his wounds we are healed. We all, like sheep, have gone astray, each of us has turned to our own way; and the Lord has laid on him the iniquity of us all.—Isa. 53:4–6

The Spirit of the Sovereign Lord is on me, because the Lord has anointed me to proclaim good news to the poor. He has sent me to bind up the brokenhearted, to proclaim freedom for the captives and release from darkness for the prisoners, to proclaim the year of the Lord's favor and the day of vengeance of our God, to comfort all who mourn.—Isa. 61:1–2

Being God's People

Then: Under Assyrian pressure, Judah could either form alliances with other nations or trust in God and believe the prophet Isaiah that God would protect them from their enemies. God was angry, disappointed, and saddened with the disobedience of his people. God's people put more trust in human power than in him. Such trust is a form of idolatry. God's anger and righteous judgment came to an unfaithful people. However, God is also merciful and compassionate and he will save his people and redeem them.

Now: So often today, we place our trust in money, possessions, weapons, governments, or our leaders. We form alliances or sacrifice our integrity instead of trusting God to provide for us and protect us. God is our rock, our fortress, our deliverer, our shield, and our salvation (Ps. 18:2). When we are in trouble, God assures us that "those who hope in the Lord will renew their strength. They will soar on wings like eagles; they will run and not grow weary, they will walk and not be faint" (Isa. 40:31).

Jesus in Isaiah

Jesus is the promised Messiah, a descendant of King David (Isa. 11:1–2). Jesus Christ fulfilled more than 50 prophecies in the book of Isaiah. Some of these prophecies are:

- The descendant of Jesse upon whom the Spirit of the Lord would rest (Isa. 11:1–2; Matt. 1).

- Born of a virgin (Isa. 7:14; Matt. 1:22–23).

- Jesus is the suffering servant who was pierced for our transgressions, crushed for our iniquities, and by his wounds we are healed (Isa. 53; 1 Peter 2:21–25).

- Jesus came to proclaim good news to the poor, bind up the brokenhearted, proclaim freedom for the captives, and release prisoners from the darkness (Isa. 61:1–2; Luke 4:14–20).

Death would not contain Jesus. In his death and resurrection, Jesus inaugurated a new kingdom—God's kingdom. When Jesus returns, there will be a new heaven and a new earth where crying and weeping will be heard no more (Isa. 65:17–19).

JEREMIAH

JUDGMENT, WRATH, DOOM, AND WEEPING

Jeremiah Lamenting the Destruction of Jerusalem by Rembrandt

Purpose

Although he did not want to be a prophet, Jeremiah brought a message of judgment against the people of Judah. He hoped that the heartfelt repentance of his people—whom he loved deeply—could possibly postpone or even cancel God's impending judgment. Early in his ministry, Jeremiah's main message was to warn people of Judah's eventual destruction because of their idolatry, unrighteousness, and smug arrogance.

King Manasseh (who ruled Judah about 697–643 BC) had violated God's covenant by encouraging the worship of many idols and other pagan practices. Manasseh's grandson, Josiah (who ruled over Judah around 641–609 BC), began several reforms to reverse his grandfather's policies. However, Josiah's efforts didn't make a lasting change in Judah. God's judgment seemed inevitable.

Convicted with courage and faith, Jeremiah spoke God's message of doom. However, his love compelled him to beg Judah to repent and weep in prayer for their forgiveness. Even after Judah's destruction and exile into Babylon, Jeremiah continued to love his people and warned them to submit to their oppressors and not to rebel. In the end, Jeremiah informed them of God's promise to redeem a remnant of his people. God would make a new covenant with his people. This new covenant would be written in their minds and on their hearts. God would be their God and they would be his people. God would show eternal grace, forgive their wickedness, and forget their sins forever (Jer. 31:33–34).

Outline

1. The Call of Jeremiah (1)

2. Condemnation and Judgment of Judah (2–11)

3. Jeremiah's Complaint and God's Answer (12)

4. Prophecy of Destruction and Captivity (13)

5. Prophecy of Drought, Famine, and War (14:1–17:18)

6. Keeping the Sabbath Day Holy (17:19–27)

7. At the Potter's House (18–19)

8. Jeremiah Placed in Stocks and His Complaint to the Lord (20)

9. Judgment Against Zedekiah, Wicked Kings, and Lying Prophets (21–23)

10. The Babylonian Exile and Those Who Opposed Jeremiah's Message (24–29)

11. Restoration, Remnant, and the New Covenant (30–33)

12. Final Warnings of Destruction (34–35)

13. The Suffering of Jeremiah (36–38)

14. The Fall of Jerusalem and Jeremiah's Flight to Egypt (39–45)

15. Judgment Against the Nations: Egypt, Philistia, Moab, Ammon, and Babylon (46–51)

16. The Destruction of Jerusalem and Jehoiachin's Release (52)

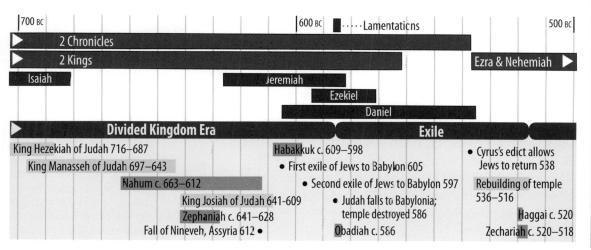

Background

Author: Many scholars agree that the prophet Jeremiah wrote most of the book, except for the final chapter, which was written later (51:64). Baruch, Jeremiah's secretary who traveled with Jeremiah to Egypt (32:11–16; 43:6–7), may have been responsible for compiling the book and writing the appendix (chapter 52).

Jeremiah was the son of Hilkiah, who was one of the priests at the town of Anathoth in the territory of Benjamin (1:1). Because King David sent the high priest Abiathar to his fields in Anathoth, some believe that Jeremiah was a descendant of Abiathar (1 Kings 2:26; 1 Chron. 15:11). Jeremiah lived at the same time as the prophets Obadiah, Habakkuk, Ezekiel, and Daniel. The Lord told Jeremiah not to marry or have children (16:1–4). Jeremiah's sole purpose was to proclaim judgment and doom to his own people. He struggled with his calling, criticized himself, and often complained to God. Accompanied by only a few friends including Ahikam (26:24), Gadaliah (39:14), Ebed-Melech (38:7–13), and Baruch, Jeremiah lived a life of depression and sorrow.

Date: Jeremiah was active during the reigns of Josiah, Jehoiakim, Johoiachin, and Zedekiah, kings of Judah. Jeremiah received his call in 626 BC, and wrote until approximately 582 BC.

Setting: King Hezekiah of Judah (716–687 BC) made several reforms and sought more independence for Judah. When the Assyrian King Sennacherib attacked Judah, God saved Jerusalem. The people of Judah believed that the temple and Jerusalem could never be destroyed. This belief, known as the "inviolability of Zion," gave the people a lazy attitude toward obeying God.

However, Hezekiah's son, King Manasseh (697–643 BC), became a loyal vassal to Assyria. The next two Assyrian kings, Esarhaddon (680–669 BC) and Ashurbanipal (668–627 BC), conquered Egypt and eventually sacked the ancient Egyptian capital of Thebes in 664 BC. This signaled the height of the Assyrian empire. King Manasseh of Judah instituted pagan worship, supported sacred prostitution in the temple area, and implemented human sacrifice. Manasseh's evil doings greatly contributed to Judah's demise.

Assyria expanded its borders too far, and it had difficulty maintaining control. Assyria began to weaken on all sides. In 628 BC, Manasseh's grandson, Josiah (641–609 BC), began to make sweeping reforms. Shortly after Josiah started his reforms, Jeremiah began his ministry. The Babylonians grew in power, and Nabopolassar the Babylonian (625–605 BC) sacked the Assyrian capital of Nineveh and conquered it in 612 BC. Assyria was never again a major world power.

Baruch Bulla. In 1975 a seal impression—known as a bulla—with the name of Baruch, appeared in Israel. The inscribed lines read, "belonging to Berachyahu, son of Neriyahu, the scribe." The seal has produced much debate among scholars. Some scholars argue that the seal belonged to Baruch, Jeremiah's secretary (Jer. 36:4).

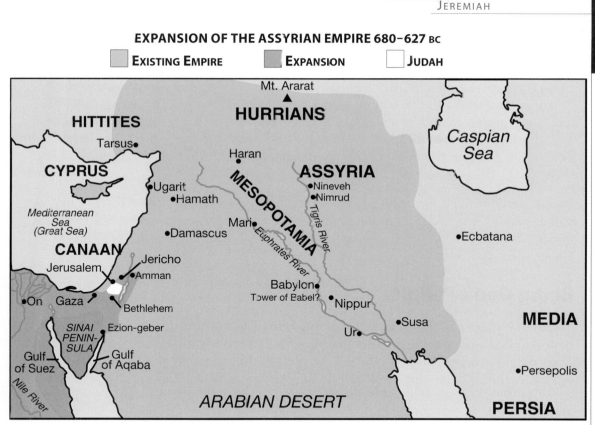

EXPANSION OF THE ASSYRIAN EMPIRE 680–627 BC

EXISTING EMPIRE · EXPANSION · JUDAH

Assyrian Kings: Esarhaddon (680–669 BC); Ashurbanipal (668–627 BC)

After King Josiah was killed by Pharaoh Necho II in 609 BC, his son Johoiakim was placed on the throne of Judah. Johoiakim didn't maintain the polices and reforms of his father. In this context, Jeremiah began his ministry in Jerusalem and preached judgment, doom, and called his people to repentance.

Themes

Judgment. Sin, idolatry, and rebellion will be punished by God. Jerusalem and Judah will be destroyed.

Restoration. After a time of exile, God will restore his people.

The New Covenant. When God restores his people, he will make a new covenant. In the new covenant, the law of God will be written upon their hearts and God will forgive and forget his people's sins.

Key Verses

Let not the wise man boast of his wisdom or the strong man boast of his strength or the rich man boast of his riches, but let him who boasts boast about this: That he understands and knows me, that I am the LORD, who exercises kindness, justice and righteousness on the earth, for in these I delight.—Jer. 9:23–24

"For I know the plans I have for you," declares the LORD, "plans to prosper you and not to harm you, plans to give you hope and a future."—Jer. 29:11

"This is the covenant I will make with the people of Israel after that time," declares the LORD. "I will put my law in their minds and write it on their hearts. I will be their God, and they will be my people. No longer will they teach their neighbor, or say to one another, 'Know the LORD,' because they will all know me, from the least of them to the greatest," declares the LORD. "For I will forgive their wickedness and will remember their sins no more."
—Jer. 31:33–34

In those days and at that time I will make a righteous Branch sprout from David's line; he will do what is just and right in the land. In those days Judah will be saved and Jerusalem will live in safety. This is the name by which it will be called: The LORD Our Righteous Savior.—Jer. 33:15–16

Being God's People

Then: The people of Judah believed that no one and nothing could defeat them—they believed that God would bless them and protect them regardless of how they behaved. They disobeyed God and worshiped the gods of their neighbors. Judah's attitude offended God, and he did not continue to bless them. Instead, God judged them severely with destruction and exile. Yet, he had compassion and promised to rescue and restore them.

Now: The letter of James reminds us that, "faith by itself, if it is not accompanied by action, is dead" (James 2:17). Faith in Christ and the grace we receive through that faith do not provide us with the freedom to openly sin and disobey God. The apostle Paul wrote, "Shall we go on sinning so that grace may increase? By no means! We are those who have died to sin; how can we live in it any longer?" (Rom. 6:1–2). Jeremiah's prophecy is a powerful reminder that faithfulness and obedience are not optional.

Jesus in Jeremiah

In Jeremiah, the Messiah is foretold as a righteous Branch from the line of David— and he would be called "The LORD Our Righteous Savior" (Jer. 23:5–6). On the night Jesus was betrayed, our Lord and Righteous Savior shared the Passover meal with his disciples. As he sat at the table, he took the cup and referenced Jeremiah 31:31 saying, "This cup is the new covenant in my blood, which is poured out for you" (Luke 22:20). Jesus' death and resurrection instituted the new covenant Jeremiah prophesied.

The Holy Spirit, who comes to every believer, writes God's law in our hearts (2 Cor. 3:3; Heb. 10:15–18). Through Jesus—his death and resurrection—we receive all the benefits of the new covenant. "For this reason Christ is the mediator of a new covenant, that those who are called may receive the promised eternal inheritance— now that he has died as a ransom to set them free from the sins committed under the first covenant" (Heb. 9:15).

LAMENTATIONS

GOD HEARS OUR DESPERATE CRY

Purpose

This short book is a cry of grief and despair over the destruction of Jerusalem and the temple. When the Babylonians attacked Jerusalem, they destroyed the city and the temple, and exiled many of the dwellers of the city. Although they had been warned many times by many prophets, the people could not believe that God would allow the destruction of the temple. However, their sin caused the destruction. The book of Lamentations allows the people to offer a cry of repentance and sorrow over the national sins and to pray for forgiveness and restoration.

Outline

1. The City: First Lament over Jerusalem (1)

2. God's Anger: Second Lament over Jerusalem (2)

3. The Prophet: Personal Lament and Prayer (3)

4. The Sins: Lament over the people of Judah (4)

5. The Prayer: Lamentation of Repentance (5)

Background

Author: The book is anonymous. However, Jewish and Christian traditions attribute the book to Jeremiah the prophet. Jeremiah is said to have composed other lamentations (2 Chron. 35:25) and the book appears to have been written by an eyewitness of the destruction of Jerusalem. Although not certain, it is plausible that Jeremiah wrote the book.

Date: Assuming that Jeremiah wrote the book, then it probably was written soon after the fall of Jerusalem to King Nebuchadnezzar (586 BC). However, it is not possible to set a definite date.

Five Poems

The book of Lamentations is composed of a series of five poems. All five poems have 22 verses or a multiple of 22 (poem 3 has 66 verses). Poems 1 through 4 are acrostics: Each verse begins with a new letter of the Hebrew alphabet in poems 1, 2, and 4; in poem 3 there are three verses for each letter of the alphabet. The Hebrew alphabet has 22 letters. So this poetical technique—the acrostics—would be an aid to memorization.

Themes

■ Sin has inevitable consequences (1:8,14; 2:14; 3:39, 42; 5:7).

■ God is holy and good (1:5; 2:17; 3:19–58).

■ God's compassion and faithfulness never fail (3:21–26).

Key Verses

Because of the LORD's great love we are not consumed, for his compassions never fail. They are new every morning; great is your faithfulness.—Lam. 3:22–23

Though he brings grief, he will show compassion, so great is his unfailing love.—Lam. 3:32

Let us examine our ways and test them, and let us return to the LORD.—Lam. 3:40

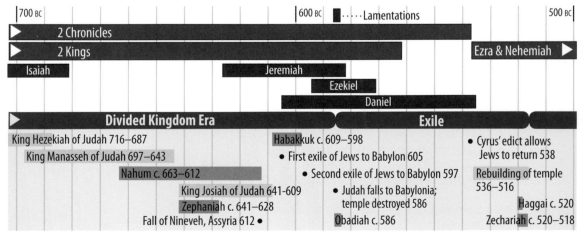

Being God's People

Then: Babylon's destruction of Jerusalem and exile of many of its dwellers was an emotional and spiritual trauma. The book accepts the reasons for the horrific punishment and expresses deep regret, sorrow, pain, and repentance. Their lament remembers that God is compassionate and good, so their hope is in God's mercy and salvation (Jer. 3:21–33).

Now: Jesus did not promise that being his followers would be a walk in the park. He promised persecutions and suffering (John 15:18–16:4). However, he also promised to send the Holy Spirit to his followers, and asked the Father, "protect them by the power of your name" (John 17:11).

Jeremiah by Michelangelo

Jesus in Lamentations

So where is Christ to be found in this book? In the pain and the suffering itself. The language of verses 2:15–16 and 3:15—"he has filled me with bitter herbs and given me gall to drink"—appears at the cross—"There they offered Jesus wine to drink, mixed with gall" (Matt. 27:34; see also Mark 15:29; Luke 23:35). The apostle Paul references Lamentations 3:45—"You have made us scum and refuse among the nations"—in 1 Corinthians 4:13 to describe the ongoing suffering of believers. God knows our suffering! The language of Lamentations expresses Christ's anguish and sorrow over sin and its terrible price.

EZEKIEL

THE PRESENCE OF GOD

The Vision of Ezekiel (Valley of Dry Bones; Ezek. 37:1–14) by Francisco Collantes

Purpose

The book of Ezekiel deals with one of the most important questions for God's people, both then and now: Is God present with us or has he abandoned us?

The Israelites had become rebellious and disobedient. They took for granted God's blessings and presence, and they were disloyal to the God of their ancestors. Yet, for many years, and through many prophets, God warned them and called them back to himself.

At one point, in 597 BC, God's judgment arrived with terrible consequences. Babylonian King Nebuchadnezzar conquered Jerusalem and carried away many of the leaders of the nation—among them, King Jehoiachin, other government officials, and priests. That group of people, even as they were marched to Babylon 800 miles (1,287 km) away, continued to think that God would destroy the Babylonians shortly and make things right again. To them, a self-deluded people, God sent a prophet. Ezekiel, who came from a priestly family, received his calling from God in 593 BC.

Throughout his long ministry, and in many creative ways, Ezekiel explained to the Israelites the meaning of God's presence with them. When God's people are faithful and humbly walk before God, God's presence is a source of blessing, peace, and fruitfulness. However, when God's people are disloyal, rebellious, and adulterous, God's presence is a terrifying thing because it means judgment and correction. However, because God is merciful and compassionate, his presence also means forgiveness, salvation, restoration, and hope.

Outline

The Prophet Ezekiel

Ezekiel

The name is a two part Hebrew name composed of *Yehazaq* ("He will make strong") and *El* ("God"). The whole name means "God will strengthen."

Background

Author: The prophet Ezekiel of the priestly line of Buzi wrote this book (1:3). Being from the temple priests of Jerusalem, Ezekiel was taken with the exiles to Babylon in 597 BC. Ezekiel lived with his wife (24:15–27) along with many exiles by the "River Kebar" (1:1) near the Babylonian city of Nippur.

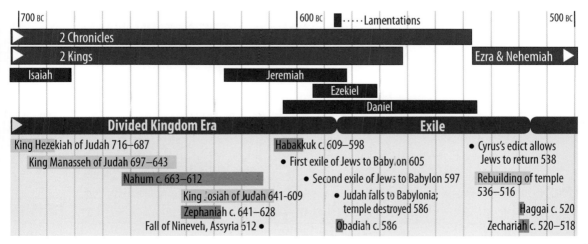

700 BC		600 BC	■····Lamentations		500 BC
▶ 2 Chronicles					
▶ 2 Kings				Ezra & Nehemiah ▶	
Isaiah		Jeremiah			
			Ezekiel		
			Daniel		

▶ Divided Kingdom Era		Exile	
King Hezekiah of Judah 716–687	Habakkuk c. 609–598	• Cyrus's edict allows Jews to return 538	
King Manasseh of Judah 697–643	• First exile of Jews to Babylon 605		
Nahum c. 663–612	• Second exile of Jews to Babylon 597	Rebuilding of temple 536–516	
King Josiah of Judah 641-609	• Judah falls to Babylonia; temple destroyed 586	Haggai c. 520	
Zephaniah c. 641–628			
Fall of Nineveh, Assyria 612 •	Obadiah c. 586	Zechariah c. 520–518	

Most scholars agree that Ezekiel received his call from God when he was thirty years old, the age he would have began his ministry as a priest (Num. 4:3). His ministry could be seen as bizarre: Ezekiel lied motionless for long periods (4:4–7), was mute (3:24–27; 24:25–27; 33:22), did not mourn the death of his wife (24:15–27), received strange and vivid visions (1–3; 8–11; 15–18; 21; 23–24; 37–48), and behaved in unusual ways, such as shaving his head with a sword and burning, cutting, or scattering the hair around the city (5:1–4; 4:12; 12:3–5). The strangeness of his ministry pointed to the terrible times God's people were experiencing, their stubbornness and rejection of God's exhortations to repentance, and the years of exile, suffering, and punishment they would experience.

Date: The book contains dates for many of the oracles Ezekiel received. We can date his first vision to 593 BC (1:1–3) and his last one in 571 BC (29:17), which means Ezekiel's ministry lasted about 22 years. Ezekiel may have written his book shortly after the end of his public ministry.

Setting: The events and prophecies of the book occurred during the period when different groups of people from Judah were forced on the long march to Babylon. The Assyrian empire had taken the northern kingdom of Israel captive over 100 years earlier. Prominent people in Judah were taken into exile in Babylon over a period of several years. Ezekiel himself was taken captive.

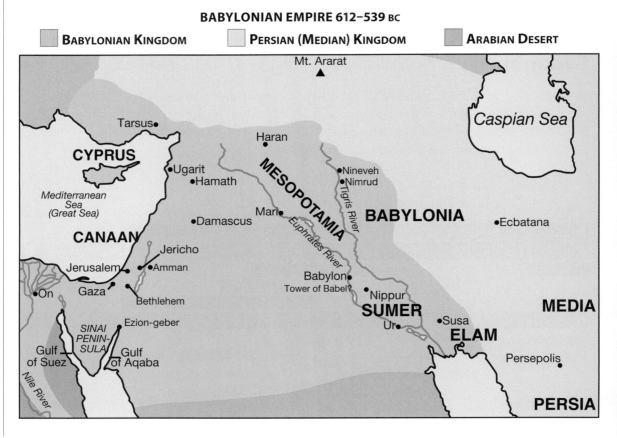

BABYLONIAN EMPIRE 612–539 BC

BABYLONIAN KINGDOM   PERSIAN (MEDIAN) KINGDOM   ARABIAN DESERT

People, Places, and Nations in Ezekiel's Prophecies

Subject	Text in Ezekiel	Description	Prophecy
Israel	4:1–5; 6–7; 12:18–28; 18:1–21:32; 23:1–10, 36–49	Northern Kingdom of Israel	The end has come for the kingdom of Israel.
Judah	4:6; 12:18–28; 18:1–21:32; 23:1–4, 11–49	Southern Kingdom of Judah	The nation of Judah will fall to Babylon.
Jerusalem	4:7–17; 8:1–11:15; 12:18–28; 15:1–17:24; 22:1–31; 24:1–27	Jerusalem, capital city of Judah	Jerusalem will be besieged and destroyed. The temple will be desecrated.
Prince in Jerusalem	12:1–16; 21:25–27	Zedekiah, the last king of Judah	Zedekiah will be captured and taken to Babylon where he will die, but he will never "see" Babylon. Ezekiel's words were precisely fulfilled (Jer. 39:1–7).
Ammon	25:1–7	Lands to the east across the Jordan river from Israel and Judah	Although their ancestors made them close relatives of Israel, these nations were hostile to Israel and Judah. God will judge them.
Moab	25:8–11		
Edom	25:12–14		
Philistia	25:15–17	Lands to the immediate north, south and west of Israel and Judah	God will judge the neighboring nations and city-states around Israel and Judah who were hostile or led Israel to worship idols.
Tyre	26:1–28:19		
Sidon	28:20–26		
Egypt	29:1–32:32		
Gog of Magog	38:1–39:29	Lands to the far north, south, east and west of Israel and Judah	God rules over all nations. Not only will Israel and Judah be judged along with their neighbor nations, but so will the nations to the north, south, east, and west.
Persia	38:5		
Cush	38:5		
Put	38:5		
Sheba	38:13		
Dedan	38:13		
Tarshish and the coastlands	38:13; 39:6		

Themes

God is the Sovereign Judge. He will judge rightly all people and nations.

Individual Responsibility. God does not punish individuals for other people's sins.

The Grace and Mercy of God. God in his mercy will rescue a remnant from the coming destruction. God stands ready to forgive any who will truly turn to him and repent.

Hope for the Future. The faithful will receive God's coming kingdom in all its glory.

Key Verses

Therefore, you Israelites, I will judge each of you according to your own ways, declares the Sovereign LORD. Repent! Turn away from all your offenses; then sin will not be your downfall. Rid yourselves of all the offenses you have committed, and get a new heart and a new spirit. Why will you die, people of Israel? For I take no pleasure in the death of anyone, declares the Sovereign LORD. Repent and live!—Ezek. 18:31–32

I will give you a new heart and put a new spirit in you; I will remove from you your heart of stone and give you a heart of flesh. And I will put my Spirit in you and move you to follow my decrees and be careful to keep my laws.—Ezek. 36:26–27

Being God's People

Then: Despite the many warnings through prophets, most Israelites did not believe that God would allow an evil people to conquer Jerusalem and destroy the temple. Even when the Babylonians conquered Jerusalem and exiled a portion of the population to Babylon, those people who were exiled still believed that God would destroy Babylon and rescue them sooner rather than later. Ezekiel's prophecy proved sadly true when Nebuchadnezzar destroyed Jerusalem and the temple in 586 BC. Yet, God's presence did not abandon his people. Rather, as Ezekiel saw in a vision, God went to Babylon to be with his people. In addition, Ezekiel saw that God's presence would remain with his people.

Apocalyptic Images

Apocalyptic literature—from a Greek word meaning "unveiling, uncovering"—in biblical times arose during periods of great suffering and persecution. When Babylon had conquered Jerusalem and destroyed the temple, God's people needed assurance and comfort. Ezekiel's prophecies included language that pointed to the future, in vivid and poetic images, and reassured the people that God would restore them and do justice in the world.

The book of Revelation in the New Testament picks up many of those images to present a vision of God's plan for the world:

- Living Creatures and the Throne of God (Ezek. 1:4–28; Rev. 4:1–11)

- Eating a Scroll (Ezek. 2:9–3:15; Rev. 19:1–11)

- God's Glory and the Temple (Ezek. 10:1–22; Rev. 11:19)

- A Prostitute (Ezek. 16:1–59; 23:1–49; Rev. 17:1–18:24)

- Gog and Magog (Ezek. 38:1–39:29; Rev. 20:7–10)

- The New Jerusalem (Ezek. 40:1–48:35; Rev. 21:1–22:6)

Now: Those who believe in Jesus as their King and Savior have God's presence with them always through the Holy Spirit. The Holy Spirit renews our hearts so we can be obedient and faithful to God. The book of Ezekiel is a reminder not to become complacent, taking for granted God's grace and blessings. The New Testament reminds us that we must grow in our faith (Heb. 5:12–14; 1 Peter 2:2), to work on our salvation (Phil. 2:12), to live like children of light (Eph. 4:17–5:14), and to be doers of the Word (James 1:19–27).

Jesus in Ezekiel

The New Testament quotes or alludes to the book of Ezekiel over sixty times—about forty times in the book of Revelation. Some of the most important imagery that Jesus used to explain his ministry to his disciples comes from the book of Ezekiel: Jesus is the true temple because he is Emmanuel, meaning "God with Us" (Matt. 1:23; John 1:14), he is the Shepherd King that Ezekiel spoke about (Ezek. 34), and Jesus is the source of living waters (Ezek. 47:1–2; John 4:10–14; 7:38–39).

Symbolism	Scripture	What It Points To
Son of Man	Ezek. 2:1; Matt. 8:20	The term means "human" as it is used in Ezekiel, but it takes on a more Messianic meaning in Daniel 7:13–14. Jesus is both truly human and the heavenly Messiah.
The Grape Vine and Its Wood	Ezek. 15:1–8; John 15:1–8	The vine is a frequent prophetic image of God's people. The fruit bearing portion is true believers; the dead wood refers to pretenders. Jesus is the true vine.
"The lowly will be exalted and the exalted will be brought low."	Ezek. 21:25–26; Matt. 23:12 (see also Gen. 49:10)	Kingship is redefined as service to others, and Jesus is therefore the King of kings by right.
Shepherd, Sheep and Goats One Flock, One Shepherd	Ezek. 34:1–31; Matt. 25:31–46; John 10:1–18 Ezek. 37:15–28; John 10:16	God is the true and good shepherd. David was a shepherd-king. Jesus is both David's son and God in the flesh. He will bring together all God's people.
Opened Graves and a Resurrected People	Ezek. 37:1–14; John 5:24–29; 11:25–26	Jesus gives new life to those who believe in him.

DANIEL

LIFE IN EXILE

Daniel in the Lions' Den by Peter Paul Rubens

Purpose

The book of Daniel has two sections and two purposes.

■ The first part of the book tells about the life of Daniel and his friends in the Babylonian court (chapters 1–6). The purpose of this section is to teach the exiled Israelites in Babylon how to live as God's people in a foreign, hostile land.

■ The second part of the book includes several visions and dreams that tell about future world events and how they affect God's people (chapters 7–12). The purpose of this section is also to encourage God's people in times of suffering and persecution by reassuring them that history in under God's control. In fact, God will do wonders that will dwarf anything he had done before.

The two sections, although very different, have a common theme: God rules over all. The book of Daniel urges us to remember that if God has been faithful in history, then we can rest assured that he continues to be faithful. And the future, which Daniel reveals in part, is victorious for God and his people.

Outline

1. Daniel and His Friends (1–6)
   a. Daniel and his friends in the Babylonian court (1)
   b. Nebuchadnezzar's dream about the statue (2)
   c. Nebuchadnezzar's image and the fiery furnace (3)
   d. Nebuchadnezzar's dream of a tree (4)
   e. Belshazzar and the fall of Babylon (5)
   f. Daniel and the lions' den (6)

2. Daniel's Visions (7–12)
   a. Vision of the four beasts (7)
   b. Vision of the ram and the he-goat (8)
   c. Vision of the seventy sevens (9)
   d. Vision of the future of Israel (10–12)

Background

Author: The authorship of the book of Daniel has been much disputed. Traditionally, Daniel is regarded as the author. Although some scholars have disagreed and brought up some historical issues, a careful analysis of the book, along with historical and archaeological discoveries, strongly suggest that the traditional view is correct.

Most of what we know about Daniel comes from this book. He was part of the first wave of exiled people from Jerusalem who were deported to Babylon in 605 BC. He was a member of the ruling or religious class of Jerusalem, who were the first groups to be deported. Having arrived in Babylon as a young man, Daniel and his friends were trained as court officials. Because of God's blessing, he rose quickly and became "the third highest ruler in the kingdom" (Dan. 5:29). From the dates in the book, Daniel ministered from the first year of Nebuchadnezzar's reign (605 BC; Dan. 1:1) to Cyrus's third year (535 BC; Dan. 10:1).

Date: Although impossible to peg a date, the writing of the book of Daniel probably took place sometime during Daniel's ministry, around 605–535 BC.

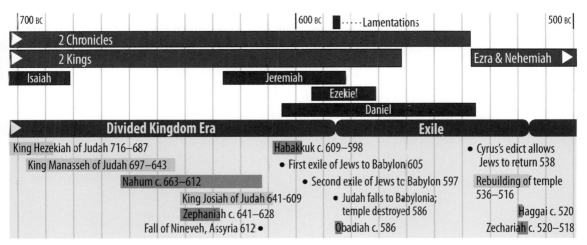

Themes

An Active God. The book of Daniel reveals that God is not merely a passive "Lord of heaven." He is the dynamic Lord of all and closely involved in the lives of his people (2:20–23, 47–49; 3:28–30; 9:15–19).

A Saving and Judging God. As Ruler of the universe, God is the righteous Judge of kings, nations, and history. He is also the powerful and compassionate Savior of his people (2:47; 3:28–29; 4:1–3, 34–37; 5:22–30; 6:25–27; 7:13–14).

A Sovereign God. God rules over history. The future is no accident to God. He knows it and is intimately involved in working out his plans (7:23–27; 8:19).

God is Breaking through in History. God will send his Man. The designation "Son of Man" as a title for the coming Messiah is first revealed in Daniel. This was Jesus' favorite term for himself (7:13–14; 9:25–26).

God and Resurrection. Though hinted at in other books (Psalms, Job, Ezekiel), Daniel is the first to speak clearly about the hope of resurrection (12:1–2, 13).

Belshazzar

At one time it was thought that the book of Daniel was in error listing Belshazzar as the last king of Babylon (5:30–31) because it was known that Nabonidus was the last monarch of the Babylonian empire. Later archeological discoveries revealed Belshazzar's name and identity as the coregent son of Nabonidus. Nabonidus was the king and Belshazzar a co-king under his father. This discovery clarified why Belshazzar offered Daniel the place of "third highest ruler in the kingdom" (5:16, 29).

Key Verses

Praise be to the name of God for ever and ever; wisdom and power are his. He changes times and seasons; he sets up kings and deposed them. He gives wisdom to the wise and knowledge to the discerning. He reveals deep and hidden things; he knows what lies in darkness, and light dwells with him.
—Dan. 2:20–22

"If we are thrown into the blazing furnace, the God we serve is able to deliver us from it, and he will deliver us from Your Majesty's hand. But even if he does not, we want you to know, Your Majesty, that we will not serve your gods or worship the image of gold you have set up."—Dan. 3:17–18

In my vision at night I looked, and there before me was one like a son of man, coming with the clouds of heaven. He approached the Ancient of Days and was led into his presence. He was given authority, glory and sovereign power; all peoples, nations and men of every language worshipped him. His dominion is an everlasting dominion that will not pass away, and his kingdom is one that will never be destroyed.
—Dan. 7:13–14

Multitudes who sleep in the dust of the earth will awake: some to everlasting life, others to shame and everlasting contempt.
—Dan. 12:2

A Dream and a Vision

Nebuchadnezzar's dream about the statue and Daniel's vision of the four creatures from the sea refer to the same historical events but use very different images.

Nebuchadnezzar's Dream of the Statue (Dan. 2)	Daniel's Vision of the Four Creatures (Dan. 7)	The Kingdoms (Dates kingdom occupied Judah)
Head (Fine Gold)	Lion with eagle's wings	Babylonia; King Nebuchadnezzar to Belshazzar (605–539 BC)
Chest and Arms (Silver)	Bear raised on one side; three ribs in its mouth	Medo-Persia; King Cyrus to Darius III (539–332 BC)
Belly and Thighs (Bronze)	Leopard with four wings and four heads	Greece; Alexander the Great and the Four Divisions (332–63 BC)
Legs (Iron) and Feet (Iron and Clay)	Beast with iron teeth, ten horns; small horn with eyes and mouth	A Divided Kingdom; Many scholars believe this kingdom to be Rome (63 BC–time of Jesus)
Stone (Cut out, not by human hands)	Son of Man (Jesus Christ)	The Everlasting Kingdom of God

Being God's People

Then: For many years, being God's people meant enjoying the Promised Land, worshiping God at the temple, and learning and following the law. After the people were captured and exiled to Babylonia, God preserved them. How could they learn to be God's people, loyal and obedient, while living as a minority in a foreign land? How could they worship and honor God without the temple? The book of Daniel shows through the life of Daniel and his friends, and through the powerful prophecies about the future, what it meant to be God's people and how to be faithful to the God of their ancestors.

Now: Christians all over the world today continue to live in a foreign land because our "citizenship is in heaven" (Phil. 3:20). The lives of Daniel and his friends remind us that God is with us, that his promises are reliable, and that he is in control because God is King. Moreover, although we still suffer in this world, we know that Daniel's visions about the future ensure that justice will be vindicated, that evil will be destroyed, and that "at the name of Jesus every knee should bow, in heaven and on earth and under the earth, and every tongue acknowledge that Jesus Christ is Lord" (Phil. 2:10–11).

Jesus in Daniel

The phrase "son of man" is just the Hebrew way of saying human being (8:17). But the name takes on a special significance in Daniel 7:13–14 where it describes someone who rides on the clouds, is given an everlasting kingdom, and is worshiped. The term became a title that referred to the coming Messiah. It was the title Jesus most preferred when speaking of himself.

Daniel uses other titles and imagery for the Messiah that are reflected in the New Testament.

A Bilingual Book

Daniel is one of the few books in the Old Testament that is written in two languages. Most of the Old Testament was written in Hebrew, the language of Israel. However, significant portions of Daniel (2:4b–7:28) are written in a language known as Imperial Aramaic. Because this was the language of much of the ancient Near East, the Babylonian empire used it for official communications.

Titles and Imagery of Jesus	Book of Daniel	New Testament
The rock that became a mountain	Dan. 2:34–35, 44–46	Luke 20:17–18; 1 Peter 2:8
The fourth man like "a son of the gods" / Angel of the Lord	Dan. 3:24–28 (See also Ex. 23:20–21)	Matt. 26:63–64, 27:54
The finger/hand of God	Dan. 5:5	Luke 11:20; John 8:6
One like a son of man	Dan. 7:13–14; 8:15; 10:16, 18	Mark 14:61–62
Prince of the Host	Dan. 7:13–14; 8:15; 10:16, 18	Rev. 19:11–16
The Anointed One (Messiah/Christ)	Dan. 9:25–26	Luke 24:25–27
A man dressed in linen, gold belt, face like lightning, eyes like torches, arms and legs like burnished bronze and a voice like a multitude	Dan. 10:4–11	Rev. 1:13–18

HOSEA

A SPIRITUALLY ADULTEROUS NATION

Purpose

The book of Hosea emphasizes the importance of the covenant and the results of breaking the covenant. Hosea is a window into the heart of God. Israel's desire to seek other gods and maneuver politically is spiritual adultery and breaks God's heart. Hosea's faithfulness toward his unfaithful wife is an illustration of God's commitment to his covenant and his beloved. The book of Hosea anticipates God's judgment against Israel for breaking the covenant. The prophecy also calls the people of Israel to repent and renew their relationship with God.

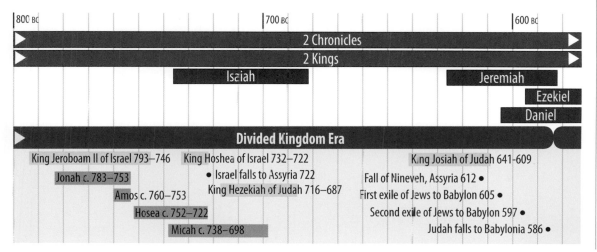

800 BC | 700 BC | 600 BC

2 Chronicles

2 Kings

Isaiah

Jeremiah

Ezekiel

Daniel

Divided Kingdom Era

King Jeroboam II of Israel 793–746 | King Hoshea of Israel 732–722 | King Josiah of Judah 641-609

Jonah c. 783–753

• Israel falls to Assyria 722

Fall of Nineveh, Assyria 612 •

Amos c. 760–753 | King Hezekiah of Judah 716–687 | First exile of Jews to Babylon 605 •

Hosea c. 752–722 | Second exile of Jews to Babylon 597 •

Micah c. 738–698 | Judah falls to Babylonia 586 •

Outline

1. Hosea and His Unfaithful Wife (1–3)

2. The Unfaithfulness of Israel (4–8)

3. The Judgment of Israel (9–10)

4. God Expresses His Love for Israel (11:1–11)

5. God Expresses His Anger against Israel's Sin (11:12–13:16)

6. The Restoration of Israel (14)

*The Prophet Hosea
by Duccio di Buoninsegna*

Background

Author: Hosea, the son of Beeri, was a prophet during the decline and fall of the northern kingdom of Israel (also known as Samaria). Hosea was married and fathered three children. His name means "salvation."

Date: Hosea began his prophetic career during the reign of King Jeroboam II of Israel (793–746 BC) and some scholars believe that he continued to prophesy for about 30 years until the fall of Samaria (722 BC).

Audience: Hosea's primary audience was the northern kingdom of Israel. Since Ephraim was a central and influential tribe in the northern kingdom, Hosea often addresses his audience as "Ephraim."

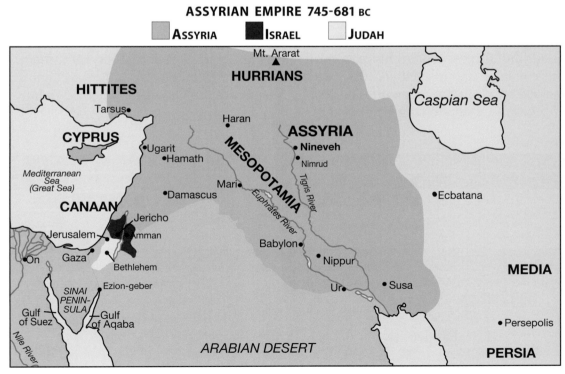

ASSYRIAN EMPIRE 745-681 BC

ASSYRIA ISRAEL JUDAH

Setting: After many decades of peace and prosperity for Israel, Assyria began to emerge as a powerful empire in the 800s BC. Expanding westward, the Assyrian empire imposed their power on Israel and Israel's neighbors by forcing them to submit and pay tribute.

In 743 BC, Tiglath-Pileser III of Assyria put into effect a policy that would deport conquered peoples from their native lands and then bring other exiles from other nations to take their place. This policy was supposed to prevent rebellion from the conquered peoples. Israel tried to form many alliances with Assyria, neighboring nations, and Egypt. Those alliances expressed their lack of trust in God and led them to idolatry.

Themes

- Disobedience separates us from God.
- God judges and punishes disobedience.
- God is faithful and his love is everlasting.
- God calls us to repentance.
- God promises redemption and reconciliation.

Marriage in Hosea

Many scholars believe that Hosea was the first Hebrew prophet to use marriage as a metaphor to compare Israel's covenantal relationship with God.

Key Verses

I will plant her for myself in the land; I will show my love to the one I called 'Not my loved one.' I will say to those called 'Not my people,' 'You are my people'; and they will say, 'You are my God.'—Hos. 2:23

I desire mercy, not sacrifice, and acknowledgment of God rather than burnt offerings.—Hos. 6:6

When Israel was a child, I loved him, and out of Egypt I called my son.—Hos. 11:1

Being God's People

God will never give up on us, and he will always be faithful to his promise to be our God and to provide for us. Despite Israel's unfaithfulness, God's love led him to keep a remnant safe. Through that remnant, God sent his Son, the Messiah. God calls us to repentance and wants us to trust in him alone. Trusting in ourselves, our families, or our money to provide protection or sustenance is spiritual adultery. We are challenged to transfer our loyalties from our power and possessions back to God.

Jesus in Hosea

Matthew quotes Hosea 11:1, "out of Egypt I called my son," when Jesus escaped Herod's persecution (Matt. 2:13–18). Jesus fulfilled Hosea's prophecy by redeeming a people who broke God's heart through unfaithfulness. Jesus delivered God's people from the slavery of sin and death, often equated to the bondage the Israelites experienced in Egypt. Jesus, the Lion of Judah, roars upon his victory over the grave that delivers us from our *Egypts* and *Assyrias*, from all those places in our lives that hold us captive.

JOEL

THE GREAT AND DREADFUL DAY OF THE LORD

Purpose

The book of Joel calls the people of Judah to repentance and warns them—and their neighbors—of a future time when God will judge them. The book of Joel speaks of the "day of the Lord." In that day, God will pour out his Spirit on the nations. The day is also one of judgment against God's enemies. Joel assures Judah's future safety from these threats, and promises full redemption.

Outline

1. The Plague of Locusts and a Call to Repentance (1:1–20)

2. The Army from the North and a Call to Repentance (2:1–27)

3. The Day of the Lord (2:28–3:21)

Background

Author: Joel, whose name means "Yahweh is God," is identified as the son of Pethuel (1:1). Nothing else is known about him.

Date and Audience: The exact date for the book of Joel is unknown and debated. Some scholars understand Joel as prophesying to the people of Judah between 609 BC and 586 BC just before their exile to Babylon, while others suggest a date following the exile, as early as 515 BC or as late as 350 BC.

Themes

- Repent and return to the Lord to avoid judgment.
- God will judge all nations on the day of the Lord.
- God will bring salvation to his people and pour out his Spirit.

Key Verses

"Even now," declares the LORD, "return to me with all your heart, with fasting and weeping and mourning."
—Joel 2:12

And afterward, I will pour out my Spirit on all people. Your sons and daughters will prophesy, your old men will dream dreams, your young men will see visions. Even on my servants, both men and women, I will pour out my Spirit in those days.—Joel 2:28–29

Being God's People

In uncertain times—when God's people were threatened and surrounded by their enemies—God promised to bring salvation to his people and empower them with his Holy Spirit. God has poured his Holy Spirit upon every believer, allowing us to be adopted into God's family and empowering us to be God's holy nation and royal priesthood (1 Peter 2:9).

Jesus in Joel

The prophet Joel anticipated the day of the Lord as a great and dreadful day. It was a day of salvation and judgment. Jesus came to the world to save it (John 3:16) and, one day, will come to judge it (Acts 10:42; 17:31). The prophet visualized a day to come. Yet, Jesus is fulfilling the prophecy in two parts: in his first coming about 2,000 years ago and when he returns in power, glory, and victory.

Pentecost

Joel's prophecy regarding the pouring out of God's Spirit was fulfilled at Pentecost (Acts 2:17–21). The coming of the Spirit upon all of God's people, without distinction of gender, age, nationality, or social standing, was part of the great "day of the LORD" (Joel 2:28–31).

AMOS

SOCIETY GONE AWRY

Purpose

Amos prophesied against Israel during a time of great material prosperity and peace. He brought words about God's imminent judgment upon Israel. This judgment came because the people of Israel had corrupted the worship of God, treated the poor and the weak with injustice, and betrayed their covenant vows with God. The result of their disobedience and lack of mercy would be their destruction at the hands of a foreign nation.

However, God is merciful. Judgment is never God's last word. Amos provided them with a glimmer of hope: God would preserve and restore a remnant in Israel who would return to the Promised Land and would remain in Israel forever (9:15).

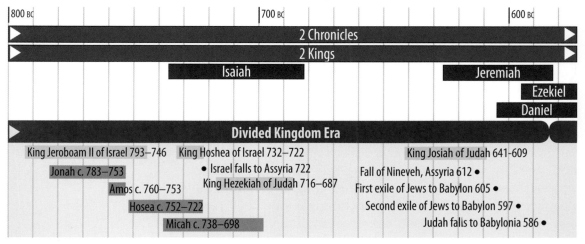

800 BC	700 BC	600 BC
2 Chronicles		
2 Kings		
Isaiah	Jeremiah	
	Ezekiel	
	Daniel	
Divided Kingdom Era		

King Jeroboam II of Israel 793–746   King Hoshea of Israel 732–722   King Josiah of Judah 641-609
    Jonah c. 783–753   • Israel falls to Assyria 722   Fall of Nineveh, Assyria 612 •
        Amos c. 760–753   King Hezekiah of Judah 716–687   First exile of Jews to Babylon 605 •
        Hosea c. 752–722   Second exile of Jews to Babylon 597 •
            Micah c. 738–698   Judah falls to Babylonia 586 •

Outline

Background

Author: Amos was from Tekoa, a small village in Judah—probably about six miles (10 km) south of Bethlehem—where he was a shepherd, a herdsman, and cultivator of sycamore-fig trees (1:1; 7:14–15). Amos's name means "burden" or "burden bearer." Amos definitely had a burden to bear—informing the prosperous nation of Israel that they would surely meet their impending doom.

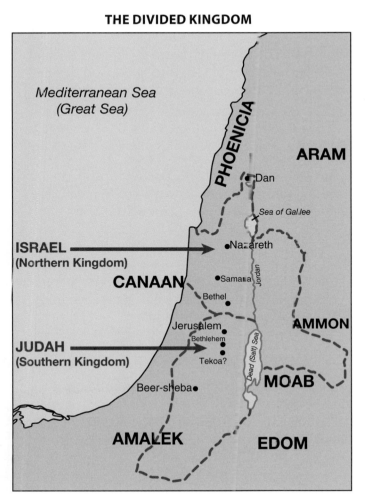

THE DIVIDED KINGDOM

Date: Amos was a prophet during the reigns of King Uzziah over Judah (792–740 BC) and King Jeroboam II over Israel (793–746 BC). Most scholars agree that the book of Amos was written sometime between 760 BC and 753 BC, approximately 32–38 years before Israel's Assyrian captivity.

Audience: Even though Amos was from the kingdom of Judah, he was prophesying and writing to the kingdom of Israel. His prophetic ministry centered in Bethel—the location of the king's temple in the northern kingdom of Israel (7:13).

Setting: During the reign of the evil King Jeroboam II (793–746 BC; 2 Kings 14:24), the kingdom of Israel was enjoying a prosperous period—they were wealthy, with a significant military and political power in their region. As a result, many individuals in the kingdom—especially high-ranking officials—were living luxuriously, indulging in idol worship and immoral behavior, and mistreating the poor.

As prosperity increased in Israel, so did their immorality and injustices. Israel believed that because they were prosperous, they were within God's graces. God sent Amos to correct this misinterpretation.

The Prophet Amos by Gustave Dore

Day of the Lord

The Israelites expected the day of the Lord to be only a day of redemption in which God would defeat Israel's enemies (Amos 5:18). The prophets, however, turn the day upside down: instead of light, there will be darkness; instead of redemption, there will be judgment (Amos 5:18, 20). The day of the Lord is a day of salvation and condemnation—the "great and dreadful day of the LORD" (Joel 2:28–31).

Themes

Social Justice. The consistent message of the Scriptures is that God's people ought to care for the poor, the widow, and the weak (Ex. 22:21–27; Deut. 23:19; 24:6–17; Amos 2:6–7; 5:11–12). The Old Testament prophets treated social injustice as seriously as idolatry, as Amos shows in his prophecy (Amos 2:6–7; 5:11–12; 8:4–6).

Proper Worship. God does not desire meaningless ritual and heartless performance of religious rites. God desires mercy, justice, righteousness, obedience, and heartfelt worship.

Key Verses

Seek good, not evil, that you may live. Then the LORD God Almighty will be with you, just as you say he is. Hate evil, love good; maintain justice in the courts. —Amos 5:14–15a

Being God's People

God's call to Israel in Amos's time is just as relevant today. Amos challenged people to worship with their hearts and to be compassionate to those in weak social positions. As God's people, we are called to seek justice and care for the poor.

Jesus in Amos

Jesus echoes Amos continuously throughout his teaching. Jesus commanded his followers to feed the hungry, to clothe the naked, to welcome the outcasts, to care for the sick, and to visit the imprisoned (Matt. 25:31–46). Jesus also criticized the religious leaders for offering "lip service" to God, but not truly living a fruitful and God-pleasing life (Matt. 15:1–20).

OBADIAH

A VISION AGAINST EDOM

Wadi Rum Valley in Southern Jordan

Purpose

The book of Obadiah—the shortest book in the Old Testament—judges the people of Edom for their disregard and mistreatment of the people of Judah. God will destroy Edom—as a people and a nation. The book of Obadiah assures the people of Judah that God will keep his promises and give them their inheritance.

Outline

1. God's Judgment of Edom (1–9)

2. Edom's Violations (10–14)

3. Israel's Victory (15–21)

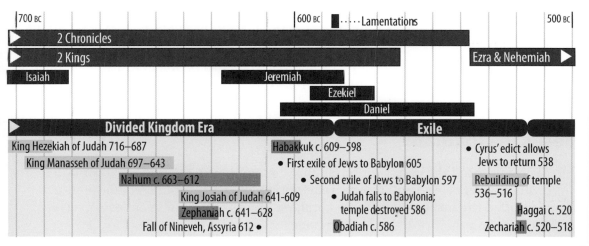

700 BC		600 BC ■····Lamentations	500 BC
▷ 2 Chronicles			
▷ 2 Kings			Ezra & Nehemiah ▷
Isaiah	Jeremiah		
		Ezekiel	
		Daniel	
▷ Divided Kingdom Era		Exile	

King Hezekiah of Judah 716–687
King Manasseh of Judah 697–643
Nahum c. 663–612
King Josiah of Judah 641-609
Zephaniah c. 641–628
Fall of Nineveh, Assyria 612 •

Habakkuk c. 609–598
• First exile of Jews to Babylon 605
• Second exile of Jews to Babylon 597
• Judah falls to Babylonia; temple destroyed 586
Obadiah c. 586

• Cyrus' edict allows Jews to return 538
Rebuilding of temple 536–516
Haggai c. 520
Zechariah c. 520–518

Background

Author: Obadiah's name, which means "servant of Yahweh" or "worshiper of Yahweh," is a common name in the Old Testament. Nothing else is known about him.

Date: Many scholars conclude that Obadiah prophesied against Edom shortly after Jerusalem fell to the Babylonians. The reasons this date is preferable are:

1. Obadiah describes God's judgment against Edom for "standing aloof while strangers [the Babylonians] carried off his [Judah's] wealth and foreigners entered his gates and cast lots for Jerusalem" (Obad. 11).

2. Obadiah goes on to describe the Edomites harassing the people of Judah on the day of their destruction, trouble, disaster, and calamity (the destruction of Jerusalem and the temple by the Babylonians).

Audience: Obadiah's vision of judgment targets the people of Edom and the promises of hope and victory are for the people of Judah.

Who Was Edom?

Edom was a small kingdom southwest of the Dead Sea and south of Moab. The name of the kingdom derives from Esau, whose name was Edom (Gen. 25:30). The Edomites were Esau's descendants. Although related to the Israelites, the Edomites were often hostile to the Israelites. From the time of the exodus, the Edomites refused to allow the Israelites to pass through their territory (Num. 20:14–21). Later, they made alliances against Israel and Judah (2 Kings 16:6). In time, the Babylonian empire conquered and destroyed the Edomite kingdom (Jer. 27:3, 6).

Themes

- Judgment against Edom
- God's promises and Israel's inheritance
- Hope that God will restore his people and keep his promises

Key Verses

Because of the violence against your brother Jacob, you will be covered with shame; you will be destroyed forever.—Obad. 10

But on Mount Zion will be deliverance; it will be holy, and Jacob will possess his inheritance.—Obad. 17

Being God's People

God kept his promises to Abraham: "and whoever curses you I will curse" (Gen. 12:3). His kingdom will come and reign supreme. God judges those who stand in the way of his purpose and persecute his people. We are challenged to endure persecution and are encouraged to remain patient through life's difficulties knowing that God is for us.

Jesus in Obadiah

Obadiah promised the people of Judah that God will keep the promise he made to Abraham. His people will receive redemption and their promised inheritance. Jesus fulfilled the promises made to Abraham. Those who believe in Jesus receive redemption and their promised inheritance (Col. 1:9–14; Heb. 9:15).

JONAH

A GRACIOUS AND COMPASSIONATE GOD

Purpose

This is a short and powerful book. The book illustrates how one cannot hide from God. Jonah tried to flee from God. However, God knows all things and is all-powerful.

The book of Jonah shows that God's mercy and compassion extend to all nations, even to those who appear to be beyond redemption. God is the one and only God for all people, and God's love and mercy are not exclusive.

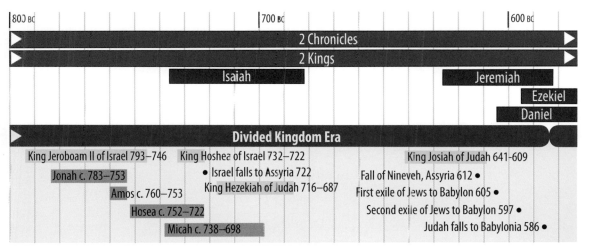

800 BC			700 BC			600 BC	
▷ 2 Chronicles ▷							
▷ 2 Kings ▷							
		Isaiah			Jeremiah		
						Ezekiel	
						Daniel	
▷ Divided Kingdom Era							

King Jeroboam II of Israel 793–746 King Hoshea of Israel 732–722 King Josiah of Judah 641-609

Jonah c. 783–753 • Israel falls to Assyria 722 Fall of Nineveh, Assyria 612 •

Amos c. 760–753 King Hezekiah of Judah 716–687 First exile of Jews to Babylon 605 •

Hosea c. 752–722 Second exile of Jews to Babylon 597 •

Micah c. 738–698 Judah falls to Babylonia 586 •

Outline

1. Jonah Flees from the Lord (1:1–16)

2. Jonah's Prayer (1:17–2:10)

3. Jonah Goes to Nineveh (3:1–10)

4. Jonah Resents God's Mercy (4:1–11)

Background

Author: Jonah was the son of Amittai and was from Gath Hepher in Zebulun. Jonah is mentioned in the book of 2 Kings where he prophesies about King Jeroboam II restoring the boundaries of Israel (14:25).

Date: According to 2 Kings 14:25, Jonah lived during the reign of King Jeroboam II of Israel (793–746 BC). Many scholars agree that Jonah was written sometime between 783 BC and 753 BC.

Audience: Jonah's message of repentance was for Nineveh. However, the message of God's compassion and mercy was also intended for the people of Israel and Judah.

Setting: During the reign of Jeroboam II, the kingdom of Israel was enjoying a prosperous period. Assyria was still a threat, but the people of Israel were under the impression that God was exclusively blessing and protecting them. Several events that occurred in Assyria from 765 BC to 755 BC, including a solar eclipse and two plagues, may have explained why the Ninevites were so open to Jonah's message of repentance.

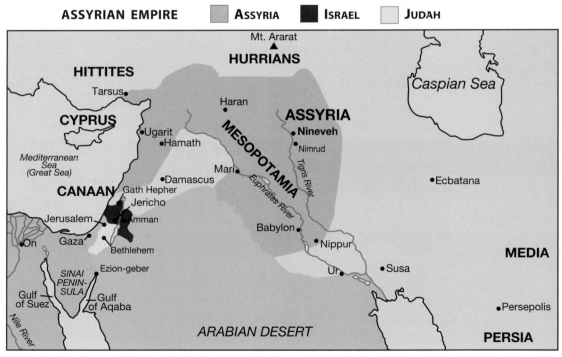

Themes

God's Omniscience and Omnipresence. God is everywhere and knows our every move. One cannot hide from God.

God's Compassion and Mercy. God will judge the disobedient. However, when one genuinely repents, God is compassionate and merciful.

God's Universal Sovereignty. God is the one and only God and is the true God for all people.

Key Verses

"In my distress I called to the LORD, and he answered me. From deep in the realm of the dead I called for help, and you listened to my cry."—Jonah 2:1

"I knew that you are a gracious and compassionate God, slow to anger and abounding in love, a God who relents from sending calamity."—Jonah 4:2b

Being God's People

God loves all people, everywhere. God's love is not exclusive; it's universal and timeless. God will show compassion and mercy to *anyone* who repents and asks for forgiveness.

Nineveh was the capital city of the nation that threatened to destroy Israel. Jonah tried to run away. He didn't even want to preach repentance to his enemy, he wanted God to judge them harshly, not forgive them. The message of Jonah challenges us to love our enemies and pray for those who persecute us. It also assures us that we can't run away from God.

Jesus in Jonah

Jesus compared himself to Jonah (Matt. 12:40–41). First, Jonah spent three days and three nights in the belly of a great fish and Jesus spent three days in the belly of the earth. Second, Jonah preached repentance to the Gentiles in Nineveh and God showed them mercy. In the same way, the gospel of Christ will be preached to the Gentiles and they too will receive the grace and mercy of God.

Big Fish Stories

The Hebrew word *dag gadol* literally means "great fish." The Hebrews didn't have a word for "whale" so they may have used *Dag* to refer to whales and fish.

Some people see Jonah as an allegory in which the big fish represents Babylon swallowing up God's people in exile only to spit them back into the Promised Land after a time of repentance and purification. Others read Jonah as a parable illustrating God's authority, compassion, and mercy for all nations. Conservative scholars agree that Jonah was a historical person and the book reports his experience as history.

MICAH

SEEK JUSTICE, LOVE MERCY, WALK HUMBLY

Micah Preaching to the Israelites by Gustave Dore

Purpose

Micah prophesied against the leaders of his people for their injustice, greed, and lack of humility. Micah brought word about God's justice, the destruction of Samaria the capital of Israel, and the fall of Jerusalem the capital of Judah.

However, the prophet also proclaimed a vision of redemption and forgiveness. Micah promised that a remnant would return, regain their inheritance, and worship the Lord. True worship looks a certain way: "To act justly and to love mercy and to walk humbly with your God" (Mic. 6:8).

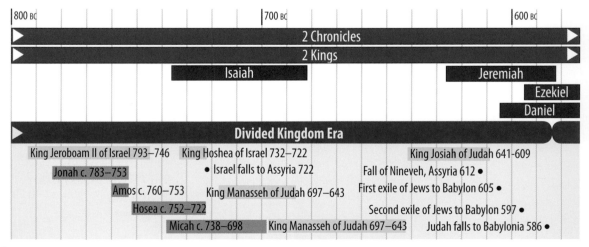

800 BC	700 BC	600 BC
2 Chronicles		
2 Kings		
	Isaiah	Jeremiah
		Ezekiel
		Daniel
Divided Kingdom Era		

King Jeroboam II of Israel 793–746   King Hoshea of Israel 732–722   King Josiah of Judah 641-609

Jonah c. 783–753   • Israel falls to Assyria 722   Fall of Nineveh, Assyria 612 •

Amos c. 760–753   King Manasseh of Judah 697–643   First exile of Jews to Babylon 605 •

Hosea c. 752–722   Second exile of Jews to Babylon 597 •

Micah c. 738–698   King Manasseh of Judah 697–643   Judah falls to Babylonia 586 •

Outline

1. Judgment of Israel and Judah (1:1–2:11)

2. Restoration of Israel and Judah (2:12–13)

3. Leaders and Prophets Rebuked (3:1–12)

4. Hope and Redemption (4:1–5:15)

5. God's Case against Israel (6:1–7:7)

6. The Final Restoration of Israel (7:8–20)

THE DIVIDED KINGDOM

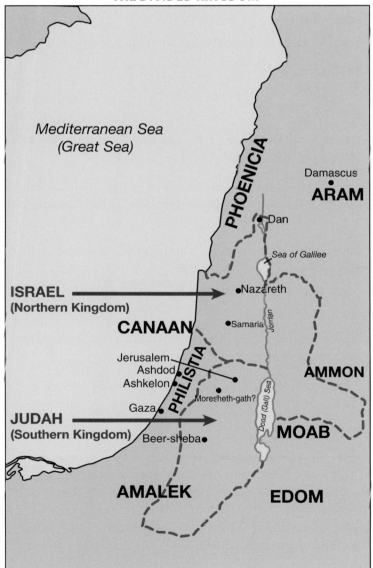

Background

Author: Micah, whose name means "who is like Yahweh," was from the town of Moresheth, often identified with Moresheth-gath located southwest of Jerusalem. The prophet's name is a reminder of the confession: "Who is a God like you…" (Mic. 7:18). He lived at the same time as Isaiah and was mentioned later by Jeremiah (Jer. 26:18).

Date: Micah began his prophetic career during the reign of King Jotham (750–732 BC), through the reign of King Ahaz (735–716 BC), and completed his prophecies during the reign of King Hezekiah (716–687 BC). Many scholars suggest a date for his ministry, and perhaps the book, from 738–698 BC.

Audience: Micah was from a town in Judah, but his primary audience was the northern kingdom of Israel (Samaria) and the city of Jerusalem.

Setting: From 734–732 BC, Assyrian King Tiglath-Pileser III defeated Aram (Syria), Philistia, Ashkelon, and Gaza. The kingdoms of Judah, Ammon, Edom, and Moab were forced to pay tribute to Assyria. In 722 BC, Samaria fell and Assyria conquered the northern king of Israel. All residents in Israel were deported to other nations. Ten years later, in 712 BC, Ashdod fell to King Sargon II of Assyria. In 701 BC, Judah joined an unsuccessful revolt against Assyria. Jerusalem was spared but was forced to pay tribute.

Themes

- God judges and punishes disobedience.

- God is loving and faithful to his promises.

- God hates injustice, idolatry, greed, lack of mercy, and empty ritualistic religion.

- God desires mercy, humility, and justice.

Key Verses

But as for me, I am filled with power, with the Spirit of the LORD, and with justice and might, to declare to Jacob his transgression, to Israel his sin.—Mic. 3:8

But you, Bethlehem Ephrathah, though you are small among the clans of Judah, out of you will come for me one who will be ruler over Israel, whose origins are from of old, from ancient times.—Mic. 5:2

He has shown you, O mortal, what is good. And what does the LORD require of you? To act justly and to love mercy and to walk humbly with your God.—Mic. 6:8

Being God's People

In a time of great upheaval, God promised that his kingdom would reign eternally and the Messiah would deliver and redeem his people (Mic. 5:1–4).

God calls us to true worship: to seek justice, to love mercy, and to walk humbly with God.

Jesus in Micah

Micah predicts the birthplace of Jesus in Bethlehem, but more than that, this prophecy states that this "shepherd" will lead God's people into an eternal kingdom that will reach to the ends of the earth (Mic. 5:2–5). When the angel Gabriel announced the birth of Jesus to Mary, he told her that Jesus "will reign over Jacob's descendants forever; his kingdom will never end" (Luke 1:33).

NAHUM

THE DESTRUCTION OF NINEVEH

Assyrian King Ashurbanipal, Nineveh (Iraq), c. 645–640 BC

Purpose

The primary purpose of the book of Nahum is to warn about God's judgment against the Assyrian capital of Nineveh for its cruelty, injustice, idolatry, and wickedness. God plans to destroy Nineveh, and Nahum is delivering this message.

The book of Nahum also proclaims God's mercy and kindness. God is slow to anger and abounding in love, yet God is firm and just. He will avenge his people for the cruelty they received from Assyria. God will eventually judge and destroy the wicked.

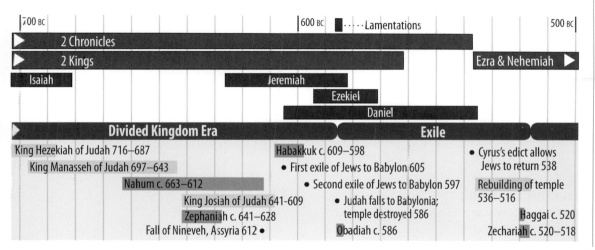

Outline

1. God Is Merciful and Just (1:1–7)

2. God Will Judge and Destroy Nineveh (1:8–2:13)

3. Woe to Nineveh (3:1–19)

Background

Author: Nahum, from the town of Elkosh, lived at the time of Zephaniah and the young Jeremiah. His name is related to the name Nehemiah, which means "the Lord comforts." The book of Nahum provided comfort for the people of Judah upon the destruction of Nineveh.

Date: The book of Nahum describes the prophet's vision regarding the events leading up to the fall of Nineveh in 612 BC. On this basis, some suggest a date from 663–612 BC for the writing of the book. The reasons this period is plausible are: (1) Nahum refers to the fall of Thebes (3:8–10), which occurred in 663 BC; and (2) Nahum details the fall of Nineveh, which occurred in 612 BC.

Audience: Although the book deals with the future of the Assyrian capital of Nineveh, Nahum's prophecy was primarily for the people of Judah. God's words were meant for God's people.

Setting: After the northern kingdom of Israel (Samaria) fell in 722 BC, the people of Judah watched as Assyria deported the people of Israel and tortured their leaders. The people of Judah also endured a century of cruelty and wicked treatment from Assyria. After the death of Assyrian King Ashurbanipal in 627 BC, the Assyrian empire began to decline rapidly. Nineveh, the capital city, fell to the Babylonians and the Medes in 612 BC.

Fall of Nineveh

The walls around Nineveh were 100 feet high (30.5 m) and wide enough to hold three chariots riding side by side. Surrounded by a moat 150 feet (46 m) wide and 60 feet (18 m) deep, Nineveh had enough supplies to survive a 20-year siege. Nahum's prophecy seemed highly unlikely. But in 612 BC, the Babylonians laid siege to Nineveh for three months. They were finally successful when the flooded Tigris River ate away at the walls allowing the soldiers to enter the city, thus fulfilling Nahum's prophecy: "but with an overwhelming flood he will make an end of Nineveh" (1:8).

*Impalement of Jews,
Neo-Assyrian relief*

Themes

- God judges the wicked, cruel, and unjust.

- God is good, slow to anger, and a refuge for those who trust in him.

- God will bring about swift justice to those who oppose him and his people.

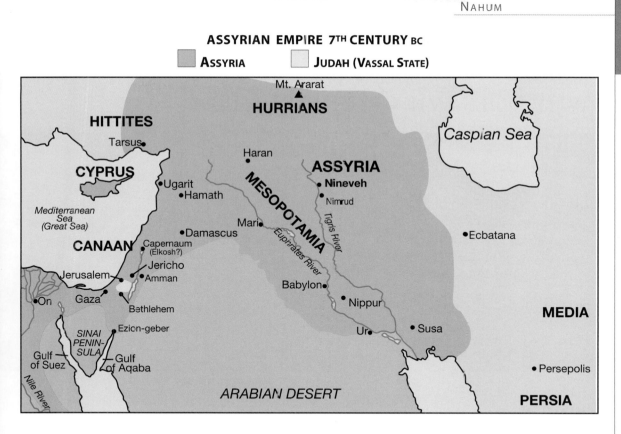

ASSYRIAN EMPIRE 7TH CENTURY BC

ASSYRIA   JUDAH (VASSAL STATE)

Key Verses

But the L ORD is slow to anger but great in power; the L ORD will not leave the guilty unpunished. His way is in the whirlwind and the storm, and clouds are the dust of his feet.—Nah. 1:3

The L ORD is good, a refuge in times of trouble. He cares for those who trust in him.—Nah. 1:7

Being God's People

God promised in Nahum to avenge his people and judge the wicked. God is both kind and stern (Rom. 11:22). When we are kind and merciful, God will show us kindness and mercy. When we are heartless, God will judge us sternly.

Jesus in Nahum

God is a stern judge, but he is also merciful. God's mercy reached its culmination with Jesus on the cross. The apostle Paul writes, "For God did not appoint us to suffer wrath but to receive salvation through our Lord Jesus Christ. He died for us so that, whether we are awake or asleep, we may live together with him" (1 Thess. 5:9–10).

Elkosh

The actual location of Elkosh is uncertain, however, some scholars believe it was located in southern Judah and later called El-Kauzeh. It has also been suggested that the Galilean city of Capernaum, which means "village of Nahum," was originally named Elkosh, but renamed Capernaum to commemorate the prophet Nahum.

HABAKKUK

WHY DOES EVIL GO UNPUNISHED?

Warriors on the Babylonian Ishtar Gate, c. 575 BC

Purpose

In the book of Habakkuk, the prophet asks, "Why does God let people get away with evil?" Habakkuk wonders why God tolerates wickedness among his people. After God answers him, the prophet is perplexed by how God allows a wicked nation like the Babylonians to impart justice upon God's own people.

The prophet Habakkuk grapples with how God's anger and justice relate to his love and mercy. Habakkuk recognizes that God is powerful and God's actions are mysterious and incomprehensible. The Lord will always render a righteous judgment. At the end of the book, the prophet rejoices and is comforted knowing that God will punish the wicked and will redeem his people.

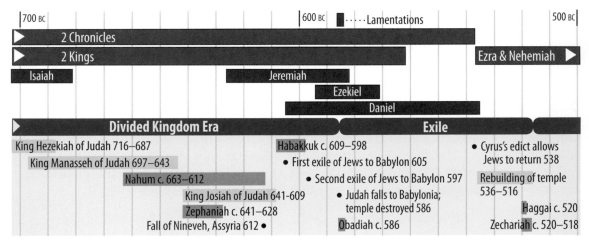

| 700 BC | | | 600 BC | ▮····Lamentations | 500 BC |

- 2 Chronicles
- 2 Kings
- Ezra & Nehemiah
- Isaiah
- Jeremiah
- Ezekiel
- Daniel

Divided Kingdom Era | **Exile**

King Hezekiah of Judah 716–687
King Manasseh of Judah 697–643
Nahum c. 663–612
King Josiah of Judah 641-609
Zephaniah c. 641–628
Fall of Nineveh, Assyria 612 •

Habakkuk c. 609–598
• First exile of Jews to Babylon 605
• Second exile of Jews to Babylon 597
• Judah falls to Babylonia; temple destroyed 586
Obadiah c. 586

• Cyrus's edict allows Jews to return 538
Rebuilding of temple 536–516
Haggai c. 520
Zechariah c. 520–518

Outline

1. Habakkuk's First Complaint: Why does evil go unpunished? (1:2–4)

2. God's Answer to the First Complaint: I will raise the Babylonians to punish the wicked. (1:5–11)

3. Habakkuk's Second Complaint: How can a loving God allow the wicked Babylonians to punish a less wicked people? (1:12–2:1)

4. God's Answer to the Second Complaint: I will eventually punish all the wicked—including Babylonia. (2:2–20)

5. Habakkuk's Prayer of Praise. (3:1–19)

Background

Author: Habakkuk lived at the time of the prophet Jeremiah. Some scholars believe that Habakkuk was a temple prophet in Judah. His name might be derived from a Hebrew word meaning "embrace."

Date: Many scholars suggest a date for the book of Habakkuk during the early reign of Johoiakim (609–598 BC) while Babylonia was advancing westward conquering nations under the leadership of Nebuchadnezzar. The reasons this period is preferable are: (1) King Johoiakim was a king who led the people of Judah to embrace the wickedness and evil described in Habakkuk 1:2–4; (2) The Babylonians were coming onto the scene as a world power and threat to Judah—as described in Habakkuk 1:5–11—shortly before the death of King Josiah in 609 BC.

Audience: Habakkuk is an unusual type of prophetic book because the prophecy itself is the prophet's own complaint to God. The dialogue between God and the prophet occurs for the benefit of God's people.

Setting: After the death of King Josiah of Judah in 609 BC, Josiah's son Jehoahaz was made king. After three months, Pharaoh Neco III deported Jehoahaz to Egypt and placed his brother Jehoiakim on the throne as a vassal to Egypt. Jehoiakim was a wicked king and evil flourished in Judah under his leadership.

The two decades after the death of King Josiah, the Babylonians rose as a world power conquering one nation after another as they swept westward from Mesopotamia. In 586 BC, the Babylonians destroyed Judah and the temple, and exiled most of Judah's inhabitants.

Figures on the Babylonian Ishtar Gate, c. 575 BC

Themes

- God's justice is mysterious.

- Why does it seem that God tolerates evil?

- God is powerful and in control.

BABYLONIAN EMPIRE 612 BC – 539 BC

BABYLONIAN KINGDOM   PERSIAN (MEDIAN) KINGDOM   ARABIAN DESERT

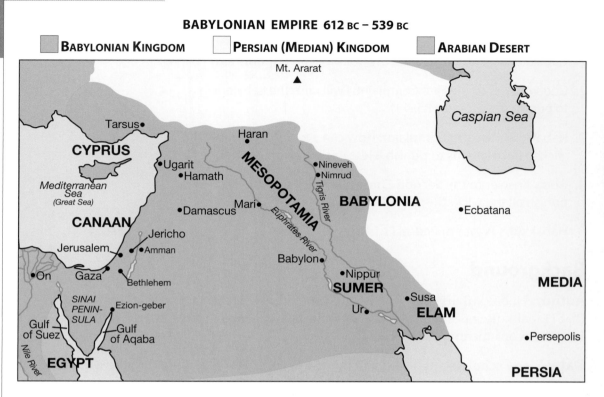

Key Verses

How long, LORD, must I call for help, but you do not listen? Or cry out to you, "Violence!" but you do not save?—Hab. 1:2

Look at the nations and watch—and be utterly amazed. For I am going to do something in your days that you would not believe, even if you were told.—Hab. 1:5

Though the fig tree does not bud and there are no grapes on the vines, though the olive crop fails and the fields produce no food, though there are no sheep in the pen and no cattle in the stalls, yet I will rejoice in the LORD, I will be joyful in God my Savior.—Hab. 3:17–18

Being God's People

God will bring justice, but his timing is not the same as ours. God's answers to Habakkuk can provide insight into our difficult questions. Sometimes it appears that God tolerates evil. How can a loving God allow the wicked to prosper and the good to suffer? Habakkuk addresses these issues and challenges us to trust in God and live in faithful obedience to him.

Jesus in Habakkuk

Habakkuk recognized that God would eventually bring justice and redeem his people (Hab. 3:13). God's ultimate redemption comes to completion in Jesus Christ. By the grace of God, Jesus crushed wickedness. On the cross, Jesus overcame sin, death, and Satan offering the world God's love, mercy, and justice (Eph. 2:1–10).

ZEPHANIAH

REPENT OR BE DESTROYED

Purpose

The book's primary purpose is to warn the people of Judah of God's impending judgment upon them and their neighbors. The doom on the coming "day of the Lord" would be devastating to Judah and their neighbors. Zephaniah appeals to Judah and calls them to repentance. Zephaniah promises that God will raise a remnant of faithful people in Judah and will restore and redeem them.

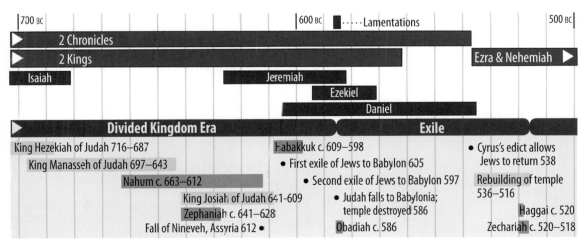

700 BC   600 BC ■······Lamentations   500 BC

2 Chronicles

2 Kings   Ezra & Nehemiah ▶

Isaiah   Jeremiah

Ezekiel

Daniel

Divided Kingdom Era   **Exile**

King Hezekiah of Judah 716–687
King Manasseh of Judah 697–643
Nahum c. 663–612
King Josiah of Judah 641–609
Zephaniah c. 641–628
Fall of Nineveh, Assyria 612 •

Habakkuk c. 609–598
• First exile of Jews to Babylon 605
• Second exile of Jews to Babylon 597
• Judah falls to Babylonia; temple destroyed 586
Obadiah c. 586

• Cyrus's edict allows Jews to return 538
Rebuilding of temple 536–516
Haggai c. 520
Zechariah c. 520–518

Outline

1. Judgment on the Day of the Lord (1:1–18)

2. A Call for Judah to Repent (2:1–3)

3. Judgment on Judah's Neighboring Nations (2:4–15)

4. Judgment on Jerusalem (3:1–8)

5. The Remnant of Israel Restored (3:9–20)

The Prophet Zephaniah

Background

Author: Zephaniah is identified as the son of Cushi, the son of Gedaliah, the son of Amariah, the son of Hezekiah (1:1). Zephaniah was most likely from Jerusalem. If he was from the royal line of King Hezekiah, then Zephaniah was familiar with the royal courts. Zephaniah lived at the time of Nahum and the young Jeremiah. The name Zephaniah means "the Lord hides" and could refer to: (1) Zephaniah was *hidden* from the evil ways of King Manasseh; (2) God will *hide* his remnant from the horror to come in the day of the Lord; (3) God remains *hidden* even though the prophet exhorts Judah to seek the Lord.

Date: Zephaniah ministered during the reign of King Josiah (641–609 BC). Many scholars suggest that Zephaniah's prophecy occurred early in King Josiah's reign (641–628 BC), since it probably occurred before the Babylonian empire conquered and destroyed Jerusalem.

Audience: The book of Zephaniah was intended for the people of Judah as a warning of God's coming judgment.

King Josiah by Julius Schnoor von Carolsfeld

While renovating the temple, the high priest found "the book of the law" and brought it to King Josiah. The king ordered it to be read to the people of Jerusalem (2 Kings 22–23).

Setting: In Judah, King Josiah was the last good king of Judah. Josiah put in place several reforms in Judah from 632 to 621 BC. He reigned during a time of political and military transition in the world around Judah. After the death of Assyrian ruler Ashurbanipal in 627 BC, the Assyrian empire began to decline rapidly. For that reason, the Babylonian empire began to increase in power and influence, overcoming Assyria and destroying the Assyrian capital of Nineveh in 612 BC.

Although Josiah was the last of Judah's good kings, Israel and Judah's many sins in the past, especially those of Manasseh (2 Kings 21:1–18), led the kingdom away from God. Because of Josiah, God delayed his just punishment of Judah. However, Zephaniah reminded them that God's punishment would come and be terrible.

Themes

- The day of the Lord.
- God will judge the nations and destroy them.
- God calls us to repent.
- God will restore a remnant of his people and keep his promises.

Key Verses

The great day of the LORD is near—near and coming quickly. The cry on the day of the LORD is bitter; the Mighty Warrior shouts his battle cry.—Zeph. 1:14

Seek the LORD, all you humble of the land, you who do what he commands. Seek righteousness, seek humility; perhaps you will be sheltered on the day of the LORD's anger.—Zeph. 2:3

The LORD your God is with you, the Mighty Warrior who saves. He will take great delight in you; in his love he will no longer rebuke you, but will rejoice over you with singing.—Zeph. 3:17

Being God's People

God kept his promises and restored a remnant of his people. Out of that remnant, God sent his only Son to redeem his people for eternity, saving us from complete destruction on the day of the Lord. One day God will judge and destroy those who live in sin and continue in their wickedness. God challenges us to avoid our sinful ways, repent, and seek his redemption found in Jesus Christ.

Jesus in Zephaniah

The day of the Lord is inevitable and on that day, God will judge the nations and make new heavens and a new earth. All who confess Jesus as their Redeemer will be saved (2 Peter 3:10–13).

HAGGAI

GIVE CAREFUL THOUGHT TO YOUR WAYS

The Temple Mount in Jerusalem where the temple once stood

Purpose

In a time of widespread indifference toward serving the Lord, the prophet Haggai challenged God's people to "give careful thought to your ways" (1:5).

In Haggai's day, the Jews had returned to Jerusalem after 70 years of exile in foreign lands. At first they enthusiastically began rebuilding God's temple, but then fell into apathy and stopped construction (1:2). God's message through Haggai challenged the people to wake up from their spiritual slumber and take on the task at hand because God Almighty is with them and will bless them when they make him their first priority.

Outline

1. Message to Rebuild the House of the Lord (1:1–11)

2. The People Respond to the Message and Resume Rebuilding (1:12–15)

3. Message to Be Strong, for God Will Fill His House with Glory (2:1–9)

4. Message to Be Holy, for God Will Bless His People (2:10–19)

5. Message to Zerubbabel of Future Blessing (2:20–23)

Background

Author: Little is known about Haggai, whose name means "festal/festival." He is mentioned in Ezra 5:1–2 and 6:14 as prophesying alongside the younger prophet Zechariah.

Date: The book of Haggai gives specific dates when "the word of the Lord came through the prophet" (1:1; 2:1, 10, 20). According to these dates, Haggai prophesied in 520 BC for a span of fifteen weeks in the sixth to the ninth months of the Babylonian calendar. This was when Zerubbabel was governor of Judah and Joshua was the high priest. The rebuilt temple was completed in 516 BC, four years after Haggai's ministry.

Audience: Haggai prophesied to the exiles who had returned to Judah, particularly in Jerusalem where the temple was to be rebuilt (Ezra 5:1–2).

Setting: The economy of this region was slow. The people worked hard, but could never seem to prosper as they had expected (Hag. 1:5–6, 9). Perhaps this is why they said, "the time has not yet come for the Lord's house to be built" (1:2). They were waiting for a time of prosperity before they would turn their attention to spiritual matters.

Themes

House of the Lord (Temple). The temple was a sign of God's presence with his people. To neglect building the temple demonstrated great apathy toward God. The people lived in their paneled houses, but the Lord's house remained in ruins (1:4, 9). Once the people responded to Haggai's message and resumed rebuilding the temple (1:14), God promised to fill his temple with glory and bless his people (2:9, 19).

Zerubbabel

As a descendant of King Jehoiachin, Zerubbabel was an heir to the throne of Judah (1 Chron. 3:17–19). Persia's King Cyrus appointed him governor of Judah when the exiles returned in 538 BC. In the books of Haggai and Zechariah, Zerubbabel, who is an ancestor of Jesus (Matt. 1:13; Luke 3:27), foreshadows the coming Messiah.

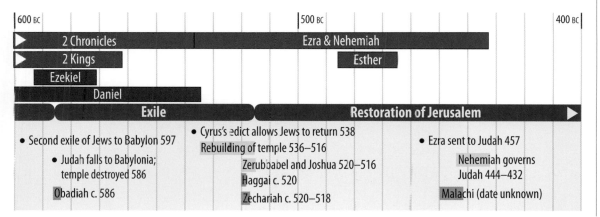

| 600 BC | | | | | | 500 BC | | | 400 BC |

| 2 Chronicles | | Ezra & Nehemiah |
| 2 Kings | | Esther |
| Ezekiel |
| Daniel |
| **Exile** | | **Restoration of Jerusalem** |

- Second exile of Jews to Babylon 597
  - Judah falls to Babylonia; temple destroyed 586
  - Obadiah c. 586

- Cyrus's edict allows Jews to return 538
  Rebuilding of temple 536–516
    Zerubbabel and Joshua 520–516
    Haggai c. 520
    Zechariah c. 520–518

- Ezra sent to Judah 457
  Nehemiah governs Judah 444–432
  Malachi (date unknown)

God Is Active in This World. In contrast to the apathy of the people, Haggai emphasizes how much God is actively involved in the world. In the book of Haggai, God sends (1:12), stirs up (1:14), shakes (2:6, 21), withholds (1:10), fills (2:7), strikes (2:17), chooses (2:23), and blesses (2:19). Just as the Lord Almighty is active, his people should also be active.

Key Verses

"Is it a time for you yourselves to be living in your paneled houses, while this [the Lord's] house remains a ruin?... Give careful thought to your ways. You have planted much, but harvested little. You eat, but never have enough. You drink, but never have your fill. You put on clothes, but are not warm. You earn wages, only to put them in a purse with holes in it."—Hag. 1:4–6

"Be strong, all you people of the land," declares the LORD,"and work. For I am with you," declares the LORD Almighty.—Hag. 2:4b

Being God's People

For Haggai, the fact that the ground produced little and that resources were scarce was not simply a matter of needing better farming methods or better planning. It was primarily a spiritual matter. The people needed God's blessing. They needed to take up the spiritual work God had called them to instead of just their own work.

Haggai's message rings just as true for us today. No matter what our financial situation may be, we must make God our first priority. When we do that, he assures us that he will be with us and will bless us.

Jesus in Haggai

The temple and Zerubbabel foreshadowed the future ministry of the coming Messiah. The Messiah would be the desire of all nations (Hag. 2:6–7), chosen, authoritative, like a signet ring on God's hand. God would once more shake the world and fill his temple with the glory of Christ (Heb. 12:26–28; Matt. 27:51–53; Luke 21:26).

ZECHARIAH

THE LORD WILL REIGN OVER ALL

Purpose

The book of Zechariah (the longest of the Minor Prophets) reminds the people that God is sovereign and faithful to his covenant with them. He is on their side. Along with the prophet Haggai, Zechariah encouraged the people who had returned to Jerusalem after many years in exile to continue rebuilding the temple. The book of Zechariah not only looks at the present situation in which the people were reestablishing their homeland and building the temple, but it also looks forward to a day when God's sovereignty will be recognized throughout the world and all peoples—Jew and Gentile—will come and worship the Lord (2:11; 6:15; 14:16).

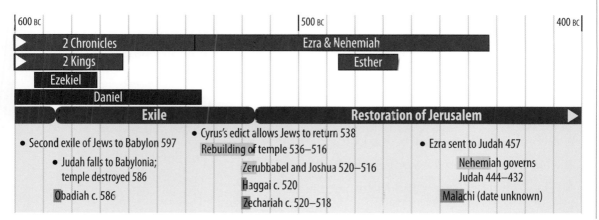

600 BC		500 BC	400 BC
▶	2 Chronicles	Ezra & Nehemiah	
▶	2 Kings	Esther	
Ezekiel			
Daniel			

Exile	**Restoration of Jerusalem**	▶

- Second exile of Jews to Babylon 597
  - Cyrus's edict allows Jews to return 538
  Rebuilding of temple 536–516
  - Judah falls to Babylonia; temple destroyed 586
    Zerubbabel and Joshua 520–516
  Obadiah c. 586
    Haggai c. 520
    Zechariah c. 520–518
  - Ezra sent to Judah 457
    Nehemiah governs Judah 444–432
    Malachi (date unknown)

Outline

1. Call for the People to Return to the Lord (1:1–6)

2. Visions and Messages for the People (1:7–8:23)
   a. Zechariah's eight visions (1:7–6:8)
   b. Zechariah told to crown the high priest Joshua (6:9–15)
   c. Zechariah's four messages (7–8)

3. Oracles against the Nations (9–14)
   a. First oracle (9–11)
   b. Second oracle (12–14)

Zechariah's vision of the lampstand and olive trees (Zech. 4:1–14)

Background

Author: Zechariah, a prophet of priestly lineage, was born in Babylon and came to Jerusalem with the exiles who returned under Zerubbabel (Zech. 1:1, 7; Neh. 12:4, 16). He is mentioned along with the older prophet Haggai in Ezra 5:1 and 6:14. Zechariah—a name shared with at least 29 other figures in the Old Testament—means "Yahweh remembers."

The Prophet Zechariah by Michelangelo

Because the content and writing style of chapters 1–8 differs so much from chapters 9–14 and because Zechariah's name is not mentioned in 9–14, it's often believed that 9–14 was not written by Zechariah but by a much later author.

Date and Audience: Zechariah prophesied to the people in Jerusalem during the time that Zerubbabel was governor of Judah and Joshua was the high priest (Ezra 5:1–2). The dates mentioned in Zechariah 1:1, 7; 7:1 place his ministry in chapters 1–8 during the early years of the reign of Persia's King Darius I (520–518 BC). The date of chapters 9–14 is uncertain, but it is sometimes dated in the 400s BC because it mentions Greece as a world power (9:13).

Themes

- Rebuilding the temple of the Lord.
- God's comfort and favor toward Israel.
- The coming Messiah and future kingdom.

Zechariah's Eight Visions

Vision	Meaning
Riders on horses (1:7–17)	Though enemy nations appear strong and secure, God will rebuild his temple and cause Jerusalem to prosper.
Four horns and four workers (1:18–21)	The mighty nations that once scattered God's people will no longer be able to do so.
Man with a measuring line (2:1–5)	Jerusalem will be rebuilt and many people—including other nations—will live there.
High priest in filthy garments (3:1–10)	God will remove his people's guilt and make them clean.
Gold lampstand and olive trees (4:1–14)	God's Spirit will empower Zerubbabel and will supply all that is needed for the temple and God's kingdom.
Flying scroll (5:1–4)	The law will purge evil doers from among God's people.
Woman in the basket (5:5–11)	Wickedness will be removed from the land.
Four chariots (6:1–8)	The Lord is mighty and sovereign over all the world.

Key Verses

"Not by might nor by power, but by my Spirit," says the LORD Almighty.—Zech. 4:6

"I will save my people from the countries of the east and the west. I will bring them back to live in Jerusalem; they will be my people, and I will be faithful and righteous to them as their God."—Zech. 8:7–8

Being God's People

Zechariah encouraged God's people to build the physical temple, but he also reminded them that they were really building a future kingdom far beyond the borders of Jerusalem in which the Messiah will reign in power.

As believers in Jesus today, we can see in the New Testament how Jesus fulfilled many of Zechariah's prophecies, yet we too await a coming day when we will see the fullness of Jesus' kingdom over all the earth.

Jesus in Zechariah

The "Servant Branch" in Zechariah 3:8 and 6:11–13 is a Messianic figure who will save his people (See Isa. 52:12; 53:8–11; Jer. 23:5; 33:15). In Zechariah 6:9–15, the Branch is described as both a priest and a king. Jesus fulfilled God's promises of the Branch by being a servant of God (Phil. 2:7) and our ultimate High Priest and King (Heb. 6:20; Luke 1:32–33).

MALACHI

THE DAY OF THE LORD IS COMING

Purpose

The prophet Malachi called for spiritual renewal among a people who had largely given up on God. Malachi lived about one generation after the prophets Haggai and Zechariah. It had been decades since the people had returned to the land and rebuilt the temple, but the promised blessings of Haggai and Zechariah had yet to materialize. The question facing the people was: Does it really matter whether we serve God or not? They shorted their tithes, brought unacceptable sacrifices, and ignored God's laws. Moreover, they seemed not to recognize their own unfaithfulness to God. In the six prophetic speeches in the book of Malachi when God lays before them the charge of how they have been unfaithful, they respond, "How have we done that?"

The book of Malachi ends with a powerful reminder that surely the day of the Lord is coming when the wicked will face judgment and the hearts of God's people will be renewed.

Outline

1. Opening (1:1)

2. Six Prophetic Speeches (1:2–3:18)
   a. First: God will punish the wicked. (1:2–5)
   b. Second: God will send a curse if unacceptable sacrifices are given. (1:6–2:9)
   c. Third: God is a witness against those unfaithful to the marriage covenant. (2:10–16)
   d. Fourth: God will meet out justice against those who wrong others. (2:17–3:5)
   e. Fifth: God will send blessing if the whole tithe is given. (3:6–12)
   f. Sixth: God distinguishes between the righteous and the wicked. (3:13–18)

3. The Day of the Lord (4:1–6)

The Prophet Malachi
by Duccio di Buoninsegna

(Note how the prophetic speeches are arranged in a *chiastic* structure common in ancient Hebrew literature. Both the first and sixth speeches address similar issues, as do the second and fifth, and the third and fourth.)

Background

Author: Nothing personal is known about the prophet Malachi. Some have speculated that Malachi may not be his proper name because *malachi* in Hebrew simply means "my messenger" (1:1).

Date and Audience: Though no dates are given in the book, it is believed that Malachi ministered to the people in Jerusalem around the same time as Ezra and Nehemiah in the mid to late 400s BC because: (1) Malachi addresses many of the same problems that faced Ezra and Nehemiah; (2) the book describes activities taking place in the temple, indicating that Malachi lived after the temple had been rebuilt; and (3) the use of a Persian term for governor (1:8) suggests a time when Persia was still in control of Judah.

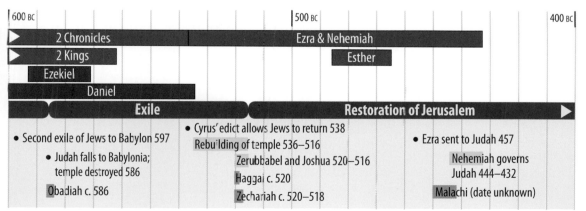

Themes

- The blessings of obedience.
- The consequences of unfaithfulness to God.
- God will judge the wicked.

Key Verses

"Bring the whole tithe into the storehouse, that there may be food in my house. Test me in this," says the LORD Almighty, "and see if I will not throw open the floodgates of heaven and pour out so much blessing that there will not be room enough to store it."—Mal. 3:10

"See, I will send the prophet Elijah to you before that great and dreadful day of the LORD comes."—Mal. 4:5

Being God's People

It can be tempting to doubt, like the people in Malachi's day, that it really makes a difference whether we serve and obey the Lord. But the book of Malachi assures us that God will act, and when he does, he will do so in power and judgment. All things will be different on the day of the Lord.

Jesus in Malachi

In Malachi, God promised to send his messenger. In fact, God would show up in the temple. God appeared in his temple in Christ (John 2:13–22). God's way was prepared by John the Baptist who came in the spirit of Elijah (Mal. 4:5; Matt. 17:11–13; Luke 1:13–17). Jesus' purpose was not merely to judge but to save. Like the sun, he rose with healing in his wings for all who revere God's name (Mal. 4:2).

Day of the Lord

In the book of Malachi, as with the other Minor Prophets, the day of the Lord was a time of judgment and deliverance. It was a day of reckoning in which God would visit his people to punish the wicked and to deliver those who remained faithful to him. In the New Testament, the day of the Lord became associated with the second coming of Christ (2 Peter 3:10–13; 1 Thess. 5:2).

THE NEW TESTAMENT

Between the Old and the New Testaments

An approximate 400-year gap divides the events in the Old Testament and the birth of Jesus in the New Testament. The Old Testament ends around 400 BC when many Jews returned to Jerusalem from their exile in Babylon. They returned to rebuild the city and the temple.

This 400-year gap is known as the Intertestamental Period (meaning "between the testaments") or the Second Temple Period (referring to the time after the temple was rebuilt). We learn about this era through a few important sources: the Apocryphal and the Pseudepigrapha books, the Dead Sea Scrolls, and the writings of Josephus.

- **The Apocrypha** – The Apocrypha, which in Greek means "the hidden books," are not considered inspired by God, and were written during the Intertestamental Period, often in Greek, though some might have been written in Hebrew. These books—like Tobit, 1–2 Maccabees, and 1–2 Esdras—reveal a great deal about this period even if they are not part of the divine revelation.

- **The Pseudepigrapha** – The word means "false name," and it is used for books written in the Intertestamental Period whose authors falsely attribute the books to famous names, like Moses, Enoch, and Isaiah.

- **The Dead Sea Scrolls** – Discovered in the mid-twentieth century near the Dead Sea, these writings contain the oldest copies of portions of the Old Testament, and also include other writings that give us insight into the religious and cultural life of the Intertestamental Period and the time of Jesus.

- **Josephus** – He was a first-century Jewish historian who wrote extensively on the history of the Jewish people and the struggles between the Romans and the Jews. His writings provide us with a portrait of first-century Judaism during the time of Jesus.

Historical Background to the New Testament

When dealing with the background to the New Testament, it is impossible to avoid important changes in the culture, politics, religion, and language in what had once been the kingdom of Israel. In the 500s BC when the Jews left Babylon to return to Jerusalem, the Persian Empire ruled from the borders of India to the eastern Greek islands. However, the Persian dominance did not last very long.

Alexander the Great, from Macedonia, a small kingdom to the North of Greece, began a campaign of expansion that overtook Greece and moved to the east to the very borders of India. In a few years, Alexander established an enormous kingdom.

However, he died at the peak of his power and abilities in 323 BC. The kingdom was divided among four of his generals. However, the cultural Greek influence was long-lasting. That was the beginning of the Hellenistic Period (331–146 BC).

Greek became the language of education and trade. As Greek expanded its influence, Greek culture also influenced and changed many other cultures; this became known as Hellenism. Alexander founded many cities, such as Alexandria in Egypt and Bactria in Central Asia—modern day Afghanistan—that became centers of Hellenic culture and influence.

Jerusalem and its surroundings were also under the influence of Hellenism. Both Ptolemies from Egypt and Seleucid from Syria dynasties (323–166 BC)—descendants of Alexander's generals—ruled the area. The Second Temple Period, especially the history that the Maccabean books narrate, occurred under the Seleucid kings, most notably Antiochus IV Epiphanes. The title Epiphanes means "god manifest," which shows his increasing megalomania during his rule (175–164 BC).

The Jews revolted and sought independence, which they achieved under the Maccabees and the Hasmonean dynasty, which ruled from 164–63 BC. As it was in the time of Ezra and Nehemiah, the Jews and their faith were once again under siege from the powerful and pervasive Hellenic influence. Under these difficult cultural conditions, the people of the land developed a tough and often legalistic understanding of religion. It became a fight for their cultural and religious survival.

Pharisees, Sadducees, and Essenes

From this time, three distinct groups emerged (there might have been more groups, but these three have survived the passing of time):

- Pharisees: The name probably means "set apart, be separated." The group appears to have emerged during the religious and social reforms under the Maccabees. Without a king, the temple was even more important for the religious practices of the Jews. However, besides the temple, Judaism was practiced and studied in smaller houses of worship, the synagogues. Whereas the priests controlled life at the temple, the synagogues became the province of scribes and teachers of the Law, the Pharisees.

- Sadducees: The name means "the righteous ones," and probably was a way to connect the group with Zadok the priest (2 Sam. 8:17). This group was in charge of the temple. The temple became the most important political symbol, and the group in charge of the temple dominated the political life of the region.

■ Essenes: The name might be connected to a self-description in the Dead Sea Scrolls as "observers of the law." Not much is known about this group. It appears that they followed a communal life, with a severe self-discipline and abstinence, daily cleansing rituals, and dedication to study the Law.

The Roman Empire

This period, the Hasmonean period, ended when the Romans conquered the region and imposed a regional government (63 BC–AD 324). The Romans governed the region first through King Herod and his successors, then through prefects (such as Pontius Pilate in Jerusalem). In time, the Jews revolted against the Roman yoke in AD 66, but this resulted in the Roman destruction of Jerusalem and the temple in AD 70.

Looking for a Messiah

The events in the New Testament take place in a time of political difficulties. The Roman Empire had tightened its fist around regions like Judea, with people unwilling to bow down to the Roman emperors. Many Jews hoped and prayed for a liberating Messiah to come and drive the Romans away from Jerusalem and rebuild the kingdom of David. God did send the Messiah, but he was not the Messiah they were expecting. He is much more than a political leader: he is the Savior who conquered death, defeated evil and sin, allows us a direct relationship with God, and offers eternal life. The New Testament tells us the story of this Messiah, Jesus Christ, his life, teachings, death, and resurrection.

In the Old Testament, we find God's revelation through his works of creation and redemption of Israel, as well as through the law and the prophets. In the New Testament, God "has spoken to us by his Son, whom he appointed heir of all things, and through whom also he made the universe" (Heb. 1:2).

In Jesus, God reveals the fullness of his plans for humanity. God also establishes a new way of relating to people. This new relationship does not occur through the Sinai covenant but through the new covenant in Jesus' blood. This new covenant, as God promised through the prophets, is now written in our hearts and sealed by God himself, the Holy Spirit. Through the ministry of Jesus and the Holy Spirit, God has created for himself a people, the body of Christ, the church.

The Beginning of the Church

The New Testament also tells the story of this new people, the church. It gives guidance, instruction, exhortations, and encouragement for the long journey home, for the mission that Jesus gave to his disciples, and for the times of persecution and trials.

In the New Testament, we find what it means to be God's people—the body of Christ, the purpose of our existence as Christ's body, and the ultimate goal of each believer and the whole creation. In the New Testament we learn about God's final solution to rescue humanity from sin and death.

Books of the New Testament

The New Testament consists of twenty-seven books. The four Gospels narrate the life of Jesus Christ and Acts tells the story of the first Christians. The twenty-one epistles are letters from early church leaders to churches and believers. Letters from the apostle Paul make up most of the epistles in the New Testament. The book of Revelation is unique in the New Testament because it is the only book that is written in an apocalyptic style; in other words, the book relates its message through signs, symbols, dreams, and visions.

Gospels & Acts		The Epistles & Revelation
Gospels:	*Paul's Epistles:*	*General Epistles:*
Matthew	Romans	Hebrews
Mark	1 Corinthians	James
Luke	2 Corinthians	1 Peter
John	Galatians	2 Peter
	Ephesians	1 John
Acts	Philippians	2 John
	Colossians	3 John
	1 Thessalonians	Jude
	2 Thessalonians	
	1 Timothy	Revelation
	2 Timothy	
	Titus	
	Philemon	

New Testament Time Line

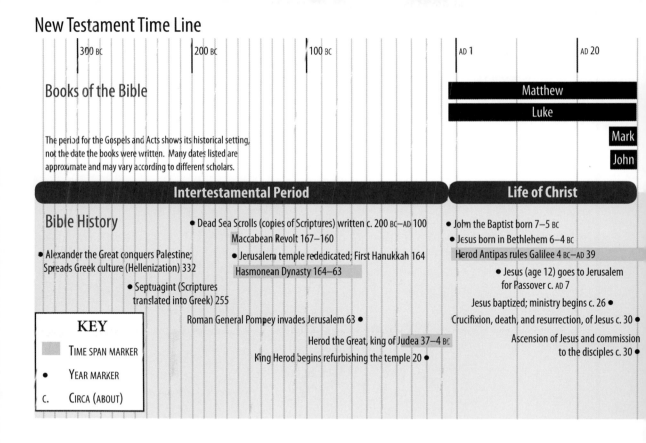

300 BC	200 BC	100 BC	AD 1	AD 20

Books of the Bible

Matthew
Luke
Mark
John

The period for the Gospels and Acts shows its historical setting, not the date the books were written. Many dates listed are approximate and may vary according to different scholars.

Intertestamental Period

Life of Christ

Bible History

- Dead Sea Scrolls (copies of Scriptures) written c. 200 BC–AD 100
- Maccabean Revolt 167–160
- Jerusalem temple rededicated; First Hanukkah 164
- Hasmonean Dynasty 164–63

- Alexander the Great conquers Palestine; Spreads Greek culture (Hellenization) 332
- Septuagint (Scriptures translated into Greek) 255

Roman General Pompey invades Jerusalem 63 ●

Herod the Great, king of Judea 37–4 BC
King Herod begins refurbishing the temple 20 ●

- John the Baptist born 7–5 BC
- Jesus born in Bethlehem 6–4 BC
- Herod Antipas rules Galilee 4 BC–AD 39
- Jesus (age 12) goes to Jerusalem for Passover c. AD 7

Jesus baptized; ministry begins c. 26 ●

Crucifixion, death, and resurrection, of Jesus c. 30 ●

Ascension of Jesus and commission to the disciples c. 30 ●

KEY

Time span marker

● Year marker

c. Circa (about)

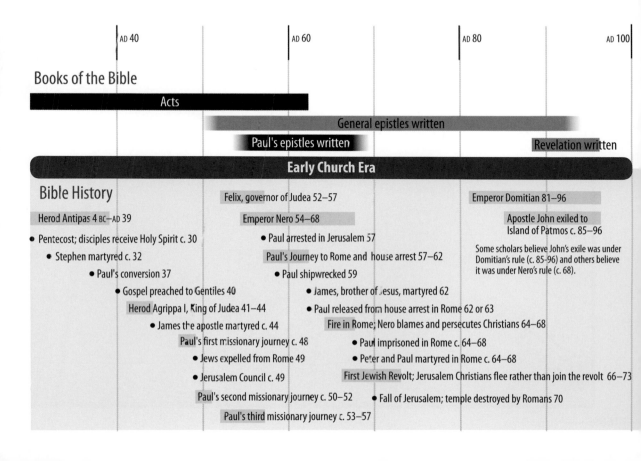

AD 40	AD 60	AD 80	AD 100

Books of the Bible

Acts

General epistles written

Paul's epistles written

Revelation written

Early Church Era

Bible History

Herod Antipas 4 BC–AD 39

- Pentecost; disciples receive Holy Spirit c. 30
- Stephen martyred c. 32
- Paul's conversion 37
- Gospel preached to Gentiles 40
- Herod Agrippa I, King of Judea 41–44
- James the apostle martyred c. 44
- Paul's first missionary journey c. 48
- Jews expelled from Rome 49
- Jerusalem Council c. 49
- Paul's second missionary journey c. 50–52
- Paul's third missionary journey c. 53–57

Felix, governor of Judea 52–57
Emperor Nero 54–68

- Paul arrested in Jerusalem 57
- Paul's Journey to Rome and house arrest 57–62
- Paul shipwrecked 59
- James, brother of Jesus, martyred 62
- Paul released from house arrest in Rome 62 or 63
- Fire in Rome; Nero blames and persecutes Christians 64–68
- Paul imprisoned in Rome c. 64–68
- Peter and Paul martyred in Rome c. 64–68
- First Jewish Revolt; Jerusalem Christians flee rather than join the revolt 66–73
- Fall of Jerusalem; temple destroyed by Romans 70

Emperor Domitian 81–96

Apostle John exiled to Island of Patmos c. 85–96

Some scholars believe John's exile was under Domitian's rule (c. 85-96) and others believe it was under Nero's rule (c. 68).

NEW TESTAMENT HOLY LAND

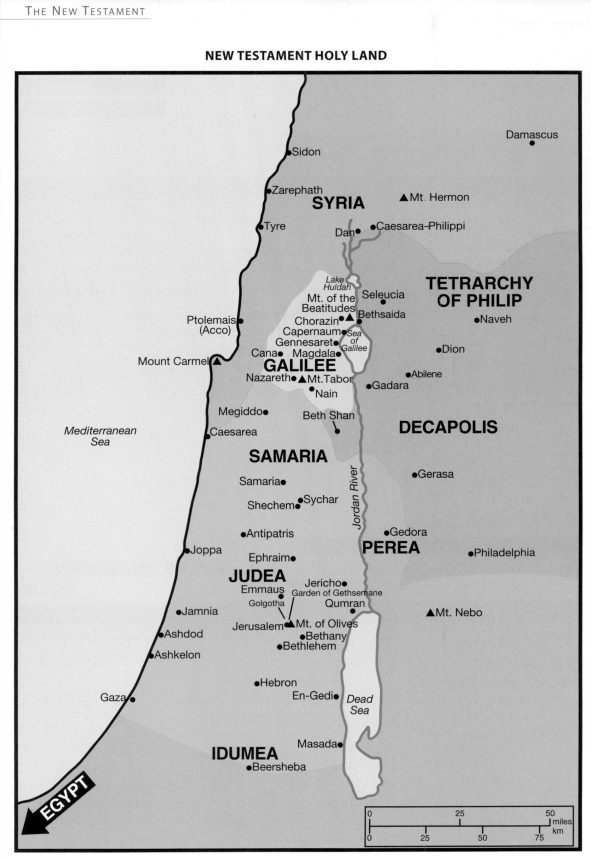

GOSPELS & ACTS

THE LIFE THAT BRINGS NEW LIFE

What Are the Gospels?

The term *gospel* was used in the Roman world as an imperial proclamation, the good news of the deeds of the Caesar. However, in the New Testament, the good news these books present is about "Jesus the Messiah, the Son of God" (Mark 1:1). The Gospels tell a story about the actions and teachings of Jesus. In his life and words, Jesus proclaimed the coming of God's kingdom. God's promises to his people in the Old Testament are now fulfilled in Jesus.

However, we do not find just one story about Jesus. Rather we find four similar yet distinctive stories. Matthew, Mark, Luke, and John tell us about Jesus' life and work from four related perspectives. Why are there four Gospels instead of just one? One answer is that it takes four points of view to get the whole story about Jesus. Some might argue that one authoritative story should be enough. However, God chose to reveal himself using four Gospels. The Gospel of John begins with these words: "In the beginning was the Word … and the Word became flesh (1:1, 14). God chooses as his preferred method of communication to speak to humans by means of the human. This is true of the Bible and it is supremely true of Christ whom we are told is God in the flesh (John 1:14–18). So then, the Gospels are, like Jesus, both a Divine work as well as a human work. They have real human authors and one divine Author. They give details that might be difficult to understand, but they are never truly contradictory. They have four different points of view on the history of Jesus, but only one Divine conclusion as to his identity as the Son of God.

Gospel	Viewpoint	Audience	Jesus the Son of God
Matthew	Palestinian Jewish	A Jewish cultural world	Is he the Messiah the King of Israel?
Mark	Hellenistic Jewish	A Greek cultural world	Is he the power of God active in the World?
Luke	Greek-Roman	A Gentile world	Is he the ideal man of God?
John	Heavenly	The whole world	Is he the Word of God?

The Synoptic Gospels and John

The word *synoptic* means "seen together." It refers to the first three Gospels: Matthew, Mark and Luke. When seen together, these Gospels often reveal related accounts in very similar language. Scholars agree there is some relationship between these three books. The exact nature of this relationship has been the subject of much debate. It seems that these three authors either read one another or some common source, which explains why so much of their content and language are so similar.

The Gospel of John, however, is different than the first three Gospels. John includes material that the other writers do not have. For example, in the feeding of the 5,000, the Synoptic Gospels show that Jesus talks to the disciples as a group, whereas the Gospel of John names specific individuals who talk with Jesus. Also the wording of some of the stories is different. John often adds details that the others do not include. For example, the name of the woman who washed Jesus' feet with her hair (John 12:3), and that John beat Peter in a foot race to the empty tomb on Easter Sunday (John 20:4). Many of these details have a personal tone. On a more theological level, whereas the Synoptic Gospels emphasize the theme of the kingdom of God, the Gospel of John focuses on the concept of eternal life. In the Synoptic Gospels, Jesus' miracles are illustrations of how the kingdom of God has already arrived through Jesus' ministry. In the Gospel of John, miracles (there are no exorcisms in this Gospel) show that Jesus' ministry is superior to Jewish institutions.

The Book of Acts

The book of Acts is a natural continuation of the Gospels. The good news of Jesus continues in the work of Jesus' disciples in Jerusalem and throughout the world. In the book of Acts we find God's plan for humanity being played out in the life of the early Christians, who embodied Jesus' ministry and announced the good news of salvation to all peoples. Similar to the Historical Books in the Old Testament, the book of Acts gives identity to God's people today by showing us how God's mission spread to all people and nations of the world.

Although the apostles Peter and Paul play a significant role in the book, the main characters of the book are God and the church. The apostles Paul and Peter lay the foundations for the spread of the gospel and illustrate the ministry of the Holy Spirit through the apostles. Acts tells about the spread of the gospel. For that reason, some knowledge of the places Christians visited and of the cultures in those places helps us to better understand the importance of the book.

In a very real sense, the book of Acts is about us because we are members of Christ's body. Understanding the book of Acts helps us understand our missions as followers of Christ.

MATTHEW

JESUS IS THE CLIMAX OF PROPHECY

Sermon on the Mount (Matt. 5–7) by Henrik Olrik

The Kingdom of Heaven

Unlike the other Gospels that use the expression "the kingdom of God," the Gospel of Matthew uses "the kingdom of heaven." Since Matthew was probably writing to Christian Jews, he avoids using the name of God out of respect, as Jews continue to do to this day. However, both expressions refer to the same reality: the kingdom that Jesus set in motion through his birth, life, teaching, death, and resurrection.

Purpose

The Gospel of Matthew presents the life and ministry of Jesus as a fulfillment of the long awaited Messiah, David's son, and heir to the kingdom. More than the other Gospels, Matthew focuses on the many ways that Jesus fulfilled the Old Testament promises and God's grand plan of salvation for Israel and the world. In Greek, the first two words of the Gospel, often translated as "a record of genealogy," can also be translated as "the book of genesis." These words introduce Jesus' royal line back to David and Abraham. Matthew presents Jesus as the true Israel in whom God's promises are being fulfilled.

The Gospel focuses on both the life and the message of Jesus Christ. The overall structure of the book gives us a narrative of Jesus' life as he traveled from Galilee to Jerusalem. Within this narrative of his life, Matthew includes Jesus' five sermons about the kingdom of heaven. These "discourses" reveal the centrality of the kingdom in Jesus' teaching and ministry.

Outline

1. Preparing the Way (1:1–4:11)
   a. Birth (1:1–24)
   b. Infancy (2:1–23)
   c. John the Baptist (3:1–12)
   d. Baptism (3:13–17)
   e. Temptation (4:1–11)

2. A Great Light Shown in Galilee (4:12–18:35)
   a. Beginning of ministry and calling of disciples (4:12–25)
   b. First Discourse: The Morality of the Kingdom—The Sermon on the Mount (5:1–7:29)
   c. Miracles and teaching (8:1–9:38)
   d. Second Discourse: The Proclamation of the Kingdom—The Commission of the Twelve (10:1–42)
   e. Opposition to the Messiah (11:1–12:50)
   f. Third Discourse: The Mysteries of the Kingdom—Parables of the Kingdom (13:1–52)
   g. Rejection in Nazareth and death of John the Baptist (14:1–12)
   h. Miracles and teaching (14:13–15:39)
   i. Opposition of Pharisees and Sadducees (16:1–12)
   j. Peter's confession and Jesus predicts his own death (16:13–20)
   k. The transfiguration: Jesus reveals his glory (17:1–13)
   l. Miracles and teaching (17:14–27)

3. Jesus in Judea and Jerusalem (19:1–27:66)
   a. Fourth Discourse: Life in the Kingdom (18:1–35)
   b. Jesus' ministry in Judea and Perea (19:1–20:34)
   c. Triumphal entry, the temple (21:1–17)
   d. Controversies with Pharisees (21:18–23:39)
   e. Fifth Discourse: The Final Coming of the Kingdom—The Olivet Discourse (24:1–25:46)
   f. Prediction and the plot to kill Jesus (26:1–16)
   g. Lord's Supper, Peter's denial predicted and Gethsemane (26:17–46)
   h. Arrest, trial, and Peter's denial (26:47–75)
   i. Judas' suicide (27:1–10)
   j. Jesus before Pilate (27:11–31)
   k. Crucifixion, death, burial, and the guard (27:32–66)

4. Triumph and Mission to All the World (28:1–20)
   a. Resurrection (28:1–10)
   b. Report of the guard (28:11–15)
   c. Great Commission (28:16–20)

St. Matthew and the Angel by Rembrandt

Background

Author: The apostle Matthew, also known as Levi (Mark 2:14), was a tax collector, a Jewish citizen working for the Romans. When he identified himself as a tax collector, he lumped himself in with "sinners," and he showed that it was not a very popular occupation (Matt. 9:9–13; 10:3).

Date: Determining when the book was written is difficult. Scholars suggest dates that range from the late AD 50s to the late 70s. There is no conclusive evidence to determine the date. Many people prefer an early date, some time around AD 60.

Audience: The emphasis on fulfilled prophecy, the use of the expression "the kingdom of heaven," and a lack of explanation of Jewish customs suggest that Matthew might have had a Jewish Christian audience.

Themes

- Jesus announces the arrival of kingdom of heaven (4:17; 7:21; 11:11–12; 18:1–4,23; 25:1, 14).

- Jesus' authority and preeminence over the law (5:21–22, 27–28), the temple (12:6), the Sabbath (12:8), the prophets (12:41), wisdom (12:42), and heaven and earth (28:18).

- Jesus' reference to God as Father (5:45; 6:4–9; 7:11; 11:25–27; 12:50; 16:17; 18:10–19; 28:19).

Key Verses

"But seek first his kingdom and his righteousness, and all these things will be given to you as well."—Matt. 6:33

"All things have been committed to me by my Father. No one knows the Son except the Father, and no one knows the Father except the Son, and those to whom the Son chooses to reveal him. Come to me, all you who are weary and burdened, and I will give you rest."—Matt. 11:27–23

"All authority in heaven and on earth has been given to me. Therefore go and make disciples of all nations, baptizing them in the name of the Father and of the Son and of the Holy Spirit, and teaching them to obey everything I have commanded you. And surely I will be with you always, to the very end of the age."—Matt. 28:18–20

Messiah

Derived from a Hebrew word, the word Messiah, as the Greek word Christ, means "anointed." In the Old Testament, some people chosen for special tasks, such as kings, priests, and prophets, were anointed with oil. In time, as the prophets warned the Israelites about God's judgment and promised God's eventual restoration, the term Messiah referred to one who would come to rule Israel, restore the kingdom of David, and bring peace and prosperity to God's people. Most Jews at the time of Jesus expected a military hero who would liberate them from Rome. However, Jesus was an unexpected Messiah. He did liberate people but not from Rome; rather from sin and death.

Prophecy — God's Promises Fulfilled

The Gospel of Matthew more than the other Gospels focuses on God's Old Testament prophecies being fulfilled in Jesus. Jesus fulfilled more than 100 Old Testament prophecies.

Old Testament Prophecy	Fulfillment in Matthew
A virgin shall bear a son who is "God with Us." Isa. 7:14	Jesus was born of a virgin. 1:23
He will be the "Branch" from David's line. Ps. 80:15; Isa. 4:2; 11:1; Jer. 23:5; 33:15; Zech. 3:8; 6:12	Jesus came from Nazareth. The name Nazareth comes from the word for branch or shoot. 2:23
The northern territory of Israel will see the revelation or his coming. Isa. 9:1–2	Jesus ministered in Galilee. 4:15–16
His life and death will be healing to people. Isa. 53:4	Jesus saved and healed people. 8:17
He will be kind, gentle, and humble. Isa. 42:1–4	Jesus was incredibly kind, gentle and humble. 12:18–21
He will speak and many will not understand. Isa. 6:9–10	Jesus spoke in parables. 13:35
He will be struck and his followers will be scattered. Isa. 53:4–5; Zech. 13:7	Jesus' was arrested and his disciples fled. 26:31–56

Being God's People

As Christians, we are followers of Jesus and citizens of the kingdom of heaven. To us, God revealed the morality of the kingdom of heaven, commissioned us to spread the good news of the kingdom, revealed the mysteries of the kingdom, instructed us to live in the kingdom, and encouraged and comforted us with the promise that the kingdom of heaven will take over all of life when Jesus returns. As people of the kingdom, we serve the King of kings and Lord of lords, before whom "every knee should bow, in heaven and on earth and under the earth" (Phil. 2:10).

MARK

JESUS IS THE HUMBLE SERVANT

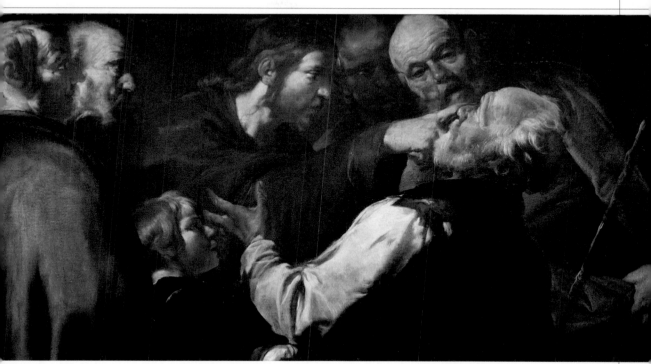

Christ Healing the Blind Man (Mark 8:22–25) by Gioacchino Assereto

Purpose

The Gospel of Mark presents "the beginning of the good news about Jesus the Messiah, the Son of God" (1:1). Mark's Gospel, then, is the starting point of the good news (the gospel) that the awaited Messiah has come. This Messiah is the Son of God. In Mark, a variety of characters identify Jesus as the Son of God:

- God the Father (1:11; 9:7)

- The demons (3:11; 5:7)

- Jesus himself (13:32; 14:61)

- The Roman centurion (15:39)

Mark's main interest is to present the good news. Jesus' first words in the Gospel introduce the good news: "The kingdom of God has come near. Repent and believe the good news!" (1:15). Mark shows that the good news of God's rule over all things has come near. This rule is revealed by Jesus' teachings and miracles. Mark presents Jesus as God's active agent, his power in the world, and his means of defeating sin, death, and the Devil (1:27–28).

In Mark, Jesus, although the Messiah with divine authority (2:1–12; 9:2–8), appears in humility, weakness, and suffering. These themes suggest that Mark is probably writing to a community in distress and persecution. The Gospel of Mark, then, is an account of the good news, Jesus' life in words and actions, and is meant to encourage, comfort, and give hope to a community under duress.

Outline

1. Beginning of Jesus' Ministry (1:1–13)
   a. John the Baptist prepares the way (1:1–8)
   b. Jesus' baptism and temptation (1:9–13)

2. Jesus' Public Ministry (1:14–8:26)
   a. Calling of disciples (1:14–45)
   b. Controversies with the Jewish authorities (2:1–3:12)
   c. Teachings and power of the kingdom (3:13–6:6a)
   d. Jesus' ministry beyond Galilee (6:6b–8:26)

3. Toward Jerusalem, Passion, Death, and Resurrection (8:27–16:8)
   a. Crisis foretold (8:27–10:52)
   b. Arrest, death, and resurrection (11:1–16:8)

St. Mark by Frans Hals

A Personal Touch

Both Matthew and Mark give the name of the man who helped Jesus carry his cross, Simon of Cyrene. But only Mark names him as the father of Alexander and Rufus (15:21). Years later in Paul's letter to the Romans we hear of another Rufus and his mother in Rome (Rom. 16:13), who might be the same person Mark names in his Gospel. Mark's reference might be a personal touch naming someone whom the Roman Christians might know.

Background

Author: An early church tradition holds that John Mark, a friend of Paul and cousin to Barnabas (Acts 12:12; Col. 4:10), wrote this work after being a disciple of the apostle Peter (1 Peter 5:13). The church leaders Papias, Irenaeus, and Clement of Alexandria, in the first and second centuries AD, are the source of this tradition. The rapid-fire style of the Gospel may show some influence from Peter's own writing style. We first learn about Mark in connection to his mother. Believers met at her house to worship (Acts 12:12). He accompanied Paul and Barnabas in their first missionary journey (Acts 12:25). After deserting them in Perga (Acts 13:13), he followed Barnabas to Cyprus.

Date: Many scholars believe Mark was the first to write his Gospel. If this is true, Mark might have written the Gospel in the late AD 50s. Other scholars suggest a later date just before the destruction of Jerusalem and the temple in AD 70.

Audience: If Mark wrote his Gospel in Rome, as many scholars think, it is possible his intended audience was Roman. The theme of suffering, power of God, and hope for the future, as well as the explanation of Jewish customs, suggest that Mark's audience could have been a community of Gentile believers under persecution and suffering, such as the church in Rome.

The Son of God and Son of Man

Son of God

As Christians, when we read the words "Son of God," we immediately and correctly think of the second member of the Trinity, Jesus. However, at the time Jesus lived on earth, that was not the natural meaning of the expression.

The expression is connected to God's promise to David. God promised that one of David's descendants would be on the throne of Israel forever: "I will be his father, and he will be my son" (2 Sam. 7:14). The expression is also connected to Israel as a people. God is the "father of Israel" (Isa. 64:8; Jer. 31:9). The expression, then, "Son of God" referred back to the king; it was royal language. Initially, calling Jesus "the Son of God" meant that he was Israel's king, descendant of David, the Messiah.

Most non-Jewish people within the Roman Empire would recognize the expression "Son of God" as referring to the Caesar. By affirming that Jesus is "the Son of God," the Gospels indirectly deny that any Caesar can truly hold that title.

However, in time, the disciples and all the people realized that Jesus was more than just David's son. As the Roman centurion confessed, "surely this man was the Son of God" (Mark 15:39). Jesus is King, but he is not King of Israel alone. He is the King of kings and God himself in the flesh.

Son of Man

Mark also affirms that Jesus is the "Son of Man." This expression occurs in three different contexts:

1. Jesus' earthly ministry (Mark 2:10, 28; 8:20; 13:37; 16:13; 18:11)

2. Jesus' humiliation and suffering (Mark 8:31; 9:31; 10:33; 9:12; 10:45)

3. The future coming in judgment (Mark 8:38; 14:62)

The expression "Son of Man" is likely connected to the prophet Daniel's vision of one "like a son of man" who receives victory and dominion from God (Dan. 7:14–18). "Son of Man," then, also expresses the promise of a King, one who would defeat the forces of evil (the four beasts in Daniel) and establish God's eternal kingdom. Thus, the two expressions, Son of God and Son of Man, are complementary and point to Jesus' role as King and Messiah.

Themes

- **The Gospel.** The gospel must be preached (8:35; 10:29; 13:10; 14:9).

- **The Nature of God.** God is passionate and compassionate.

- **Jesus' Emotions.** Mark shows us Jesus' emotions: compassion (1:41; 6:34; 8:2); anger (3:5; 10:14); weariness (7:34; 8:12); overwhelming sorrow (14:33–34).

- **Jesus' Passion.** Mark focuses a major portion of his work on Jesus' Passion (his last hours and crucifixion) and the events leading up to it (chapters 10–16).

- **The Goodness of God.** God is unstoppably good. (1:32–34; 3:10–11; 5:18–20; 6:47–56; 7:33–37; 10:27; 11:22–23; 16:6–7).

- **The Messianic Mystery.** In the Gospel of Mark, Jesus warned different people to not reveal to others that he was the Messiah (Mark 1:43–44; 1:34; 3:11–12; 5:43; 7:36; 8:30; 9:9). Because first century Jews expected the Messiah to be a conquering hero, Jesus revealed slowly his true nature as the Messiah.

Curious Details

Some think that the unnamed "young man wearing nothing but a linen garment" in Mark 14:51–52 is a reference to Mark himself. This may be so, but it is certainly an example of detail that often Mark alone provides. Alternatively, the reference might be one of those curious details that an aged witness—perhaps Peter—would recall in his memoirs of those amazing events surrounding the death of Jesus.

Key Verses

"For whoever wants to save his life will lose it, but whoever loses his life for me and for the gospel will save it."—Mark 8:3

Filled with compassion, Jesus reached out his hand and touched the man.—Mark 1:41

"Don't be alarmed," he said. *"You are looking for Jesus the Nazarene, who was crucified. He has risen! He is not here."*—Mark 16:6

Being God's People

Marks presents two equally important sides of Jesus. On the one hand, Jesus is "the Son of God," full of power and authority, which he demonstrates through many miracles and teaching with authority. On the other hand, Jesus is humble, unassuming, obedient, and a servant.

With that presentation, the Gospel challenges our normal concept of leadership: to be a leader does not mean having power and being feared like the Caesars. Rather, it means to be humble, obedient, and have the heart of a servant. Jesus was a servant-leader through whom God's power shone brightly.

The Gospel of Mark presents the "beginning of the gospel ... " The gospel continues through the life and ministry of each and every Christian since Christ ascended until he returns in power and glory.

LUKE

THE GOSPEL FOR THE WORLD

Jesus' Entry into Jerusalem (Luke 19:28–43)

Luke, Mark, and Paul

Luke as the author of both the Gospel and Acts is the most prolific writer of the New Testament. Paul wrote more books, but Luke wrote more pages. Luke knew John Mark as well (Col. 4:10, 14; Philem. 24). It is a common view among scholars that Mark's Gospel was one of the source materials used by Luke (1:1–2). Many scholars point to Luke's use of Mark's basic outline of events. To this Luke adds much more material and his own insight in the development of his Gospel.

Purpose

Luke's main purpose is to show that the good news of Jesus is meant for the whole world. First, Luke addresses the book to Theophilus who was probably a Gentile, an indication that Luke saw the gospel message as not only for the Jewish people. Second, the sending of the seventy—or seventy-two—disciples occurs only in Luke (10:1–24). For many rabbis, seventy was the number of languages of the world. Sending seventy disciples meant that the gospel was being preached to the whole world.

In addition, Luke, who is also thought to be the author of the book of Acts, wants to show how Jesus' ministry is extended to the disciples at the end of the Gospel and into Acts.

Outline

1. Prologue (1:1–4)

2. Birth of Jesus (1:5–2:52)

3. Preparation for Jesus' Ministry (3:1–4:13)

4. The Work in Galilee (4:14–9:50)
   a. Beginning of his ministry in Galilee (4:14–5:16)
   b. Beginning of conflicts (5:17–6:11)
   c. Jesus and his disciples (6:12–49)
   d. Identity of Jesus (7:1–50)
   e. Teachings of Jesus (8:1–21)
   f. The power of Jesus (8:22–56)
   g. Jesus and the twelve disciples (9:1–50)

5. The Ministry on the Way to Jerusalem (9:51–19:27)
   a. Ministry in Judea (9:51–13:21)
   b. Ministry in and around Perea (13:22–19:27)

6. The Work in Jerusalem (19:28–24:53)
   a. Triumphal entry and cleansing of the temple (19:28–48)
   b. Authority of Jesus questioned (20:1–47)
   c. The Olivet Discourse (21:1–37)
   d. Last Supper (22:1–38)
   e. Gethsemane (22:39–46)
   f. Jesus arrested (22:47–65)
   g. Jesus, Pilate, and Herod (22:66–23:25)
   h. The crucifixion (23:26–56)
   i. The resurrection and appearances (24:1–49)
   j. The ascension (24:50–53)

Theophilus

Both of Luke and Acts are addressed to a certain Theophilus whom the author calls "most excellent" (Luke 1:3; Acts 1:1) The same Greek word is applied to Felix (Acts 24:3) and Festus (Acts 26:25) both Roman governors. Theophilus may have been a Roman official. Another possibility is that he was a Christian convert who became Luke's patron. Books were expensive, and only a few people and groups were able to afford them. It was common to have a wealthy patron who would keep the books and grant access to others to read. Theophilus might have financed Luke's writing, paid for copies of the books, and granted churches access to the books.

Background

Author: Luke is thought to be the author, based on a second century (100s) tradition that names him as the author of this Gospel as well as Acts. Also, evidence from the two books and Paul's letters make that conclusion more likely. The introductions to Luke and Acts seem to connect the books; both are addressed to Theophilus (Luke 1:3; Acts 1:1).

It is likely that Luke was a Gentile, well educated, companion and friend of Paul, and possibly the same Luke the physician mentioned in Colossians 4:14. Luke followed Paul from his second missionary journey through the time of Paul's house arrest in Rome (2 Tim. 4:11).

St. Luke by James J. Tissot

Date: Tradition says that Paul was martyred sometime late in the persecution of Christians by Roman Emperor Nero (AD 64–68). Thus, Luke probably wrote both his books around AD 60–62 before the fires in Rome for which Nero falsely blamed and persecuted Christians.

Audience: The Gospel of Luke was most likely intended for a Gentile audience. It is presented as a biography similar to other works of its day. The book is historical, although not in the same way we think of a historical book. It is historical in the sense of being a character portrait of Jesus the man, his work and, if Acts is included, his continuing work in and through others.

The Gospels as Biography

Modern Biographies	Ancient Biographies
Biographies place a premium on historical sequencing. This means that the events of the subject's life are typically narrated in the order in which they happened. Beginning with the birth of the individual, relevant events and information are viewed in sequential order up to the death of the subject. While chapters may present different phases in the subject's life, these phases are arranged in the order in which they are supposed to have happened.	Ancient biographers had a general commitment to an historical sequence. They did not feel the need to place every detail in their writings in the exact order in which it happened. Much more emphasis is given to developing an accurate picture of the character of the subject. Deeds and happenings are seen as illustrative of that character no matter when they occurred.

Example:

Luke 7:36–50 is an example of the non-sequential nature of ancient biographies. This passage is Luke's account of the woman who anointed Jesus' feet. Matthew, Mark and John tell this event as part of Jesus' arrival at Bethany just before the events of Easter week. Despite Luke's care as an accurate historian (Luke 1:1–4), he places this event much earlier in Jesus' ministry.

Some have tried to resolve the difficulty by suggesting that there were two such events, two times when various women anointed Jesus' feet. But scholars think that the details of Luke's account too closely resemble the other Gospel accounts to make it a separate incident.

It is possible that Luke (and so the Holy Spirit) placed this event out of historical sequence to illustrate the coming of the kingdom of God through the Messiah Jesus. This story, like the stories before it, illustrate the kind of Messiah Jesus is: one who heals—like the story of the centurion and the widow's son show—and one who forgives, as the story of the woman who anoints Jesus' feet shows. For Luke, this story helps demonstrate who the Messiah is, which was more important than placing the story in historical sequence as the other Gospels do.

Themes

- The presence and ministry of the Holy Spirit (1:15; 1:35; 3:22; 4:1, 14, 18; 10:21; 24:49).

- Luke, like Matthew, lays emphasis on the kingdom and Jesus as king (4:43; 6:20; 7:28; 9:2; 10:9–11; 12:32; 13:18–29; 14:15–24; 17:20–21; 18:15–17; 19:11–27).

- Luke focuses on the spiritual realm with frequent references to angels (more than twenty times) and the hidden reality of God (1:11, 26; 2:9, 13; 9:28–36; 22:43; 24:15–31).

- God's care for the poor and the disadvantaged in society (5:12–14; 6:17–26; 8:36–50; 13:10–17; 18:9–17; 19:1–10; 21:1–4).

- Jesus as the perfect spiritual man (3:23, 38).

Gospel

The word *gospel* translates the Greek word *euangelion*, which means "good news." Around the time Jesus was born, the term *euangelion* was used to announce the birth of the emperor's (Caesar's) son and future Caesar. The Roman empire promised a *pax romana*, a Roman peace, that would benefit all peoples. Caesar was regarded as the son of the gods, divinely chosen to rule the world. The gospel in the New Testament refers to the birth of the true King, one who came first to be a humble servant and a savior, and then he will rule as the rightful King of all forever. The gospel is the good news about Jesus' life, death, and resurrection, and the new life that he offers to all who repent and believe in him as their King and Savior.

Key Verses

"The Spirit of the Lord is on me, because he has anointed me to preach good news to the poor. He has sent me to proclaim freedom for the prisoners and recovery of sight for the blind, to release the oppressed, to proclaim the year of the Lord's favor."—Luke 4:18–19 (Isa. 61:1–2)

"Blessed are you who are poor, for yours is the kingdom of God."—Luke 6:20

The centurion, seeing what had happened, praised God and said, "Surely this was a righteous man."—Luke 23:47

Being God's People

The Gospel of Luke presents the ongoing importance, relevance, and necessity of the good news for all humans. The presence of the kingdom of God now is seen the work of the Holy Spirit who equips, guides, and empowers believers to continue the work that Jesus began. Besides the wondrous salvation Jesus accomplished on the cross, Jesus was also an example of what it means to live and serve God in his kingdom. Empowered and led by the Holy Spirit, all Christians are entrusted to continue Jesus' ministry until he returns, as he promised.

JOHN

THE WORD BECAME FLESH

The Descent from the Cross (John 19:31–42) by Peter Paul Rubens

Purpose

The Gospel of John makes its purpose clear: "But these are written that you may believe that Jesus is the Messiah, the Son of God, and that by believing you may have life in his name" (John 20:31).

The Gospel of John seems to have two main purposes:

1. For teaching, in that it presents Jesus as the Messiah, the Son of God in the flesh and helps believers to continue exercising their faith in Christ.

2. For evangelism, in that it leads people to have faith in Jesus the Messiah.

In addition, the Gospel of John also seems to argue against the view that the material world is evil and worthless. By showing Jesus, the Word, becoming flesh, the Gospel of John shows that the material world, although sinful and dominated by the powers of evil, is worth redeeming and is valuable to God.

Outline

1. Prologue: The Word of God Becomes Flesh (1:1–18)

2. Preparation and Start of Ministry (1:19–2:11)
   a. John the Baptist and Jesus' baptism (1:19–34)
   b. Beginning of discipleship (1:35–51)
   c. First miracle in Galilee (2:1–2:11)

3. First Passover—First Year (2:12–4:54)
   a. Cleansing the temple (2:12–25)
   b. Jesus and Nicodemus (3:1–21)
   c. Jesus and John the Baptist (3:22–36)
   d. Jesus and the Samaritan woman (4:1–42)
   e. Healing at Cana (4:43–54)

4. Second Passover—Second Year (5:1–6:2)
   a. Healing at the pool (5:1–15)
   b. Opposition from the Jewish leaders (5:16–47)
   c. Miracles in Galilee (6:1–2)

5. Third Passover—Third Year (6:3–11:57)
   a. Jesus the bread of life (6:3–71)
   b. Jesus the living water—Feast of Tabernacles (7:1–8:11)
   c. Jesus the light of the world (8:12–41)
   d. Jesus the I AM (8:42–59)
   e. Jesus heals a blind man (9:1–41)
   f. Jesus the gate of the sheepfold and good shepherd (10:1–21)
   g. Jesus and the Father are one—Feast of Dedication (10:22–42)
   h. Jesus the resurrection and life (11:1–11:57)

6. Last Passover—Easter Week (12:1–19:42)
   a. Jesus anointed at Bethany (12:1–11)
   b. Triumphal entry into Jerusalem (12:12–19)
   c. Jesus predicts his death (12:20–50)
   d. Jesus in the upper room with his disciples (13:1–17:26)
   e. Jesus' arrest, trial, and crucifixion (18:1–19:42)

7. The Resurrection and Appearances (20:1–31)

8. Epilogue (21:1–25)

John, "the disciple whom Jesus loved"
Mosaic of the Last Supper of Christ

Background

Author: The authorship of this Gospel has raised much discussion among scholars. According to a well-known tradition of the church, John the apostle wrote this book. This view is based on the witness of Irenaeus and other second-century church leaders. Irenaeus had close contact with at least two disciples of John. He affirmed that John wrote his Gospel after all the others had written theirs. Other scholars have suggested that there was another John, John the Elder, who may have been responsible for the Gospel. The Gospel itself refers to "the disciple whom Jesus loved" (John 13:23; 19:26; 20:2; 21:7), who probably is John, the author of the book. It is likely that John also wrote the letters of 1, 2, and 3 John and the book of Revelation.

Date: Some scholars have suggested this Gospel was written first because it is so very different and independent of the other three, but most consider the work later than the Synoptic Gospels—Matthew, Mark, and Luke. With that assumption, a likely period for the writing is AD 85–95.

Audience: Tradition holds that John wrote his Gospel while living in Ephesus. Ephesus was a cosmopolitan port city of great importance. It already had a Jewish presence including followers of John the Baptist early on in the days of Paul's missionary work (Acts 19:1–12). The apostle John's care in describing Jesus' ministry and the ministry of John the Baptist (1:19–37; 3:22–36) may reflect the apostle's concern for his Jewish audience. But John's Gospel also appealed to Gentiles by using the term "Word" (*Logos*), which for the larger Gentile audience would have carried the idea of "the Divine Mind" behind creation.

Themes

The Persons of the Trinity. John shows the relationship of Jesus to the Father through the Spirit (1:1–18; 3:13–21; 4:21–26; 5:16–47; 6:32–63; 7:28–29; 8:14–58; 10:17–18, 22–39; 12:44–50; 14:1–31; 15:1–16:33). The Gospel focuses on Jesus' connection to the Father. It is this relationship in the power and love of the Holy Spirit that is at the center and foundation of everything else from creation to salvation.

Contrasting Realities. Unlike the other Gospels that focus on the contrast between the present and the future, the Gospel of John focuses on two realities: the heavenly and the worldly realities (8:23; 16:11; 18:36). John makes this contrast using several important images:

1. Darkness and Light (1:5; 8:12; 9:5; 12:35–36)
2. Flesh and Spirit (1:13; 3:6; 4:24; 6:63)
3. The Old and the New (2:1–25)

The heavenly realm refers to God's rule, which is characterized by light, life, and the presence of the Spirit.

Logos

The Greek word *logos* was an important word in the Greek understanding of the world at the time. Based on a philosophy called Stoicism, many Greeks believed that the world was in constant change (just like the water of a river going under a bridge). However, the universe had an eternal principle (the *logos*) that gave order, meaning, and allowed morality to be possible. It is likely that John referred to this concept when using the term for Jesus (1:1). Most Gentile believers would have known about the Greek *logos* and understood how John was using the term.

It is also likely that John had in mind an Old Testament usage of the term. *Logos* can also simply mean "word." The Greek translation of the Old Testament—the Septuagint—uses *logos* to translate the Hebrew for "the word of the LORD." The expression refers to the active and revealing activity of God. Jesus reveals the Father (John 17:6; Heb. 1:2). In fact, Jesus affirms that "this is eternal life: that they know you, the only true God, and Jesus Christ, whom you have sent" (John 17:3).

The worldly realm—the "world" in the Gospel—refers to the usurping rule of Satan, which is characterized by darkness, death, and sin. One of Jesus' missions was to unmask Satan as the false ruler he is. Jesus is the only rightful ruler of the whole world (*kosmos* in Greek).

The Seven "I Am's"

1. "I am the bread of life" (6:35)
2. "I am the light of the world" (8:12; 9:5)
3. "I am the door" (10:7, 9)
4. "I am the good shepherd" (10:11)
5. "I am the resurrection and the life" (11:25)
6. "I am the way, the truth, and the life" (14:6)
7. "I am the true vine" (15:1)

Love. Love is a central theme in the writings of John: the Gospel and the letters of John.

Identity of Jesus. Jesus' teachings about himself reveal that he is God's Son (6:35; 7:37–38; 8:12, 58; 10:1–21; 13:12–17; 14:6; 18:36–37). He came to the world for two main reasons: to reveal the Father and to die for the world. In the book of John, Jesus teaches the famous seven "I am's" to illustrate with powerful images who he is. All the images come from the Old Testament. In them, Jesus identifies with God because he is God.

The Holy Spirit. Although the other Gospels also teach about the Holy Spirit, the emphasis in the Gospel of John is unique. The Holy Spirit is sent as a result of Jesus' death and resurrection. The Holy Spirit's ministry anticipates the full coming of the kingdom (chapters 14–16).

Jesus and Miracles. Jesus' miracles are signs of his identity as the Incarnate Son of God (2:11; 4:46–54; 5:1–15; 6:1–21; 9:1–41; 11:1–45; 20:1–31).

Key Verses

In the beginning was the Word, and the Word was with God, and the Word was God.... The Word became flesh and made his dwelling among us. We have seen his glory, the glory of the one and only Son, who came from the Father, full of grace and truth.—John 1:1, 14

For God so loved the world that he gave his one and only Son, that whoever believes in him shall not perish but have eternal life. For God did not send his Son into the world to condemn the world, but to save the world through him.—John 3:16–17

"I am the vine; you are the branches. If you remain in me and I in you, you will bear much fruit; apart from me you can do nothing."—John 15:5

Being God's People

The Gospel of John reveals God's wonderful promise of a new birth into an abundant life. God challenged his people to take hold of that promise offered in his Son Jesus. As Jesus prepared his disciples to continue his ministry, he promised to send the very same Spirit that empowered him to be their teacher, counselor, and comforter.

ACTS

THE STORY OF THE EARLY CHURCH

Apostle Paul Preaching on the Ruins by Giovanni Paolo Pannini

Purpose

The book of Acts continues where the Gospel of Luke left off, with Jesus' resurrection. In the Gospel of Luke we meet the Word of God—Jesus—acting through the power of the Holy Spirit. Jesus, the Messiah, fulfills God's promises to Israel and brings good news to all people from all walks of life. In the book of Acts, Luke continues the story about God's work in history. Acts tells the story of what the disciples did as a response to Jesus' commissioning (Acts 1:4–5, 8). Through the power of the Holy Spirit, the apostles continued the work that Jesus began.

Luke presents not a history in the academic sense that we use that word today. He presents a selective history, a history that helps him accomplish several important purposes:

1. *A Proclamation Purpose:* The book of Acts proclaims the good news of Jesus. In the narration of events, and in the speeches, we find a basic presentation of the good news that was pivotal for the life of the early church and is still useful today.

2. *An Apologetic Purpose:* Judaism was a legal religion in the Roman empire. This means that the Jews were free to practice their religion as they saw fit. At first, Christianity was seen as a division of Judaism. However, both Jews and Christians

soon separated themselves from each other. Christians had to show the citizens of Rome that Christianity was not dangerous, but rather a source of blessings for all. This apologetic purpose is best seen in the speeches of Peter (2:14–40; 3:12–26; 4:8–12), Stephen (7:1–53), and Paul (13:10–42; 17:22–31; 20:17–25; 21:40–22:21; 23:1–6; 24:10–21; 26:1–29), and the encounters with the Roman government officers (13:4–12; 18:9–17; 22:22–23:11; 24:1–27; 25:1–26:32).

3. *A Unifying Purpose:* As the church was growing out, numerically and geographically, the issue of how to include Gentiles came to the forefront.

Although both the Gospel of Luke and the book of Acts emphasize the mission to the Gentiles, the work among the Jews was equally important. By focusing both on Peter who ministered primarily in Jerusalem and Paul who ventured to spread the gospel to the Gentile world, the book of Acts shows the importance of preaching the gospel to Jew and Gentile alike.

4. *A Teaching Purpose:* The book of Acts was meant to be a book of instruction for the many new believers throughout the Roman empire. Believers needed to know the origin of their faith (Gospel of Luke) and the way the power of the gospel spread through the empire (book of Acts). As believers could trace God's actions in the Old Testament, they could also trace the actions of the Holy Spirit in their time. The history of the book of Acts is the history of God's people, and it shows how the Holy Spirit is moving throughout the world through believers' words and actions.

Pentecost (Acts 2) by Titian

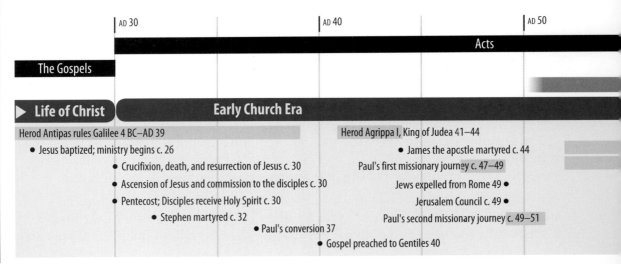

AD 30	AD 40	AD 50

Acts

The Gospels

▶ Life of Christ　　　　　　　Early Church Era

Herod Antipas rules Galilee 4 BC–AD 39　　　　　　Herod Agrippa I, King of Judea 41–44

• Jesus baptized; ministry begins c. 26　　　　　　　　• James the apostle martyred c. 44

• Crucifixion, death, and resurrection of Jesus c. 30　　Paul's first missionary journey c. 47–49

• Ascension of Jesus and commission to the disciples c. 30　Jews expelled from Rome 49 •

• Pentecost; Disciples receive Holy Spirit c. 30　　　Jerusalem Council c. 49 •

• Stephen martyred c. 32　　　　　　　Paul's second missionary journey c. 49–51

• Paul's conversion 37

• Gospel preached to Gentiles 40

Outline

1. The Work of Jesus Continues with the Apostles (1:1–11)

2. The Mission in Jerusalem (1:12–8:3)
   a. The ministry of Peter (1:12–5:42)
   b. The ministry of Stephen (6:1–8:3)

3. The Mission in Samaria and Judea (8:4–11:18)
   a. The ministry of Philip (8:4–40)
   b. The conversion of Saul (Paul) (9:1–31)
   c. The ministry of Peter continues (9:32–11:18)

4. The Mission to the Ends of the Earth (11:19–28:31)
   a. The ministry of Barnabas (11:19–30)
   b. The conclusion of Peter's ministry (12:1–19a)
   c. The death of Herod Agrippa I (12:19b–25)
   d. The ministry of Paul and Barnabas: First missionary journey (13:1–14:28)
   e. The Jerusalem Council (15:1–35)
   f. The ministry of Paul and Silas: Second missionary journey (15:36–18:22)
   g. The ministry of Paul: Third missionary journey (18:23–21:14)
   h. Paul in Jerusalem (21:15–23:10)
   i. Paul in Caesarea (23:11–26:32)
   j. Paul taken to Rome (27:1–28:29)
   k. Conclusion: The gospel preached throughout the world (28:30–31)

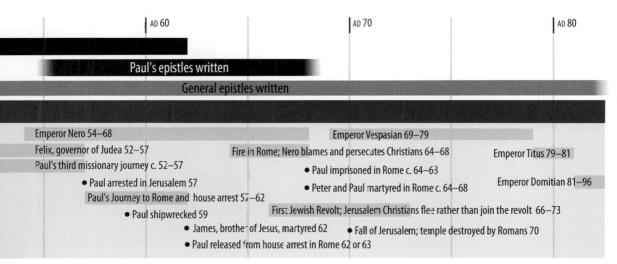

AD 60　　　　　　　　　　AD 70　　　　　　　　　　AD 80

Paul's epistles written

General epistles written

Emperor Nero 54–68　　　　　　　　　Emperor Vespasian 69–79
Felix, governor of Judea 52–57　　　　Fire in Rome; Nero blames and persecutes Christians 64–68　　　Emperor Titus 79–81
Paul's third missionary journey c. 52–57
　　　　　　　　　　• Paul imprisoned in Rome c. 64–63
　• Paul arrested in Jerusalem 57　　　　　　　　　　　　　　Emperor Domitian 81–96
　　Paul's Journey to Rome and house arrest 57–62　　• Peter and Paul martyred in Rome c. 64–68
　　　• Paul shipwrecked 59　　　First Jewish Revolt; Jerusalem Christians flee rather than join the revolt 66–73
　　　　　• James, brother of Jesus, martyred 62　　• Fall of Jerusalem; temple destroyed by Romans 70
　　　　　• Paul released from house arrest in Rome 62 or 63

Background

Author: An early church tradition names Luke as the author of Acts as well as the Gospel that bears his name.

Determining the authorship of an anonymous text is very difficult. However, there seems to be enough internal evidence between the two books and Paul's letters to make Luke a plausible suggestion. Acts 28:16–31 suggests that the author of the book came to Rome with Paul. From Paul's prison epistles written from Rome a list of those who were with him there can be assembled: Epaphras, Epaphroditus, Timothy, Tychicus, Aristarchus, Mark, Jesus called Justus, Demas, and Luke. The first two did not arrive with Paul when he came to Rome. The next four on the list are ruled out because the author mentions them by name in Acts. Demas deserted Paul later, which makes him an unlikely candidate, leaving only Jesus-Justus and Luke. No tradition exists in favor of authorship by Jesus-Justus. Also, some medical terminology appears in both the Gospel of Luke and the book of Acts, and Paul mentions a Luke in Colossians 4:14 who was a physician.

Date: Because of the historical sequence found in the Gospel and Acts, it is likely that Acts was written after the Gospel. If Luke wrote the Gospel around the years 60–62, it is possible that Acts was written shortly after that period.

Audience: Both Luke and Acts address a certain Theophilus. He is addressed as "most excellent" (Luke 1:3), a common way of addressing socially important people. Some scholars have suggested that Theophilus was an important Roman noble, perhaps a member of the government.

Others suggest that he could have been a Christian convert who became Luke's patron. Books were expensive, and only a few people and groups were able to afford them. It was common to have a wealthy patron to write books for who would keep them and grant access to others to read. If Theophilus was a wealthy patron, then it is possible that he financed Luke's writing, paid for copies of the book, and granted churches access to the book.

Acts was meant for several audiences: first, the book is addressed to an individual— Theophilus; second, it's for other people like him—perhaps Romans who were intrigued by Christianity; and third, it's for all Christian believers—Jews and Gentiles alike.

Philip Baptizes the Ethiopian Eunuch
(Acts 8:26–40) by Rembrandt

Themes

Commission to the Disciples. Jesus' mission continues through the acts of his disciples. Jesus sent his disciples to be his witnesses "in Jerusalem, and in all Judea and Samaria, and to the ends of the earth" (1:8).

The Coming of the Holy Spirit. When Jesus sent his disciples to proclaim the gospel, he promised to send them the Holy Spirit: "But you will receive power when the Holy Spirit comes on you" (1:8).

The Cost of Discipleship. Because of his mission, Jesus suffered greatly. Suffering and rejection continue in the mission of the disciples (1:3; 14:22; 28:17–31).

The Spread of the Gospel. The book of Acts tells about the fulfillment of Jesus' orders to his disciples. They preached the gospel throughout the known world.

The Leadership of the Church. Leadership in the church was vital during the early formative years of the church. Although there are many important leaders—Stephen, James, Barnabas and Silas, and many more—the book of Acts focuses on two main leaders: Peter and Paul. Peter, who appeared as the natural leader of the apostles, enters the scene first and dominates the book early on. A bit surprisingly, the focus then shifts to Paul, and his story goes on much longer. However, the book of Acts makes parallel affirmations about both apostles that place them on equal footing. In addition, these parallels show that Paul, although not an apostle when Jesus was on earth, became an apostle just like Peter.

Parallels between Peter and Paul in Acts

Action	Peter	Paul
Healed a lame man	3:2–8	14:8–10
Performed a miracle at a distance	5:15	19:12
Exorcised evil spirits	5:16	16:18
Defeated sorcerers	8:18–24	13:6–11
Raised the dead	9:36–43	20:9–12
Defended themselves against Jewish authorities	4:8–12; 5:27–32	22:3–21; 23:1–6; 28:25–28
Received heavenly visions	10:9–16	16:9
Involved in giving the Holy Spirit upon new believers	8:14–17	19:1–7
Miraculously released from prison	5:19; 12:7–11	16:25–27
Proclaimed the same message	2:27	13:35

The Gospel in the Book of Acts

In the book of Acts, we find a basic presentation of the gospel. It is not the only presentation of the gospel, but it is a message that appealed to Jews and Gentiles. The basic outline was helpful for Christians then and is helpful for Christians today.

1. God's promises to Israel are now fulfilled with the coming of Jesus, the Messiah (2:30; 3:19, 24; 10:43; 26:6–7, 22).

2. God anointed Jesus as his Messiah during his baptism (10:38).

3. Jesus began his ministry in Galilee after his baptism (10:37). His ministry showed God's power with words and actions.

4. Jesus, the Messiah, suffered and died on the cross according to God's own plan (2:23; 3:13–15, 18; 4:11; 10:39; 26:23).

5. God raised Jesus from the dead. Jesus appeared to his disciples (2:24, 31–32; 3:15, 26; 10:40–41; 17:31; 26:23).

6. God exalted Jesus and gave him the name of "Lord" (2:25–29, 33–36; 3:13; 10:36).

7. God sent the Holy Spirit to create a new community, the church (1:8; 2:14–18, 38–39; 10:44–47).

8. Jesus will come back one day to judge all people and to make all things new (3:20–21; 10:42; 17:31).

9. The good news of Jesus is for all people. The gospel urges all people to hear the message, repent, and be baptized (2:21, 38; 3:19; 10:43, 47–48; 17:30; 26:20).

The Movement of God in Luke-Acts

Tracking God's movement through the books of Luke and Acts is an interesting exercise. God moves from the outside in and then from the inside out, much like the Spirit's movement in individual lives.

● God invades planet earth from the outside in as a baby (Luke 1:5–4:13).

● Jesus invades Galilee of the Gentiles first (Luke 4:14–9:50).

● Jesus invades Samaria and Judea (Luke 9:51–19:27).

● Jesus invades Jerusalem at Passover (Luke 19:28–22:46).

CRUCIFIXION AND RESURRECTION (Luke 22:47–Acts 1:11).

● The Holy Spirit takes Jerusalem at Pentecost (Acts 1:12–7:60).

● The Holy Spirit takes Judea and Samaria (Acts 8:1–40).

● The Holy Spirit takes the nations (Acts 9:1–28:31).

● The Holy Spirit takes the world from the inside out through the body of Christ.

Key Verses

In my former book, Theophilus, I wrote about all that Jesus began to do and to teach until the day he was taken up to heaven, after giving instructions through the Holy Spirit to the apostles he had chosen. After his suffering, he showed himself to these men and gave many convincing proofs that he was alive. He appeared to them over a period of forty days and spoke about the kingdom of God.—Acts 1:1–3

[Christ's promise to his disciples:] *"But you will receive power when the Holy Spirit comes on you; and you will be my witnesses in Jerusalem, and in all Judea and Samaria, and to the ends of the earth."*—Acts 1: 8

[Paul's address to King Agrippa II:] *"Short time or long—I pray God that not only you but all who are listening to me today may become what I am [a Christ-follower], except for these chains."*—Acts 26:29

Being God's People

Jesus promised that the presence and power of his Spirit would be with his disciples so that all of them would be able to carry on Jesus' mission to spread the good news throughout the world. Although proclaiming the gospel can be dangerous, the Holy Spirit is present to comfort and guide us. The history of Acts shows Jesus' faithfulness to the promises he made to his disciples.

The book of Acts challenges believers to remain faithful to Jesus' commands. It teaches us what it means to be Jesus' disciples and how to carry on with Jesus' mission.

View of the Areopagus (Mars Hill) from the Acropolis onto the city of Athens, Greece.
The apostle Paul preached the gospel to a group of Greeks at the Areopagus (Acts 17:19–34).

Luke as a Historian

One of the interesting details of Luke as a careful historian comes out in his proper use of titles for the many and varied Roman officials. This could not have been done easily by someone writing much later since provincial boundaries and terms often changed. The use of these titles reveals an eyewitness account, someone with first hand knowledge.

Book of Acts	Title	Comment
13:7; 18:12	Proconsul: Used of Sergius Paulus of Cyprus and Gallio of Achaia.	Title for the ruler of a senatorial province.
16:20, 22, 35–38	Magistrates: Used of the authorities in Philippi, a Roman colony.	Though the technical Roman term for those in charge of a colony was *duumviri*, Luke used a popular term here showing his familiarity with the area.
17:6, 8	City Officials: Used of the leaders of the city of Thessalonica.	The strange term *politarch* Luke used here was thought to be an error, until an inscription on the city gate was unearthed using the same word.
19:35	Clerk: Used of an official in Ephesus.	This is the same word that is used in other places for "scribe." In Ephesus it meant the town recorder.
23:24, 26, 33–34; 24:1, 10; 26:30	Governor or Procurator: Used of Felix and Festus in Palestine.	Title for the ruler of an imperial province or a ruler with certain authority from the emperor.
28:7	Chief Official: Used of Publius, governor of Malta.	This term seemed like a very general term, but inscriptions found on the island of Malta show it was the title used.

The Gallio Inscription. A stone found in Delphi, Greece, mentions a Roman governor (proconsul) named Gallio of the province of Achaia. Dating to around AD 52, the name quite possibly refers to the governor in Acts 18:12.

The Politarch Inscriptions. Thirty-two inscriptions have been found with the term *politarch* ("city officials"). At least three of them date from Paul's time. Until their discovery, there were no other documents with the same term for city officials. These inscriptions confirm Luke's use the term in Acts 17:6, 8.

Paul's Missionary Journeys

Paul's First Missionary Journey • AD 47–49 • Acts 13:1–14:28

TRAVELERS: Paul, Barnabas, John Mark

MAIN ROUTE: Cyprus and Turkey (1,400 miles; 2,253 km)

CITIES/PLACES:

1. **Antioch in Syria:** The Holy Spirit sets apart Paul and Barnabas to be missionaries. John Mark goes along as their helper.

2. **Sailed from Seleucia to Salamis and Paphos (on Cyprus):** Paul confronts a sorcerer named Elymas and blinds him. (From this point the Bible calls him Paul, rather than Saul.)

3. **Perga in Pamphylia:** John Mark deserts the group and returns to Jerusalem.

4. **Antioch of Pisidia:** Paul preaches his longest recorded sermon, and many respond. Jewish leaders drive them out of the city. The Lord calls Paul to focus his ministry on Gentiles. The Gentiles are glad and many become believers.

5. **Iconium:** More plots force them to flee.

6. **Lystra:** When Paul heals a lame man, the townspeople think he and Barnabas are Greek gods. Jews from Antioch stir up the crowd, and Paul is stoned and left for dead. But Paul survives and goes back into the city.

7. **Derbe:** Paul preaches and many disciples are added to the church.

8. **Lystra, Iconium, Antioch of Pisidia, Pamphylia, Perga, Attalia:** On the return trip, Paul and Barnabas appoint elders in the churches they had planted.

9. **Antioch (Syria):** Paul remains there for a while, reporting what God had done. (Possibly writes Galatians from here.)

10. **Jerusalem, via Phoenicia and Samaria:** In AD 49, Paul and Barnabas report to the leaders of the Jerusalem church. This meeting is known as the Jerusalem Council (Acts 15:1–35).

Paul's Second Missionary Journey • AD 49–51 • Acts 15:36–18:22

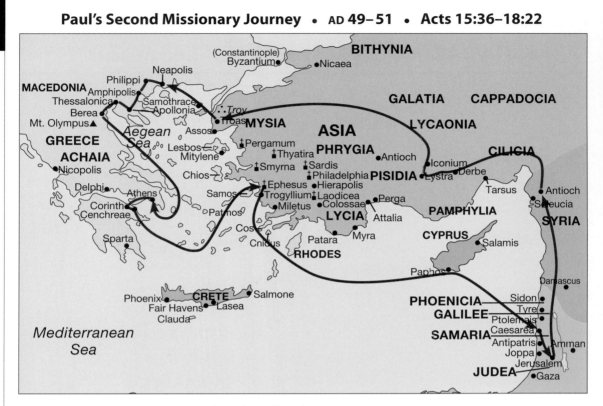

TRAVELERS: Paul, Silas, Timothy, Priscilla and Aquilla, Luke

MAIN ROUTE: Syria, Turkey, Greece, Jerusalem (2,800 miles; 4,506 km)

CITIES/PLACES:

1. **Antioch in Syria:** Paul and Barnabas decide to visit the churches again, but disagree about who should go with them. Barnabas takes John Mark with him to Cyprus. Paul takes Silas.

2. **Syria and Cilicia:** Paul and Silas take a letter from the Jerusalem church for the churches in this region.

3. **Derbe, Lystra, Iconium:** While visiting these churches, Timothy joins them.

4. **Troas:** While in this seaport, Paul has a vision of a man from Macedonia calling him to come help them.

5. **Samothrace, Neapolis, Philippi:** Lydia, a wealthy businesswoman, is converted in the Macedonian city of Philippi, and the group stays in her house. When a fortune-telling slave girl is converted, her owners start a riot, and Paul and Silas are thrown in jail. After an earthquake, Paul and Silas stay in their cells. The jailer is converted.

6. **Amphipolis, Apollonia, Thessalonica:** Jews in Thessalonica try to have Paul and Silas arrested after they gain some converts.

7. **Berea:** The people in the synagogue receive the message eagerly. Silas and Timothy stay here while Paul goes on.

8. **Athens (Mars Hill/Areopagus):** Paul sees an altar to an unknown god, and preaches to the thinkers of Athens. A number of them believe.

9. **Corinth:** Paul meets Aquila and Priscilla, who join him. People try to get Paul arrested, but the authorities refuse. He writes 1 and 2 Thessalonians here.

10. **Cenchrea:** Paul gets his hair cut because he had taken a vow (Acts 18:18). No more details are given.

11. **Ephesus:** Paul leaves Priscilla and Aquila here.

12. **Caesarea in Syria, Jerusalem, Antioch in Syria:** After visiting these churches, Paul returns to his home base of Antioch.

Paul's Third Missionary Journey • AD 52–57 • Acts 18:23–21:16

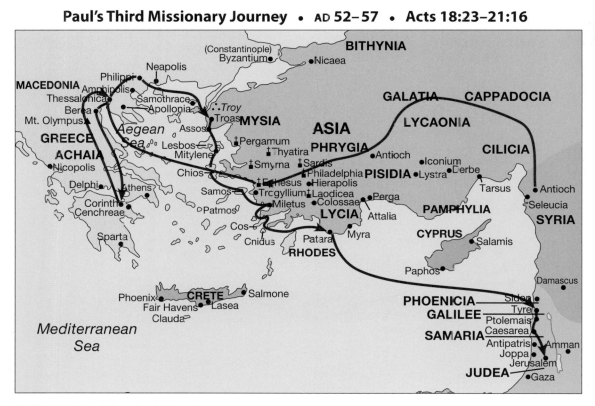

TRAVELERS: Paul, Timothy, Luke, others

MAIN ROUTE: Turkey, Greece, Lebanon, Israel (2700 miles; 4,345 km)

CITIES/PLACES:

1. **Region of Galatia and Phrygia:** Paul decides to visit the churches again.

2. **Ephesus:** Paul stays here two years. He writes 1 Corinthians. So many people convert that the silversmiths who manufacture idols start a riot.

3. **Macedonia and Greece (Achaia):** Paul writes 2 Corinthians and Romans.

4. **Philippi (Macedonia) and Troas:** While Paul is preaching, a young man falls asleep, falls from a third-story window, and dies. Paul revives him.

5. **Assos, Mitylene (near Chios), Samos, Miletus:** Elders from Ephesus meet the ship at Miletus; Paul tells them he expects to be imprisoned in Jerusalem.

6. **Cos, Rhodes, Patara, Tyre:** Disciples warn Paul not to go to Jerusalem.

7. **Ptolemais and Caesarea:** A prophet predicts that Paul will be imprisoned and handed over to the Gentiles.

8. **Jerusalem:** The missionaries report to the church leaders, who urge Paul to participate in a purification ritual at the temple to counteract rumors that Christianity is anti-Jewish.

Paul's Journey to Rome • AD 57–62 • Acts 21:17–28:31

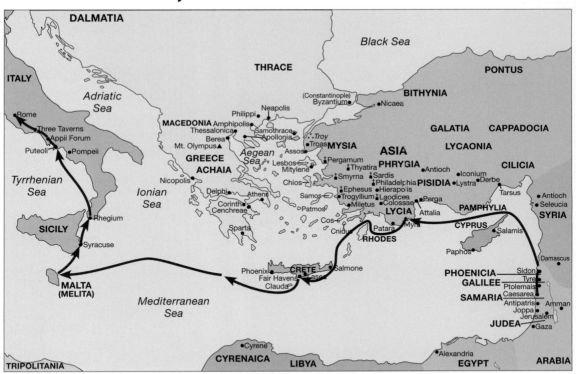

TRAVELERS: Paul, Roman guards, Luke, others

MAIN ROUTE: Israel, Lebanon, Turkey, Crete, Malta, Sicily, Italy (2,250 miles; 3,621 km)

CITIES/PLACES:

1. **Jerusalem:** The Roman commander arrests Paul to save him from a Jewish mob. When the commander learns of a death threat against Paul, he orders an armed escort to take him to Caesarea.

2. **Antipatris and Caesarea:** Paul is tried before Felix, the governor of Judea. Felix leaves Paul in prison for two years, and he is tried again before Festus, who was appointed governor after Felix. The Jews try to get Paul transferred to Jerusalem where they plan to have him killed. Paul demands his right as a Roman citizen and appeals his case to Caesar. King Agrippa II visits Festus, and Paul appears before him as well.

3. **Sidon:** The centurion in charge of Paul lets him visit with friends here. Then Paul boarded a ship, and set sail for Italy.

4. **Myra, Cnidus, Fair Havens (Crete):** Paul recommends that the ship stay in safe harbor, but the centurion orders the ship to sail on.

5. **Clauda and the Island of Malta (shipwrecked):** After a two-week storm, the ship is wrecked near the island of Malta. Everyone on the ship makes it to shore after the shipwreck. While putting wood on a campfire, Paul is bitten by a venomous snake, but it does not harm him.

6. **Syracuse (Sicily), Rhegium, Puteoli:** Paul stays with believers for seven days.

7. **Appii Forum, Three Taverns:** Paul is met by Christians from Rome.

8. **Rome:** Paul remains under house arrest for two years, where he writes Ephesians, Colossians, Philemon, and Philippians.

GUIDANCE FOR THE JOURNEY

The Epistles

The epistles (or letters) make up twenty-one of the twenty-seven books in the New Testament. They contain vital information for Christians and their journey through life. Whereas the Gospels present the good news of Jesus—his life and ministry—the epistles explain the effects of Jesus' ministry, the coming of the Holy Spirit, and the spread of the gospel through Jerusalem, Judea, Samaria, and the Gentile world.

The epistles are traditionally grouped into two sections: Paul's Epistles which are the thirteen letters written by the apostle Paul, and the eight General Epistles which are letters written by other apostles or early church leaders.

There are different kinds of epistles in New Testament:

1. Personal letters, such as Philemon which is written to a specific individual.

2. Circular letters, such as Ephesians which was a letter meant to be circulated among several churches in a region.

3. Letters to a specific congregation, such as 1 and 2 Corinthians which were written to the church congregation in the city of Corinth.

4. Other letters do not name the author or the recipients, such as Hebrews which does not name its author and 1 John which does not indicate to whom it is written. Others look only in a very general way like a letter at all (James).

However, all the letters share some important features. The first, and most important, is that they are divine communications for God's people in the early church and throughout history. Another important consideration about these New Testament letters is that they are *occasional documents*. This means that each letter was written to address a specific set of issues, at a specific time, and in a specific place. This point is important to keep in mind because it highlights the value in knowing as much about the context of the letter as possible. It also reminds us that none of the letters, or even all of them put together, represents the full theology of Paul, Peter, or John. Rather, they were addressing specific issues. Those issues determined the content of each letter. However, understanding the issues that each letter addresses is not easy. Often, reading the letters can feel like listening in on a person's phone conversation; we know only half of it.

Paul's Epistles

Romans
1 Corinthians
2 Corinthians
Galatians
Ephesians
Philippians
Colossians
1 Thessalonians
2 Thessalonians
1 Timothy
2 Timothy
Titus
Philemon

General Epistles & Revelation

Hebrews
James
1 Peter
2 Peter
1 John
2 John
3 John
Jude
Revelation

Epistle	Author	Date	Audience	Major Themes
James	James	49	Christian Jews in and around Jerusalem	A faith in action
Galatians	Paul	48–49 or 54–55	Churches in the Roman province of Galatia	Justification by faith through Christ alone
1 Thessalonians	Paul	50–52	Church in the city of Thessalonica	Encouragement during persecution
2 Thessalonians	Paul	50–52	Church in the city of Thessalonica	The second coming of Christ and the end times
1 Corinthians	Paul	55–56	Church in the port city of Corinth	Unity of the body of Christ, freedom and mature behavior of a godly lifestyle, the nature of love, and the centrality of Christ's resurrection
2 Corinthians	Paul	56	Church in the port city of Corinth	Humility and power, tough love, and the new creation
Romans	Paul	57	Church in Rome	God's power, justification, sin, and holy living
Philippians	Paul	60–62	Church in the important Roman colonial city of Philippi	Servant leadership, unity of believers, joy in the Lord
Colossians	Paul	60–62	Church in Colossae (in modern day Turkey)	The supremacy of Christ, community life in Christ
Philemon	Paul	60–62	Philemon, a leader at the church in Colossae	Forgiveness and Christian love
Ephesians	Paul	60–62	Church in the Hellenistic cultural center of Ephesus	God's gracious salvation in Christ, unity and diversity of the church, and the Christian life
1 Timothy	Paul	62–66	Timothy, one of Paul's disciples, who was ministering in Ephesus	Encouragement in the face of false teaching, instruction on worship, organization, and care within the church
Titus	Paul	64–66	Titus, one of Paul's disciples, who was ministering on the island of Crete	Encouragement for Titus, warning against false teachings, doing good
1 Peter	Peter	64–65	Churches in Roman provinces of Asia Minor (modern day Turkey)	Suffering and Christian witness
2 Peter	Peter	64–65	Churches in Roman provinces of Asia Minor (modern day Turkey)	God's revelation and warning against false teachings
2 Timothy	Paul	66–67	Timothy, one of Paul's disciples, who was ministering in Ephesus	Personal appeals to Timothy, encouragement to proclaim the gospel at all times, and encouragements for the church
Jude	Jude	60s–80s	Unknown. Perhaps addressed to Jewish Christians.	Christ's faithfulness and God's judgment
Hebrews	Unknown	60–69	Jewish Christians	The superiority of Christ
1 John	John	85–95	Churches in Asia Minor	The love of God
2 John	John	85–95	Probably to a house church in Asia Minor	Warning against false teachings
3 John	John	85–95	Gaius, a Christian in a church in Asia Minor	The Christian life

THE WORLD OF THE FIRST CHRISTIANS

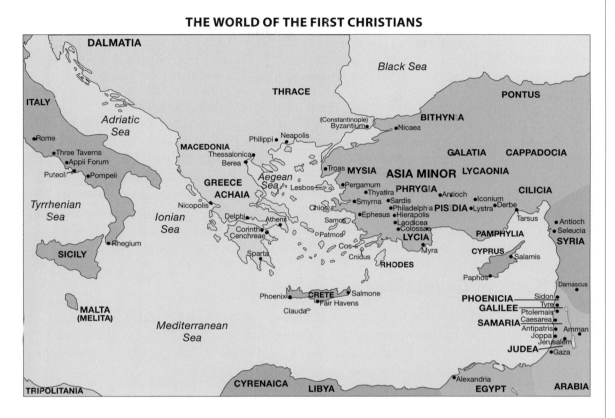

Who Was Paul?

Paul was an enemy of Christianity, who became the greatest Christian missionary of all time. He authored more books of the Bible than anyone else. He is better known as the "apostle to the Gentiles."

Paul came from a well-respected family in Asia Minor (Turkey today) where his father was an official. He excelled in his studies and became a devout Pharisee. As a young man Paul—whose Jewish name was Saul—was sent to Jerusalem to study under the great teacher Gamaliel. He hated Christians and participated in the first execution of a Christian leader, a man named Stephen. Paul was determined to murder all those who followed Jesus, not just in Jerusalem, but elsewhere (Acts 7:54–8:3).

Paul asked the chief priest in Jerusalem to give him authorization to arrest any follower of Jesus in Damascus (about 100 miles away). On his way from Judea to Damascus, a light from heaven blinded him. He fell to the ground and a voice said, "Saul, Saul, why do you persecute me?" He answered, "Who are you?" The voice said, "I am Jesus, the one you are persecuting. Get up! Go into the city, and you will be told what to do." Paul was told to go to a house and wait for a Christian man named Ananias to come restore his sight (Acts 9:1–12).

The Lord spoke to Ananias and said that Paul was chosen to take the Lord's name to Gentiles, their kings, and to the Jews. Ananias placed his hands on Paul and his sight was restored. Paul was filled with the Holy Spirit and was baptized. He started speaking in synagogues and convincing people that Jesus was the Messiah.

During the early years of Christianity, most of the converts were Jewish. Jesus' disciples preached only to Jews. Yet as Jewish people scattered throughout the Roman empire, they told their neighbors about Jesus. Many of these Gentiles (non-Jews) became followers of Jesus too (Acts 11:19–21). Traveling all over the Roman empire, the apostle Paul preached and ministered to Gentile Christians. Paul became one of God's powerful tools to spread the good news of Jesus. Eventually it would cost him his life. According to tradition, Paul was martyred during Emperor Nero's fierce persecution of Christians in Rome. Yet Paul's God-inspired writings have provided guidance, comfort, exhortation, and assurance to millions of Christians throughout history.

The Book of Revelation

The book of Revelation is not an epistle. Rather it belongs to a special category or *genre* of writing, known as apocalyptic literature. *Apocalyptic* is a type of literature that reveals God's plans that had been hidden to humanity. The message is conveyed through signs, symbols, dreams, and visions.

Interpreting the book has always been a great challenge for Christians. However, its message is much too important to simply ignore it. We must approach the book with a sense of respect and wonder, but also with the confidence that God's message in the book is still relevant to all believers today.

Despite the many disagreements about the meaning of the book, there are important agreements among Christians:

- The message of the book is relevant for Christians today, as it was for Christians in the times of the apostles.

- The main purpose of the book is to provide *hope* and *encouragement* for believers at all times, especially in times of persecution or suffering.

- The message of the book is clear on at least three points: (1) Christ is coming back and will judge humanity; (2) the powers of evil are doomed before Christ; and (3) God promises a wonderful future for all who believe in Christ.

ROMANS

THE POWER OF THE GOSPEL

Purpose

The epistle to the Romans is Paul's most theological and complex letter. The letter has at least three important purposes:

- **Missionary.** Paul's ministry was at its core missionary—spreading the gospel throughout the world. His travels present us with an apostle profoundly involved with Jesus' commission to spread the gospel. The epistle to the Romans reveals Paul's heart for missions. The apostle had not visited the church in Rome, yet he wanted to make it his church base for launching a missionary effort that would reach the end of the known world: Spain. Paul might have wanted to explain to the Roman believers what the content of his missionary preaching was—in other words, the message of the gospel.

- **Teaching.** Paul explained in detail many crucial topics of the Christian faith. The letter to the Romans is not a complete handbook of Christian beliefs. Rather, the book reveals an interest in themes like the human need for salvation, the relationship between Jewish and Gentile Christians, the death and resurrection of Jesus as the way of salvation, justification by faith alone, and the role of faith in people's lives.

- **Pastoral.** This is not just a doctrinal letter; it is a personal letter. The apostle Paul sends personal greetings to many people and shows that he is aware of the different house churches in Rome. He is also aware of potential divisions and troubles. With pastoral love, he writes to encourage and exhort Roman believers to unity and wisdom.

Outline

1. Introduction, Greeting, and Preface (1:1–17)

2. The Righteous Anger of God (1:18–3:20)
   a. Against the Gentile world
   b. Against the Jewish world
   c. Against the whole world

3. Justification by Faith in Christ (3:21–5:21)

4. Sanctification through Union with Christ (6:1–8:17)

5. Glorification in Conquering with Christ (8:18–39)

6. Election (9:1–11:36)

7. A Living Sacrifice (12:1–15:13)

8. Conclusion, Personal Greetings, and Doxology (15:14– 16:27)

Election

Election (Rom. 9–11) is best thought of as a compelling love story in which God's love seeks a specific beloved (the church in Christ) and we are individually and as a group drawn compulsively into that love revealed in Christ.

Paul's Roman Citizenship

The apostle Paul was a Roman citizen by birth (Acts 22:25–29). Access to Roman citizenship was limited and difficult to obtain. Although many people achieved, earned, or were granted Roman citizenship, their citizenship had less rights and privileges than those who were citizens by birth. In the Roman Empire, when slaves were freed, they became citizens. When people performed special duties for Rome, the emperor granted them full Roman citizenship. Many scholars believe this is how Paul's ancestors might have acquired their Roman citizenship.

Background

Author: The apostle Paul is the author of this important letter (1:1).

Date: This letter was probably written in AD 57 a little after the Corinthian letters at the time Paul was visiting the Corinthian church and just before he was headed to Jerusalem with the relief fund gathered for the believers there (Rom. 15:25–27).

Audience: Paul wrote this letter to the church in Rome. Rome was at the center of nearly all that happened in the Mediterranean world. Though there is no mention of who first brought the gospel to Rome, Christianity had spread quickly to the capital city of the Empire, probably through the natural concourse of business, political, and religious activity. By the time of the great persecution under Emperor Nero (AD 64), the historian Tacitus could say a "great multitude" of Christians lived in Rome. (Those were Nero's early days as emperor, and he had not yet turned into the cruel ruler he would become after the fires in Rome.)

The church at Rome was a mix of both Jewish and Gentile believers. There was a large Jewish presence in Rome as we learn from the expulsion order given under Emperor Claudius (Acts 18:2–3). Many believers were already there before Paul made his first journey to Rome around AD 57 (Acts 21:17–28:31).

Paul greatly desired to visit the Christians in Rome. Little did he know when he wrote this letter that he would later come in chains to the city and testify before the emperor. Nor could he know of his eventual death by beheading in Rome. What Paul did know was the power of the gospel. In Romans, we have an unmatched presentation of it.

Examples of Faith in Romans

Believers	Example	Reference in Romans
Abraham	Father of all the faithful and example of justification by faith	4:1–25
David	Knew God's justification by faith	4:6–8
Adam	Through his faithless disobedience, the punishment of death came to all humanity.	5:12–21
Sarah and her son Isaac	Examples of God's choice in Christ	9:6–9
Rebecca and her sons Jacob and Esau	Examples of God's choice in Christ	9:10–13
Moses and Pharaoh	Examples of God's choice. Moses is quoted to show the distinction between salvation by perfect obedience to the law and salvation by faith.	9:14–18 10:5–10
Phoebe	She lived in Cenchrea, the port city of Corinth and was a deaconess. She probably carried the letter of Romans (10:8).	16:1–2
Aquila and Priscilla	A husband and wife team expelled from Rome with other Jews. They met Paul at Corinth and worked the same trade with him. They risked their lives for Paul, possibly at Ephesus (Acts 19:30).	16:3–5

Themes

God's Power. The apostle Paul was writing to citizens of the most powerful city at the time. The Roman believers knew about power. God's power to save and condemn, as the righteous owner of the whole universe, was manifested in the law of Moses and in the gospel. His power, along with his justice, grace, mercy, and holiness, has reached out to save humanity from the hold of sin and evil.

Justification. In Christ, God has justified us and opened the way to serve him and love him. Justification is a word that comes from the courts of law. Paul uses this word to explain to the Romans—well acquainted with the court system—the effects of Jesus' death for believers. In Christ, God has declared us just, or acceptable, before God.

Sin. Humanity is a slave to sin, death, and evil. Through Christ's sacrifice, however, God has redeemed us—made us free—from the tyranny of sin and death. God has empowered us to live in a new way for God.

Emperors

Rome was under Nero at the time Paul wrote Romans. Roman government had descended into an empire where the Caesars were quickly becoming powerful tyrants. Caligula had already made his evil and insane mark on the office—his cruelty and sexual perversity were well known. Fortunately, the more competent and moderate Claudius had replaced him. Nero came next after his stepfather Claudius died. The sixth Caesar, Nero, was restrained at first. In time, however, Nero became so cruel and evil that his contemporaries called him the "beast." Tradition says that both Peter and Paul were martyred under the persecution of Nero.

Nero, Roman Emperor AD 54–68

Key Verses

For all have sinned and fall short of the glory of God.—Rom. 3:23

For the wages of sin is death, but the gift of God is eternal life in Christ Jesus our Lord.
—Rom. 6:23

Therefore, I urge you, brothers and sisters, in view of God's mercy, to offer your bodies as a living sacrifice, holy and pleasing to God—this is your true and proper worship.
—Rom. 12:1

Propitiation

Propitiation is a key word used in Rom. 3:25. Often translated as "sacrifice of atonement" or "expiation," the word carries the idea of "turning aside anger." It points back to Paul's opening statement in 1:18, "The wrath of God is being revealed from heaven against all the godlessness and wickedness of people."

Being God's People

Believers in Rome faced many challenges to their faith. A powerful, rich, and influential city like Rome harbored many different religions, ideas, and practices that contradicted the Christian faith. Paul's desire to present the Christian faith in some detail and his exhortations to keep the unity hint at the problems that confronted believers then. In the face of persecution, Paul reminded them that God has promised that nothing shall separate us from his love in Christ (8:28–39). The apostle Paul also reminded the Romans that the Christian faith is always a missionary faith.

The Christian faith continues to be assailed by different religions, ideas, and practices. Paul's exhortations to faithful belief and the practice of Christian unity are still important for us today. God challenges us in view of his great mercy to present ourselves as living sacrifices (12:1). The reminder that our faith is at its core missionary must shape our Christian life and practice.

Jesus in Romans

A large part of the letter includes Paul's presentation of the gospel. Jesus is the central figure and the climax of the gospel story. In his letter, Paul presents the power of God through Jesus, his full grace displayed in his sacrifice, and his justice fulfilled in his death and resurrection. The Holy Spirit, fulfilling Jesus' promise of sending the Counselor, empowers all believers to follow Jesus, do as he commanded, and work "so that all nations might believe and obey him" (16:26).

The Forum Romanum in Rome, Italy

1 CORINTHIANS

THE WAY OF LOVE

Purpose

This letter was a reply to specific problems at the church in Corinth. The apostle Paul had previously written a letter to the church addressing sexual immorality (see 1 Cor. 5:9). It appears that Paul received, perhaps, an oral report about the church having misunderstood his first letter (5:10). The letter that we know as 1 Corinthians was written to correct those misunderstandings, and also to deal with further problems of division, doctrinal confusion, and social snobbery (1:10; 5:1; 11:18).

In 1 Corinthians, the apostle Paul writes some basic teachings on Christian behavior and doctrine for this congregation, which was exhibiting some childish behavior (5:1, 6:1). Some of the doctrinal concerns the apostle addresses in the letter are spiritual gifts, the true nature of love, and bodily resurrection (12:1; 13:1–13; 15:1–8).

Outline

1. Greeting and Prayer of Thanksgiving (1:1–9)

2. Division and Harmony Addressed (1:10–4:17)
   a. Divisions in the church (1:10–17)
   b. Human wisdom is not God's way (1.18–2:5)
   c. Godly wisdom is beyond human ways (2:6–3:23)
   d. Christ is the beginning and end of all wisdom (4:1–17)

3. Church Discipline Addressed (4:18–11:33)
   a. Arrogance, immorality, and lawsuits (4:18–6:11)
   b. Human body belongs to God (6:12–20)
   c. Marriage and celibacy (7)
   d. Food sacrificed to idols (8)
   e. Rights vs. respect for the gospel's sake (9)
   f. Warnings – Israel as an example (10:1–22)
   g. Freedom and deference for the gospel's sake (10:23–11:1)
   h. Proper decorum in worship and the Lord's Supper (11:2–33)

4. Doctrinal Issues Addressed (12:1–15:58)
   a. Spiritual gifts (12)
   b. Love (13)
   c. The loving use of spiritual gifts (14)
   d. The resurrection (15)

5. Practical Issues Addressed (16:1–18)
   a. Famine relief collection for the church of Jerusalem (16:1–4)
   b. Future plans to visit by Paul and others (16:5–12)
   c. Recognition of certain leading brethren (16:13–18)

6. Final Greeting (16:19–24)

Stephanas

The household of Stephanas is mentioned twice in 1 Corinthians: once at the beginning of the letter (1:16) and then at the end (16:15). Stephanas and his family were the first converts to Christ that Paul baptized in that part of Greece. Stephanas along with two others (16:17) came to Paul from Corinth bringing greetings. These men may have also carried the letter of 1 Corinthians back with them. Paul recommended these people to the Corinthians as trustworthy leaders to be followed. In a place like Corinth, good role models were very much needed.

Background

Author: The apostle Paul is the author of this letter (1:1).

Date: Paul wrote 1 Corinthians from Ephesus (16:8) about AD 55–56. The letter may have been carried to Corinth by the three persons mentioned in 16:15–18. Clement of Rome mentioned the epistle when he wrote to the Corinthian church in AD 95.

Audience: Paul's readers were Christians in the port city of Corinth. They comprised a church that was situated at a diverse commercial crossroad. Such diversity resulted in competing ideas and factions. Lifestyle issues and basic moral questions needed to be addressed in this confusing environment. From the list of issues addressed in 1 Corinthians, the church seems to be largely Gentile, but the problem of meat sacrificed to idols may indicate a Jewish-Christian element in the congregation as well.

Themes

Unity of the Church (1:10; 12:4–26). The apostle Paul writes about the unity of the church using the image of a building. The apostles, in this case Paul, laid the foundation upon which others build up the church. Every person in the church is responsible to build up the church by being sensitive to those new in the faith (10:28–33) and using the gifts of the Spirit to strengthen other believers and the church (11:2–16; 12:12–30; 14:1–35). The celebration of the Lord's Supper is another image of the unity of the church: "Because there is one loaf, we, who are many, are one body, for we all share the one loaf" (10:17).

Freedom and Mature Behavior of a Godly Lifestyle (3:1–3; 6:12; 10:23–24). Freedom should not lead to immoral behavior. Rather, believers should use their freedom to lead a godly lifestyle, a behavior that honors God and other believers.

The Nature of Love (13:1–13). Paul writes to correct the Corinthians' view of spiritual gifts—they were emphasizing some spiritual gifts over the others—and the divisions caused by that doctrinal error. The apostle teaches that, although all spiritual gifts are equally important, they are meaningless if practiced apart from love: "Follow the way of love and eagerly desire gifts of the Spirit" (14:1). As he explains the way of love in 1 Corinthians 13, Paul presents in unforgettable words the nature of love.

The Centrality of Christ's Resurrection (15:1–58). The resurrection of Jesus is not just a teaching of the apostles; it is the very center of the Christian faith: "And if Christ has not been raised, our preaching is useless and so is your faith" (15:14). Furthermore, Christ's resurrection guarantees our own resurrection, a resurrection of our bodies (15:35–58). Because Christ rose from the dead, Paul, and all believers, can affirm: "Where, O death, is your victory? Where, O death, is your sting?" (15:55).

Key Verses

For I resolved to know nothing while I was with you except Jesus Christ and him crucified. —1 Cor. 2:2

For I received from the Lord what I passed on to you: The Lord Jesus, on the night he was betrayed, took bread, and when he had given thanks, he broke it and said, "This is my body, which is for you; do this in remembrance of me." In the same way, after supper he took the cup, saying, "This cup is the new covenant in my blood; do this, whenever you drink it, in remembrance of me." —1 Cor. 11:23–25

And now these three remain: faith, hope and love. But the greatest of these is love. —1 Cor. 13:13

For what I received I passed on to you as of first importance: that Christ died for our sins according to the Scriptures, that he was buried, that he was raised on the third day according to the Scriptures, and that he appeared to Peter, and then to the Twelve. —1 Cor. 15:3–5

Paul's Short List

In 1 Corinthians 15, Paul lists eyewitnesses to Jesus' resurrection. Along with information from the Gospels and Acts, there were at least eleven separate appearances to over 500 individuals spanning a forty-day period.

Reference	Eyewitness
John 19:1–18	Mary Magdalene
Matt. 28:8–10	The women (probably Mary Magdalene, Mary mother of James and Salome, Joanna, and others; Mark 16:1; Luke 24:10)
1 Cor. 15:5	Peter (see also Luke 24:33)
John 20:19–25	The Twelve minus Thomas (see also Luke 24:36–49)
1 Cor. 15:5	The Twelve (probably the same as John 20:26–29)
Luke 24:13–35	Two on the road to Emmaus
John 21:1–25	Seven fishing on Lake Galilee
1 Cor. 15:6	Five hundred believers (probably in Galilee—Matt. 28:7, 16–20)
1 Cor. 15:7	James the brother of the Lord
1 Cor. 15:7	All the apostles (see also Mark 16:19–20; Luke 24:50–53; Acts 1:9–11, 21–22)
1 Cor. 15:8	Paul on the road to Damascus (see also Acts 9:1–19; 22:1–18; 26:12–18)

Being God's People

God promised to bring the Corinthians into the fullness of his love. He challenged them to make their lifestyle inside and outside the church consistent with their high calling.

God still calls us to preserve the unity of Christ's body (the church). As we exercise spiritual gifts, celebrate the Lord's Supper, and deal with other believers, the apostle's advice to build up Christ's body remains as relevant for us today as ever.

Jesus in 1 Corinthians

The apostle's main interest is with the unity of Christ's body. As promised, God sent the Holy Spirit to guide and empower us to become faithful followers of Jesus. Jesus' resurrection is at the heart of the Christian proclamation of the good news and of our faith. His resurrection gives us hope in uncertain times, courage for the times of trials, and guidance when we feel disoriented.

2 CORINTHIANS

TOUGH LOVE

Purpose

The letter of 2 Corinthians is one of Paul's most personal works. His emotions of anguish, joy, stern anger, and love are clear. Much of what Paul writes about involves his ministry and personal relations with the Corinthian believers. One of Paul's main purposes in writing this letter was to clarify his first letter. The apostle wanted to reinforce what he had said in his first letter. He also wanted to help his readers understand the spirit of anguished, loving concern in which he intended his remarks (6:11–13).

The collection of money for the relief of the poor in Judea was also a major concern in this letter (8:1–9:15). Judea had undergone a food shortage that had actually been predicted earlier in the reign of Claudius (Acts 11:27–30). A collection was taken then, but this appears to be another relief collection some ten years later.

False apostles and their attempts to discredit Paul are addressed in this letter, though their teaching is not (10:1–12:13). Paul offers a passionate defense of his ministry in the face of many attacks—ministry is an important word in the letter. Paul explains in a moving and powerful way what it means to be a servant and ambassador of Christ.

Outline

The Roman fountain in ancient Corinth, Greece

Background

Author: The author of 2 Corinthians is the apostle Paul (1:1). Comparisons with the first letter to the Corinthians make it plain that the two letters have the same author.

Date: Paul wrote the letter somewhere in Macedonia, probably Philippi. The letter was written soon after 1 Corinthians, around AD 56.

Audience: Paul specifically addressed the church in the city of Corinth, but he also intended the letter to be read throughout the province of Achaia (1:1). This wider scope may have been because he desired to reach as many as possible in his collection effort for the relief of the famine stricken Christians in Judea (9:2). Alternatively, the wider scope may have been necessary in order to combat the threat of the "false apostles" and the spread of their corrupt teaching (11:10–15).

Themes

Humility and Power/Authority. The Christian life and whole way of thinking is opposite of the way the rest of the world runs and understands things. True power/authority comes with humility not pride. True success comes with suffering and service, not a life of ease. In fact, true wisdom, the wisdom of God, looks like foolishness to the rest of the world (4:7–18, 10:7–18, 11:16–32, 12:7–10).

Tough Love. God's love is not mere sentimentalism. God's love actually has a goal of healing, restoring, and transforming people. Being transformed into a follower of Christ can be a painful transformation (3:18, 5:1–4).

New Creation. God transforms us into new creations in Christ (5:16–21). Being a new creation allow us to become effective ambassadors of Christ to carry on the ministry of reconciliation.

Key Verses

For no matter how many promises God has made, they are "Yes" in Christ. And so through him the "Amen" is spoken by us to the glory of God.—2 Cor. 1:20

Now the Lord is the Spirit, and where the Spirit of the Lord is, there is freedom. And we, who with unveiled faces all reflect the Lord's glory, are being transformed into his likeness with ever-increasing glory, which comes from the Lord, who is the Spirit.—2 Cor. 3:17–18

Therefore, if anyone is in Christ, the new creation has come: The old has gone, the new is here!—2 Cor. 5:17

The weapons we fight with are not the weapons of the world. On the contrary, they have divine power to demolish strongholds. We demolish arguments and every pretension that sets itself up against the knowledge of God, and we take captive every thought to make it obedient to Christ.—2 Cor. 10:4–5

Paul's Heartfelt Language

Emotion	What Paul Says	2 Cor.
Despair	"We were under great pressure, far beyond our ability to endure, so that we despaired of life itself."	1:8
Distress, Anguish, Tears, Grief, Love	"For I wrote you out of great distress and anguish of heart and with many tears, not to grieve you but to let you know the depth of my love for you."	2:4
Confident Hope	"We are hard pressed on every side, but not crushed; perplexed, but not in despair; persecuted, but not abandoned; struck down, but not destroyed. We always carry around in our body the death of Jesus, so that the life of Jesus may also be revealed in our body."	4:8–10
Affection	"We have spoken freely to you, Corinthians, and opened wide our hearts to you."	6:11
Longing, Sorrow, Concern, Joy	"[Titus] told us about your longing for me, your deep sorrow, your ardent concern for me, so that my joy was greater than ever."	7:7
Stern Anger	"I already gave you a warning when I was with you the second time. I now repeat it while absent: On my return I will not spare those who sinned earlier or any of the others, since you are demanding proof that Christ is speaking through me."	13:2–3

Temple of Apollo in ancient Corinth, Greece

Being God's People

Despite the confusion in Corinth about Christian behavior, worship, and doctrine, God's many promises to his people were confirmed as "Yes" in Jesus (1:20). God challenged his people in Corinth to be transformed into the likeness of his Son.

God's promises are still kept to his people today even in the confusing world we live in. God challenges believers to live out the life of a new creation in Jesus.

Jesus in 2 Corinthians

The apostle Paul's ministry was modeled after Jesus' own ministry of reconciliation. His authority as an apostle does not derive from his own personal strength or abilities. Rather, in his weakness, Christ's glory is more fully displayed. Jesus shone in Paul's suffering, was revealed in Paul's preaching, and was glorified in Paul's ministry.

Mosaic at the Temple of Apollo in ancient Corinth, Greece

GALATIANS

JUSTIFICATION BY FAITH AND FREEDOM IN CHRIST

Purpose

Galatians is a strong warning against a corrupted view of the gospel. Paul is writing to the churches of Galatia in order to defend his apostolic authority and argue that justification is by *faith* alone against some "preachers" who were corrupting the gospel. These preachers were Judaizers, Jewish Christians who believed that certain Jewish rites were still necessary and should be enforced by the church. According to Judaizers, all Gentile Christians should be circumcised. Apparently, Judaizers were also questioning Paul's authority and convincing the Galatians that Paul had removed certain legal requirements in order to make the gospel more appealing to Gentiles.

In his letter to the Galatians, Paul adamantly defends his apostolic authority and the true gospel he preaches. He stresses that a person is justified by grace through faith in Jesus and only faith in Jesus. Life is renewed by grace through faith alone, and life in Christ depends on and flows from the Spirit. The Spirit shapes the life of a Christian and the fruit of the Spirit is good and beneficial to the community. The ways of the flesh—the ways of the law—do not produce good fruit and to follow these ways is futile.

Outline

1. Introduction and Warning against Other Gospels (1:1–10)

2. Paul Defends His Apostolic Call (1:11–2:21)

3. Justification by Faith (3:1–4:31)

4. Freedom in Christ (5:1–12)

5. Living by the Spirit (5:13–6:18)

Background

Author: The author of Galatians is the apostle Paul (1:1).

Date and Audience: Dating the book of Galatians depends on the audience. Paul addresses his letter "to the churches in Galatia" (modern-day Turkey). Paul traveled through the southern part of Galatia on his first and second missionary journeys, and the northern part of Galatia during his third missionary journey. If Paul was writing to churches in southern Galatia—such as Antioch, Iconium, Lystra, and Derbe—scholars suggest he wrote the letter from Syrian Antioch around AD 48–49 during his second missionary journey. If Paul was writing to churches in northern Galatia—such as Pessinus, Ancyra, and Tavium—scholars suggest he wrote from Ephesus around AD 54–55 during his third missionary journey.

The Gentile Problem

After Paul had left Galatia on one of his missionary journeys, several "preachers" arrived in Galatia and began teaching that although faith in Jesus was important, justification was not complete without obedience to the laws and rituals of Judaism. Faith in Jesus needed to be accompanied by circumcision (Gal. 5:12–13) and adherence to the Jewish calendar (4:10).

The question of whether Gentile converts should adhere to Jewish laws and rites came up over and over again in the early church. In AD 49, Paul met with the leaders in Jerusalem to discuss this issue. In response to those arguing in favor of these requirements, the apostle Peter stood up and said, "Brothers, you know that some time ago God made a choice among you that the Gentiles might hear from my lips the message of the gospel and believe. God, who knows the heart, showed that he accepted them by giving the Holy Spirit to them, just as he did to us. He did not discriminate between us and them, for he purified their hearts by faith. Now then, why do you try to test God by putting on the necks of Gentiles a yoke that neither we nor our ancestors have been able to bear? No! We believe it is through the grace of our Lord Jesus that we are saved, just as they are" (Acts 15:7–11).

Themes

■ We are saved (justified) by grace through faith alone. Doing good works or obedience to the law is not the means by which we receive salvation.

■ We are free in Christ. We are free from a strict adherence to the Old Testament ritual and purity laws. Adhering to the law in such a rigid way is the same as "slavery" (5:1).

■ Good fruit flows from the Spirit. We do good things because God saved us by his grace; we don't do good things in order to achieve salvation.

Fascinating Facts

■ Galatians is often referred to as the "Magna Carta of Christian Liberty."

■ Because Martin Luther used Galatians to support his doctrine of justification by faith alone, Galatians is often called "Luther's Book."

■ Galatia was settled by Celts around 270 BC. Celtic culture and language were still present when Paul traveled through the region.

Key Verses

A person is not justified by the works of the law, but by faith in Jesus Christ. So we, too, have put our faith in Christ Jesus that we may be justified by faith in Christ and not by the works of the law, because by the works of the law no one will be justified.—Gal. 2:16

So in Christ Jesus you are all children of God through faith, for all of you who were baptized into Christ have clothed yourselves with Christ. There is neither Jew nor Gentile, neither slave nor free, nor is there male and female, for you are all one in Christ Jesus.—Gal. 3:26–28

But the fruit of the Spirit is love, joy, peace, forbearance, kindness, goodness, faithfulness, gentleness and self-control. Against such things there is no law.—Gal. 5:22–23

Being God's People

God's promises made to Abraham were fulfilled with Christ. Just as Abraham believed God and it was credited to him as righteousness (Gal. 3:6), by God's grace, our faith in Jesus is credited to us as righteousness. We are no longer slaves to rituals, laws, and observances.

Sometimes, adherence to rituals, laws, and doing good works as our sole purpose in order to attain salvation can be tempting. Our good works are important, not because they earn us salvation, but because they show the work of the Holy Spirit in our lives.

Jesus in Galatians

By the grace of God, Jesus died so that all who believe in him are saved. To say that faith needs to be accompanied by strict adherence to the laws and rituals of Judaism is to return to the yoke of slavery from which Jesus freed us. To suggest one is justified by anything other than faith in Jesus is corrupting the grace of God that is Jesus Christ, his death, and his resurrection.

EPHESIANS

THE RICHES OF GOD'S GOODNESS

Library of Celsus in Ephesus, Turkey (c. AD 135)

A Circular Letter

Some very early manuscripts of the epistle do not contain the name Ephesus in the title. This might suggest that the letter was originally intended to be a circular letter. The name of the church would have been read or added in as the epistle made its rounds. That the name Ephesus became attached to many manuscripts may be due to the prominence of this city in the area of circulation. Perhaps since Ephesus was a port city, its ability to share this epistle with other churches throughout the growing Christian world led to this association as well.

Purpose

The apostle Paul wrote to believers in Ephesus to encourage and help them realize and lay hold of the riches of God's grace in Christ (1:3–23). The language of the letter makes it clear that Paul is enraptured by the overflowing goodness of God. His words of praise stream out like a gushing river. Paul explains to his readers the incredible gift believers have been given in Christ. In Ephesus, a city with a powerful and influential pagan cult—the worship of Diana of Ephesus—the apostle emphasizes the universal and supreme nature of Christ's power and authority.

The apostle wrote to encourage believers to live a life worthy of God's calling in a spirit of gratitude (2:8–10; 4:1). Paul had been accused of preaching a gospel that made good deeds irrelevant. However, the apostle shows that good deeds are a thankful response to what God has done for the world through Jesus. "For we are God's handiwork, created in Christ Jesus to do good works, which God prepared in advance for us to do" (2:10).

Outline

1. Greeting (1:1–2)

2. Prayer of Praise and Request (1:3–23)
   a. Praise for grace, adoption, and the Spirit (1:3–16)
   b. Request for wisdom, knowledge, and insight (1:17–23)

3. Past Position, Present Reality, and Future Intention (2:1–22)
   a. Once dead in sin (2:1–3)
   b. Now alive by grace through faith (2:4–10)
   c. Reconciled in Christ (2:11–22)

4. Paul the Prisoner (3:1– 6:20)
   a. For the sake of the gospel for the Gentiles (3:1–13)
   b. Prays for the church (3:14–21)
   c. Encourages a life consistent with Christ (4:1–6:20)

5. Conclusion (6:21–24)

Background

Author: The author of Ephesians is the apostle Paul (1:1).

Date: The letter was written sometime in AD 60–62, while he was under house arrest in Rome.

Audience: The audience was the church at Ephesus. But since Ephesus was a cosmopolitan city and probably included believers from Greek, Roman, and Jewish backgrounds, the letter was likely circulated to other churches in the area and so would have had an additional audience as well.

Ephesus (in modern-day Turkey) was an important cultural center of the ancient world, only behind Rome and Alexandria. The amazing temple to Diana of Ephesus, one of the Seven Wonders of the ancient world, dominated the social life of the city. Diana, among many other things, was the goddess of new life and birth.

It's traditionally thought that Ephesus was the home of the apostle John in the latter part of the first century.

God's Riches to Believers

In his many letters, Paul often uses the phrase, "in Christ." The letter of Ephesians contains the most examples. The phrases "with Christ" and "through Christ" are also used. In Christ, believers:

- Have every spiritual blessing reserved in heaven (1:3).
- Are chosen before the creation of the world to be holy and blameless (1:4, 11).
- Are predestined to be adopted as children of God (1:5, 11).
- Are given grace, have redemption and forgiveness, and receive wisdom (1:6–8).
- Are marked with God's seal of the promised Holy Spirit as a guarantee (1:13–14).
- Have resurrection power (1:19–20).
- Are made alive (2:5).
- Are created anew (2:10, 15–16).
- Are brought near to God (2:13).
- Have access to the Father through the Spirit (2:18).
- Are built and joined together into a spiritual temple (2:21–22).
- May approach God with freedom and confidence (3:12).

Themes

God's Gracious Choice to Save Believers in Christ (1:4–5, 11; 2:4–10). Salvation is all about what God does. Believers do well to remember that there can be no boasting or pride about what they have done to "get right with God." All praise is due to the Father, Son, and Spirit.

The Richness of What We Have and Will Inherit in Christ (1:3–19; 2:4–7; 3:16–19). Paul tries to capture in words the magnificent treasure given to believer in Jesus. It defies description to think that every possible blessing has been given to those who are in Christ and these treasures are secure in heaven!

The Unity and Diversity of the Church (2:11–22; 4:3–16). Paul uses his famous metaphor of the body to describe how the church is made up of diverse members but is itself one organism. This unity and diversity encompasses all races and nationalities, every member working together under one head—Christ.

The Discipline of the Christian Life (4:17–6:18). The godly life requires discipline. Being disciplined is not always easy. In the end, Christian discipline is really about being a disciple and following Jesus.

Key Verses

For he chose us in him before the creation of the world to be holy and blameless in his sight. In love he predestined us to be adopted as his sons through Jesus Christ in accordance with his pleasure and will.—Eph. 1:4–5

For it is by grace you have been saved, through faith—and this is not from yourselves, it is the gift of God—not by works, so that no one can boast.—Eph. 2:8–9

Put on the full armor of God so that you can take your stand against the devil's schemes. —Eph. 6:11

Being God's People

God promises to give believers everything in Christ. Christians, as God's adopted children, can rely on God's provision for all things in life. With that in mind, the apostle Paul exhorts the Ephesians to maintain the unity of Christ's body. The letter includes practical advice for the Christian life. God challenges believers to lay hold of the grace (new life) he has given us, and then live like his workmanship. The image of the armor that equips believers in their spiritual struggle to be children of light continues to be as important today as it was for the Ephesians.

Jesus in Ephesians

Paul describes the church as the body of Christ. Our identity as believers comes by our being in and with Christ. Jesus is at the center of the identity, activity, and future of the church. God has equipped all believers to serve Christ in the world.

PHILIPPIANS

THE ATTITUDE OF CHRIST

Jesus Washing the Feet of His Disciples at the Last Supper

Purpose

The apostle Paul wrote to the Philippians to call for unity and harmony among believers based on the imitation of Christ's humble servanthood (2:1–11, 14; 4:2). As in every human institution, people in the church at Philippi did not always get along. Complaints and arguments are common occurrences, but believers are called by God to look to a higher example in Christ. Jesus put all his personal preferences aside and went to the cross, first in obedience to the Father and second in order to redeem the world. We are called to this kind of life.

The letter also warns against certain false teachings and practices (3:2–6, 18–19). False teaching under the pretense of being the real thing has plagued the church from the beginning. The Philippians are warned against teachers that wished to exchange the grace of the gospel for a merit system of religion.

Finally, this letter encourages believers to live a life worthy of their calling (2:12–16; 4:8–9). The life believers are to follow is not easy. The model for the believer is Christ, who is the highest goal of all thought and action.

Outline

1. Greeting, Thanksgiving, and Prayer (1:1–11)

2. Paul's Imprisonment (1:12–30)

3. Imitating the Incarnation (2:1–18)

4. Timothy and Epaphroditus—Paul's Envoys (2:19–30)

5. Paul's Exhortations (3:1–4:9)
   a. Warnings against Judaizers (3:1–11)
   b. Encouragement to press on (3:12–4:1)
   c. Plea for unity and high-mindedness (4:2–9)

6. Thanks and Final Greeting (4:10–23)

Background

Author: The author of Philippians is the apostle Paul (1:1).

Date: Paul wrote this letter while under house arrest in Rome, around AD 60–62.

Audience: Paul probably had a personal connection with the church at Philippi. Philippi was Paul's first stop in his preaching of the good news in Europe. The occasion of the letter centers on Epaphroditus who had been sent by the church with a financial gift for the apostle. The care that this body of believers had for Paul indicates a receptive audience.

Philippi was in northern Greece and was a Roman colonial city on the royal trade route. Though there was a Jewish presence, the population was predominantly non-Jewish and proud of its Roman connection. Although a small city, it received special favors from Rome. Roman citizenship was very important in the city, as Paul's use of citizenship as a metaphor reveals (3:20).

Epaphroditus

Epaphroditus was the Philippian believer who brought the church's financial gift to Paul. He apparently contracted a life-threatening illness while on this mission. Paul uses him as an example of someone who risked his life for the sake of the gospel (2:25–30).

Every day around the world there are believers who risk their lives for God's kingdom. It is good to remember them, and that we are all called, sometimes in simple ways, to put our lives on the line for Jesus.

Themes

Servant Leadership (2:5–11). Just as Christ humbled himself and became one of us, our relationships ought to be modeled by the same humility.

Unity of Believers (2:1–4). Humility and love must be present in all our relationships, especially with other believers. This unity reflects our submission to Christ (1:21; 3:7–14).

Rejoicing in the Lord Always (1:18; 3:1; 4:4–13). Being under house arrest in Rome made this exhortation especially relevant to the apostle. His joy springs from the conviction that Christ provides for believers (4:13).

Key Verses

... being confident of this, that he who began a good work in you will carry it on to completion until the day of Christ Jesus.—Phil. 1:6

For to me, to live is Christ and to die is gain.—Phil. 1:21

Your attitude should be the same as that of Jesus Christ: Who, being in very nature God, did not consider equality with God something to be grasped, but made himself nothing, taking the very nature of a servant, being made in human likeness. And being found in appearance as a man, he humbled himself and became obedient to death—even death on a cross! —Phil. 2:5–8

Rejoice in the Lord always. I will say it again: Rejoice! —Phil. 4:4

Do not be anxious about anything, but in every situation, by prayer and petition, with thanksgiving, present your requests to God. And the peace of God, which transcends all understanding, will guard your hearts and your minds in Christ Jesus.—Phil. 4:6–7

Fascinating Facts

■ Phil. 2:5–11 may have been an early Christian creed set in the form of a hymn. In many translations these verses are set apart in poetic style. Paul may have composed the lines himself or merely used something that was held in common already.

■ Philippians has two endings: One is in 3:1 ("Finally my brothers...") and the second at 4:8 ("Finally brothers..."). It looks like the apostle had an afterthought, what we might call a P.S.

Being God's People

God promises to honor and glorify those who serve. Paul called believers to preserve the unity of all believers in love and humility. God challenges us to work against our selfishness and put others first as we serve him.

Jesus in Philippians

The view that Paul offers of Jesus in this letter is breathtaking. The glorious Lord humbled himself to become like one of us. Such humility is best demonstrated in his obedience, which led him to a gruesome death. Yet, God lifted him up (exalted him) from his humiliation and put him above all things. The apostle Paul makes this song a paradigm (an example) for all believers to follow: "Your attitude should be the same as that of Christ Jesus" (Phil. 2:5).

COLOSSIANS

THE SUPREMACY OF CHRIST

Gnosticism

Gnosticism was a philosophy that began during the first and second centuries AD. Gnostics believed one could "escape" the evil, physical world through a special knowledge (*gnosis*) typically obtained through a connection with a transcendent Being. Early Gnostics held the heretical belief that a special knowledge revealed to only a select group of souls could help them achieve salvation, escaping from the physical world into a spiritual reality.

Purpose

The church in the city of Colossae was dealing with some false beliefs. It appears the heresy in Colossae was a mixture of Jewish legalism and an early form of Gnosticism. Jewish legalism made the observation of Jewish practices like circumcision (Col. 2:11), festivals, and dietary laws (2:16) mandatory for Gentile believers.

Paul's emphasis on Christ providing all the "understanding, mystery, and hidden treasures of wisdom" (2:2–3) seems aimed at early Gnostic beliefs. Some elements of extreme self-denying (2:21–23) and Greek philosophy (2:8) were also part of the misled beliefs of the Colossians.

Paul combats the Colossian heresy by emphasizing the supremacy and complete sufficiency of Christ while at the same time denouncing human philosophies and proving that they are inadequate.

Outline

1. Introduction, Thanksgiving, and Prayer (1:1–14)

2. The Supremacy of Christ (1:15–23)

3. Paul's Labor for the Church (1:24–2:5)

4. Freedom in Christ (2:6–23)

5. The Christian Life (3:1–4:6)

6. Final Greetings (4:7–18)

Paul Ends His Letter to the Colossians
by Julius Schnorr von Carolsfeld

Background

Author: The author of Colossians is the apostle Paul (1:1).

Date: The letter to the Colossians is one of the Prison Epistles, meaning that Paul wrote it during his house arrest in Rome, sometime between AD 60 and 62.

Audience: Paul wrote this letter to the church in Colossae (in modern-day Turkey). Prior to the first century AD, Colossae was an influential trading town in Asia Minor. However, by the time Paul wrote Colossians, the city had been on the decline for several centuries.

Themes

The Supremacy of Christ. Jesus is all that is necessary in life—over and above Jewish legalism, Gnostic beliefs, and any other human philosophy, which are empty, inadequate, and unfulfilling.

Family and Community Life in Christ. When Jesus is central, he will influence all we do and say within our families and within our societies.

The Prison Epistles

Paul had been sent to Rome where he spent two years under house arrest (AD 60–62). Paul was allowed to have visitors and share the gospel. Acts 28:30–31 reads, "For two whole years Paul stayed there in his own rented house and welcomed all who came to see him. He proclaimed the kingdom of God and taught about the Lord Jesus Christ— with all boldness and without hindrance!" Epaphras, a minister to the church in Colossae and possibly the churches in Laodicea and Hierapolis (Col. 4:13), eventually joined Paul as a prisoner (Phil. 1:23).

While under house arrest in Rome, Paul wrote the Prison Epistles: Colossians, Ephesians, Philippians, and Philemon. According to his letter to the Colossians, Paul wrote another letter from prison to the Laodiceans (Col. 4:16). This letter was never discovered.

Key Verses

The Son is the image of the invisible God, the firstborn over all creation. For in him all things were created: things in heaven and on earth, visible and invisible, whether thrones or powers or rulers or authorities; all things have been created through him and for him. —Col. 1:15–16

When you were dead in your sins and in the uncircumcision of your flesh, God made you alive with Christ. He forgave us all our sins, having canceled the charge of our legal indebtedness, which stood against us and condemned us; he has taken it away, nailing it to the cross.—Col. 2:13–14

Therefore, as God's chosen people, holy and dearly loved, clothe yourselves with compassion, kindness, humility, gentleness and patience. Bear with each other and forgive one another if any of you has a grievance against someone. Forgive as the Lord forgave you. And over all these virtues put on love, which binds them all together in perfect unity.—Col. 3:12–14

Being God's People

Jesus Christ is sufficient in all things. No power, philosophy, or practice is effective in forgiving us and redeeming us other than Jesus. Jesus is the absolute truth and we can be assured of the effectiveness of Christ's influence in our lives, the lives of our family, and the life of our community. It is important to be on guard and aware of false teachings, heresies, and idle promises from other religions and philosophies that claim salvation can be found in something or someone else besides Jesus. Unlike Gnosticism that claims to have "hidden knowledge," God has revealed in the Scriptures everything we need to know and come to him.

Fascinating Facts

■ Colossae was only 10 miles (16 km) from Laodicea and 13 miles (21 km) from Hierapolis. The three cities combined were known as the tri-city area.

■ Philemon lived in Colossae and the church met in his house.

■ Paul never visited Colossae. Many scholars believe that Epaphras planted the church in Colossae while Paul lived in Ephesus.

Jesus in Colossians

The epistle to the Colossians emphasizes Jesus' divinity in a wonderful way: "The Son is the image of the invisible God" (1:15). Since Jesus is God, he is at the center of the whole universe, and through him, God is reconciling "all things, whether things on earth or things in heaven, by making peace through his blood, shed on the cross" (1:20).

1 & 2 THESSALONIANS

HOPE, HOLINESS, AND THE SECOND COMING

Purpose

Because of violent persecution, Paul and his companion Silas had to depart Thessalonica quickly, leaving the church vulnerable to persecution and discouragement (Acts 17:1–10). Therefore, Paul spends the first three chapters of 1 Thessalonians defending his actions and his absence, as well as the actions of his traveling companions.

After explaining why he had to leave so abruptly and why he wasn't able to return (2:1–3; 2:17–3:5), Paul exhorts the Thessalonians. Paul encourages them through their persecution, provides them with instruction on how to live a holy life that is pleasing to God, and teaches them about the return of Christ and about those who die before Christ returns.

But only a few months after writing his first letter to the Thessalonians, Paul learned that they misunderstood some of the details regarding Christ's second coming, so Paul wrote back to them to correct those misunderstandings. Some individuals had been trying to convince the Thessalonians that Jesus had already returned. In response to that, several Thessalonian Christians had resorted to laziness and idle living: Why work or labor if the end is here or upon us? Paul wanted to encourage the Thessalonians to continue with their daily routines. The second letter to the Thessalonians reminded them to continue in diligence and productivity because first, Jesus had not returned at that point, and second, no one knows the hour, day, month, or year Jesus will return.

Outline

First Thessalonians

1. Introduction and Thanksgiving (1:1–10)

2. Paul's Relationship with the Thessalonians (2:1–3:13)

3. Living to Please God (4:1–12)

4. Believers Who Have Died (4:13–18)

5. The Day of the Lord (5:1–11)

6. Final Instructions (5:12–28)

Second Thessalonians

1. Introduction, Thanksgiving, and Prayer (1:1–12)

2. Man of Lawlessness (2:1–12)

3. Standing Firm and Praying through Persecution (2:13–3:5)

4. Warning against Laziness (3:6–15)

5. Final Greetings (3:16–18)

> ## Was Paul the Author?
>
> Words that only appear in 2 Thessalonians, a more formal style, and the reference to "the man of lawlessness" have made some question the authorship of the letter. Although some modern scholars believe the letter was written in the second century, the early church fathers accepted Paul as the author. For this reason, Paul's authorship continues to be the preferred option.

Background

Author: The author of 1 and 2 Thessalonians is the apostle Paul (1:1).

Date: Paul wrote the first letter to the Thessalonians during his second missionary journey while he resided in Corinth. Most scholars suggest a date for 1 Thessalonians from AD 50 to 52.

Paul wrote the second letter to the Thessalonians, also from Corinth, approximately six months after writing the first letter, most likely just after Silas and Timothy returned from delivering the first letter.

Audience: Paul wrote to the church in Thessalonica (in modern day Greece). Thessalonica was the largest city in Macedonia and the capital of that province. Thessalonica was a seaport city in the Thermaic Gulf of the Aegean Sea and a critical trading center along the great Egnatian Way, which connected Byzantium with the Greek Peninsula.

THE EGNATIAN WAY

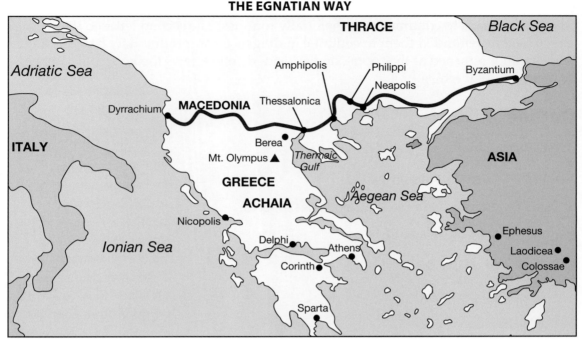

Themes

- Encouragement during persecution
- The second coming of Christ and the end times
- Instructions on holy living
- Criticism against laziness and idle living

Key Verses

For the Lord himself will come down from heaven, with a loud command, with the voice of the archangel and with the trumpet call of God, and the dead in Christ will rise first. After that, we who are still alive and are left will be caught up together with them in the clouds to meet the Lord in the air. And so we will be with the Lord forever.—1 Thess. 4:16–17

Now, brothers and sisters, about times and dates we do not need to write to you, for you know very well that the day of the Lord will come like a thief in the night.—1 Thess. 5:1–2

Rejoice always, pray continually, give thanks in all circumstances; for this is God's will for you in Christ Jesus.—1 Thess. 5:16–18

But we ought always to thank God for you, brothers and sisters loved by the Lord, because God chose you as firstfruits to be saved through the sanctifying work of the Spirit and through belief in the truth.—2 Thess. 2:13

May our Lord Jesus Christ himself and God our Father, who loved us and by his grace gave us eternal encouragement and good hope, encourage your hearts and strengthen you in every good deed and word.—2 Thess. 2:16–17

Being God's People

Jesus warned his followers to be prepared for his return (Matt. 25). Paul encouraged the believers in Thessalonica to be alert and of sober mind—to be prepared (1 Thess. 5:1–10). Paul also warned them against idle living and laziness: "We hear that some among you are idle and disruptive. They are not busy; they are busybodies. Such people we command and urge in the Lord Jesus Christ to settle down and earn the food they eat" (2 Thess. 3:11–12). The Thessalonians thought the end had either come or was coming very soon. This attitude may have contributed to their laziness. Why work if Jesus is already here or will be here tomorrow?

We can definitely expect Jesus to return. We are encouraged to endure trials and persecution while we wait for our Lord to establish his kingdom on earth. God calls everyone to contribute to his or her society, be productive, and care for the welfare of others.

Paul Preaching to the Thessalonians by Gustave Dore

Paul, Silas, and Timothy

Before Paul set out on his second missionary journey, he had a disagreement with Barnabas. As a result, Barnabas and Paul went separate ways. "Barnabas took Mark and sailed for Cyprus, but Paul chose Silas" (Acts 15:39–41).

Paul and Silas traveled to Derbe and Lystra where Timothy joined the group (Acts 16:1), and together these three companions continued on the journey to spread the gospel. While in the city of Philippi, Paul and Silas were flogged, imprisoned, and placed in stocks. Paul explains this mistreatment in his first letter to the Thessalonians in (2:2). The Philippians asked Paul and his companions to leave Philippi, so they traveled to Thessalonica to preach the gospel there (Acts 17:1). After only three weeks, Paul and his companions

were sent on to Berea (Acts 17:10), and then Paul went on to Athens alone (Acts 17:14–15). While Paul was in Athens, he sent Timothy back to Thessalonica to encourage the believers there (1 Thess. 3:1–3) and Paul went on to Corinth.

By the time Paul arrived in Corinth (Acts 18:1), Silas and Timothy rejoined him (Acts 18:5). Since Paul mentions Timothy specifically returning to him from Thessalonica (1 Thess. 3:6), it is clear that Paul wrote the first letter to the Thessalonians at that point while he was in Corinth. Paul stayed in Corinth for 18 months (Acts 18:11), and during that time wrote the second letter to the Thessalonians. After his extended stay in Corinth, Paul sailed for Ephesus with Priscilla and Aquila (Acts 18:18–19).

Jesus in 1 & 2 Thessalonians

Jesus told his disciples that he would come again (Matt. 16:27; 24:30; Mark 14:21; John 14:1–4). Back in the book of Acts, after Jesus ascended into heaven, two men dressed in white came and stood next to Jesus' disciples and said, "This same Jesus, who has been taken from you into heaven, will come back in the same way you have seen him go into heaven" (1:11). Someday, there will be a new heaven and a new earth. When Jesus returns, we will be in God's presence forever and God will "wipe every tear from [our] eyes. There will be no more death or mourning or crying or pain" (Rev. 21:4).

When Christ returns, he will put an end to all the suffering and persecution we live through now. Jesus promises us that the Holy Spirit will comfort and strengthen us through these difficult times (John 14). Paul writes in 2 Thessalonians, "But the Lord is faithful, and he will strengthen you and protect you from the evil one" (3:3). Jesus kept, and continues to keep, his promises to strengthen and comfort us until the day of his second coming.

Fascinating Facts

- Paul's first letter to the Thessalonians may be the first epistle Paul wrote. (Galatians is the other epistle sometimes thought to be earliest, AD 48–49)

- First Thessalonians is jam-packed with apocalyptic language. Paul emphasizes the end times more in 1 Thessalonians than any of the letters he wrote later in life. First Thessalonians is one of the most important books of the Bible used to support the concept of the "rapture" (see 4:16–17).

- Most scholars believe that the "man of lawlessness" mentioned in 2 Thessalonians 2:1–12 is a reference to the Antichrist. The "man of lawlessness" is also called the "Son of Perdition," the phrase assigned to Judas Iscariot (John 17:12). Who that antichrist actually was, is, or will be, is much debated among Christian scholars worldwide.

1 TIMOTHY

THE BODY OF CHRIST

The Apostle Paul

Purpose

Paul wrote to Timothy to encourage and instruct the young pastor as he faced heretical teachings in the church and within the community of Ephesus. The major heretical teachings in Ephesus were an early form of Gnosticism, Jewish legalism, and asceticism.

Most of 1 Timothy involves detailed instructions on proper worship, discipleship, leadership training, and church organization. Paul is providing Timothy with the authority to guide the growing Ephesian church through some of the basic issues any church faces as it begins to influence the community.

Outline

1. Greetings and Timothy's Charge (1)

2. Instructions on Worship and Church Order (2–3)

3. Instructions on Teaching Correct Doctrine in the Midst of False Teaching (4)

4. Instructions on Dealing with Church Members (5:1–6:2)

5. Final Instructions to Timothy (6:3–21)

Background

Author: The author of 1 Timothy is the apostle Paul (1:1).

Date: Paul wrote the first letter to Timothy approximately eight years after Paul's three-year stay in Ephesus. Most scholars suggest a date from AD 62 to 66, after Paul was released from his house arrest in Rome.

Audience: Paul is writing to the young pastor Timothy who struggled to teach and pastor the church in Ephesus.

Themes

- Encouragement against false teachings: stand firm in the presence of heresy and embrace love.

- Instructions on worship: pray for all people, continue in faith, remain holy, and love continuously.

- Instructions on organization: elders and deacons should be of quality character.

- Instructions on care for church members: love and care for children, the elderly, and widows; respect the elders of your church.

Grandmother Lois, Timothy, and Mother Eunice by Julius Schnorr von Carolsfeld

Who Was Timothy?

Timothy was from Lystra (in modern-day Turkey). His father was a Greek and his mother was a Jewish Christian (Acts 16:1). Timothy was well educated in the Old Testament (2 Tim. 3:15). Both Timothy's mother Eunice and his grandmother Lois modeled a life of sincere faith and raised Timothy to live similarly (2 Tim. 1:5)

Paul invited Timothy to travel with him when he passed through Lystra on his second missionary journey. Timothy became a pivotal missionary, evangelist, and friend to Paul as they together—with the help of several others—spread the gospel to Asia, Macedonia, and Achaia (Acts 17). Paul was very close to Timothy and referred to him as a "true son of faith" (1 Tim. 1:2).

Timothy was with Paul during his extended stay in Ephesus (Acts 19:22) and was present during Paul's first imprisonment in Rome (Phil. 1:1; Col. 1:1; Philem. 1:1). Paul entrusted Timothy to deliver six of his letters. Paul said the following about Timothy to the Philippians: "I have no one else like him, who will show genuine concern for your welfare. For everyone looks out for their own interests, not those of Jesus Christ. But you know that Timothy has proved himself, because as a son with his father he has served with me in the work of the gospel" (Phil. 2:20–22).

Key Verses

This is good, and pleases God our Savior, who wants all people to be saved and to come to a knowledge of the truth. For there is one God and one mediator between God and mankind, the man Christ Jesus, who gave himself as a ransom for all people.—1 Tim. 2:3–6

Beyond all question, the mystery from which true godliness springs is great: He appeared in the flesh, was vindicated by the Spirit, was seen by angels, was preached among the nations, was believed on in the world, was taken up in glory.—1 Tim. 3:16

Don't let anyone look down on you because you are young, but set an example for the believers in speech, in conduct, in love, in faith and in purity. Until I come, devote yourself to the public reading of Scripture, to preaching and to teaching.—1 Tim. 4:13–14

Pastoral Epistles

Paul wrote three letters in the New Testament to pastors: 1 and 2 Timothy and Titus. These three letters are called the Pastoral Epistles.

Being God's People

The message in 1 Timothy calls us, as the body of Christ (the church), to live holy lives that are pleasing to the Lord. Paul encourages Timothy to raise up leaders who are above reproach, faithful to their wives, temperate, self-controlled, respectable, hospitable, able to teach, not given to drunkenness, not violent but gentle, not quarrelsome, and not lovers of money (1 Tim. 3:2–3).

Jesus is the head of the body. All worship and organization within the body falls under Jesus' Lordship. As leaders of Christ's church today, we too keep our Lord in the forefronts of our minds as we lead and guide other members of the body.

Jesus in 1 Timothy

The letter to Timothy is a practical letter about the church, its life and teachings. Jesus is our Savior, our Mediator, and the Lord of the church. "For there is one God and one mediator between God and mankind, the man Christ Jesus, who gave himself as a ransom for all people" (1 Tim. 2:5–6). Because Jesus ransomed our sins on the cross, he can now carry those sins to God the Father and mediate on our behalf. Jesus is also the head of the body. Jesus serves as the head of the church. All worship and organization within the body falls under Jesus' Lordship.

Who Wrote 1 Timothy?

Some modern scholars question whether Paul wrote 1 Timothy because of the different vocabulary and style compared to the undisputed letters of Paul. These scholars also point out that there appears to be a more developed church structure and organization within 1 Timothy than what was actually evident in the first century. However, evidence from the letter itself and from the early church suggests that Paul was the author of the letter.

2 TIMOTHY

FINAL WORDS OF ENCOURAGEMENT

Paul in Prison by Rembrandt

Purpose

Imprisoned in Rome, the apostle Paul felt abandoned and lonely (2 Tim. 1:15; 4:16). Paul longed for Timothy, his close companion and brother in the Lord to come visit him (1:4; 4:9). Paul had been arrested in the city of Troas, in the northwestern tip of modern-day Turkey. In this second letter to Timothy, Paul asks Timothy to pick up the cloak, scrolls, and parchments that he left in Troas, and bring them with him when he comes to visit him in Rome (4:12).

Paul is also writing this letter to encourage the young pastor Timothy and the Ephesian church to persevere in the gospel through suffering and persecution, to continue preaching the gospel in all circumstances, and to guard the gospel against false teachings.

Outline

1. Greetings, Thanksgiving, and Appeal to the Gospel (1:1–2:13)

2. Encouragement against False Teachers (2:14–3:9)

3. Encouragement and Charge to Preach the Word (3:10–4:8)

4. Final Instructions and Greetings (4:9–22)

Background

Author: The author of 2 Timothy is the apostle Paul (1:1).

Date: Paul wrote the second letter to Timothy during his imprisonment in Rome. Scholars suggest 2 Timothy was written from approximately AD 66 to 67, shortly before Paul was executed in Rome.

Audience: Paul is writing to Timothy, the pastor of the church in Ephesus, as well as the Ephesian church as they continued to persevere under cruel persecution by the Roman Emperor Nero. Timothy was Paul's friend and fellow missionary. Timothy had stood by Paul through trials and persecutions and Paul longed to see his friend during the last days of his life.

Themes

▪ Appeal for Timothy to visit him in prison: Paul was lonely and felt abandoned by his friends. He hopes his apprentice and friend will visit him soon.

▪ Encouragement to proclaim the gospel in the midst of persecution, suffering, and false teaching.

▪ A final appeal to the Ephesian church to stand firm against persecution and false teachings.

Key Verses

He has saved us and called us to a holy life—not because of anything we have done but because of his own purpose and grace. This grace was given us in Christ Jesus before the beginning of time, but it has now been revealed through the appearing of our Savior, Christ Jesus, who has destroyed death and has brought life and immortality to light through the gospel.
—2 Tim. 1:9–10

All Scripture is God-breathed and is useful for teaching, rebuking, correcting and training in righteousness, so that the servant of God may be thoroughly equipped for every good work.
—2 Tim. 3:16–17

I have fought the good fight, I have finished the race, I have kept the faith. Now there is in store for me the crown of righteousness, which the Lord, the righteous Judge, will award to me on that day—and not only to me, but also to all who have longed for his appearing.—2 Tim. 4:7–8

Being God's People

Paul writes, "In fact, everyone who wants to live a godly life in Christ Jesus will be persecuted" (2 Tim 3:12). Paul also assures Christians that death is not the end for those of us who persevere in the faith and stand firm in the gospel. God will reward our faith in Christ's death and resurrection with eternal life—a "crown of righteousness" (4:7–8). The Christian life is difficult and we will encounter teachings and temptations that are contrary to the gospel. It is important to remain grounded in Scripture as our foundation for wisdom (3:16–17). It is comforting to know that even through suffering, we have hope in the reward of eternal life.

Two Magicians

Jewish tradition suggests that the two magicians who opposed Moses in Egypt (Ex. 7:11, 22) were also responsible for convincing the people to build the golden calf (Ex. 32). Even though these magicians were not named in the Old Testament, Paul repeats tradition by referencing them by name: Jannes and Jambres (2 Tim. 3:8).

Jesus in 2 Timothy

Eternal glory is the reward for all who have faith in Christ, who died and rose from the dead. Jesus is the righteous judge of everyone (2 Tim. 4:1, 8). Those who endure suffering for the sake of the gospel will someday be rewarded for their perseverance; those who live immoral lives and cause suffering to believers will be punished someday.

Paul's Last Days

Paul spent two years under house arrest in Rome and was released in AD 62. Evidence from 1 Timothy, Titus, and 2 Timothy suggest that Paul then spent several years traveling through Asia (2 Tim. 4:20), Macedonia (Titus 1:5; 3:12), and Crete (Titus 1:5). Paul was again arrested, this time in Troas (2 Tim. 4:13) and brought to Rome where he was thrown into prison to await execution. We see from his second letter to Timothy that Paul was not very optimistic about the outcome (2 Tim. 1:8, 15–18; 4:9–16).

When Paul wrote 2 Timothy, many of Paul's fellow missionaries and evangelists had already deserted him (2 Tim. 1:15; 4:10). Others were away from Paul (2 Tim. 4:10–12), leaving him lonely and desiring companionship. This second letter to Timothy—the last epistle Paul wrote—appears to be a testimony of his "final words" as the apostle Paul prepared for the end. It's traditionally thought that Paul was executed in Rome during Emperor Nero's persecution of Christians.

TITUS

RESPONDING TO THE GOSPEL

Basilica of St. Titus in Gortyn, Crete

Purpose

Paul wrote this letter to Titus to encourage him as the pastor of the churches of Crete to appoint responsible elders in the midst of false teachings and immoral behavior (Titus 1:12) and to instruct Titus on proper doctrine. Paul also instructs Titus to meet him in Nicopolis (in Greece), the city from where Paul is writing this letter (3:12).

Outline

1. Greetings and Appointing Elders (1:1–9)

2. Rebuking False Teachers (1:10–16)

3. Dealing with Church Members (2:1–15)

4. Responding to the Gospel (3:1-11)

5. Final Instructions (3:12–15)

Background

Author: The author of Titus is the apostle Paul (1:1).

Date: Titus was written sometime between AD 64 and 66, shortly before Paul spent the winter in Nicopolis (3:12). This was a few years after Paul had been released from house arrest in Rome, but just before his second arrest and confinement in a Roman prison.

Audience: Paul is writing to Titus, the pastor Paul left in charge of the churches on the island of Crete (Titus 1:5). Titus was a Greek, a Gentile convert who traveled with Paul to Jerusalem (Gal. 2:1–5) and assisted Paul during his third missionary journey. Titus assisted the Corinthian church (2 Cor. 2, 7, 8) and also traveled to Dalmatia (2 Tim. 4:10).

Crete is the fourth largest island in the Mediterranean Sea. Cretans were excellent archers and shrewd in business. But Crete had developed a bad reputation and many people considered Cretans to be immoral and lawbreakers.

Paul Writing His Epistles by Valentin Boulogne

Themes

■ Encouragement to Titus to make sure moral believers were leading and ministering to the church in Crete.

■ Warnings against false teachers and the immoral.

■ Doing good in response to our salvation in Jesus Christ.

Key Verses

For the grace of God has appeared that offers salvation to all people.—Titus 2:11

But when the kindness and love of God our Savior appeared, he saved us, not because of righteous things we had done, but because of his mercy. He saved us through the washing of rebirth and renewal by the Holy Spirit.—Titus 3:4–5

Cretans

To emphasize the difficulties facing Titus on Crete, Paul quotes the Cretan philosopher Epimenides who said of his own people, "Cretans are always liars, evil brutes, lazy gluttons" (1:12). The saying "to act the Cretan" became synonymous with "to play the liar."

Being God's People

The gospel of Jesus Christ is such great news. We are saved by the grace of God (3:3–7). When responding to the gospel we are to renew our minds and do good. This isn't how we achieve salvation, but it is our response to salvation.

Jesus in Titus

In his advice to Titus, Paul reminds us that Jesus is at the center of the gospel. Jesus is our Savior, blessed hope, and Lord. We no longer subscribe to the ways of the world. When we profess our faith in Jesus, our lives should line up according to that belief.

PHILEMON

THE PRACTICE OF FORGIVENESS AND LOVE

Purpose

Paul is writing to convince a wealthy believer, Philemon, to forgive the runaway slave Onesimus and receive him back as a brother in Christ. Onesimus may have wronged Philemon or stolen from him (Philem. 18), and according to Roman law, Onesimus could be put to death. After running away from Philemon, Onesimus met Paul, became a Christian, and wished to be reconciled with his former owner.

Outline

1. Introduction and Greetings (1–3)

2. Paul Commends Philemon's Love (4–7)

3. Paul's Appeal to Philemon (8–22)

4. Paul's Request and Final Greetings (23–25)

Paul's Tactic

Paul uses an ancient Greek prescription when writing to Philemon: flattery (4–10), persuasion (11–19), emotional appeal (20–21).

Background

Author: The author of Philemon is the apostle Paul (verse 1).

Date: Paul wrote this letter at the same time he wrote the letter to the church in Colossae—sometime during his house arrest (imprisonment) in Rome, between AD 60 and 62.

Audience: Paul is writing to Philemon, a leader at the church in Colossae and the owner of a slave named Onesimus. (The Colossian church met in Philemon's house.)

Themes

Forgiveness. Paul appeals to Philemon to forgive Onesimus.

Christian Love. Loving other believers as family will elevate a slave's status to a point in which the slave-owner distinction can be transcended.

Key Verses

Perhaps the reason he was separated from you for a little while was that you might have him back forever—no longer as a slave, but better than a slave, as a dear brother. —Philem. 15–16a

Being God's People

Philemon had every legal right to punish Onesimus, but the love and grace found in Christ can overcome anything. Paul encourages Philemon to love Onesimus. Jesus commanded his followers, "Love one another. As I have loved you, so you must love one another. By this everyone will know that you are my disciples, if you love one another" (John 13:34–35). As followers of Jesus, the outward expression of love—even toward those who have wronged us—is a sign of our obedience to God.

Jesus in Philemon

Jesus said, "I have come that they may have life, and have it to the full" (John 10:10). Jesus died to provide life and freedom to all people, so that there is neither "slave or free, but Christ is all, and is in all" (Col. 3:11).

Slavery in the First-Century

Slavery in the Roman world was unlike recent examples of slavery. Although mistreatment of slaves occurred, many slaves were too important to mistreat. Slaves owned property, could manage large portions or entire households or businesses, and, with enough money, could buy their own freedom and even Roman citizenship.

To understand Paul's views about slavery, we need to pay attention to all of his writings rather than just this letter:

■ In 1 Corinthians 7:22 Paul affirms that a slave who has become a believer is "the Lord's freed person."

■ In Galatians 3:28, the apostle affirms that all people, regardless of social standing, are one in Christ.

■ In Ephesians 6:5–9, Paul exhorts slaves to be obedient. However, he also exhorts masters to treat slaves with fairness because "you know that he who is both their Master and yours is in heaven, and there is no favoritism with him."

■ In Colossians 3:22–24 the apostle makes the extraordinary affirmation that the reward for servants' obedience comes from the Lord because "it is the Lord Christ you are serving."

HEBREWS

A SUPERIOR COVENANT

The Last Supper by Philippe de Champaigne

Purpose

The main purpose of the letter to the Hebrews was to establish the superiority of Jesus. Jesus is better than angels, the prophets of the Old Testament, Moses, the law, the old covenant, the priesthood, the tabernacle (or sanctuary), and the Jewish sacrificial system. Jesus' death on the cross fulfilled the Old Testament. Jesus reveals God in a new and more complete way.

The letter aims to guide God's people into God's rest—his promised land. This is a journey of faith. Faith is the stance God's people take as they persevere in confidence toward the goal. The letter urges all Christians to strive to be holy and be like Jesus. Suffering was a catalyst for Christ's life of obedience and perfection. As imitators of Christ, suffering can help believers on their journey toward obedience in faith and love.

Outline

1. The Superiority of Christ over Angels, Moses, and Priests (1:1–7:28)
    a. Supremacy of Christ's revelation (1:1–4)
    b. Supremacy over angels (1:5–2:18)
    c. Supremacy over Moses (3:1–4:13)
    d. Supremacy over priests (4:14–7:28)

2. The Superiority of Christ as the High Priest of the New Covenant (8:1–13)

3. The Superiority of the New Tabernacle (9:1–12)

4. The Superiority of Christ's Sacrifice (9:13–10:18)

5. A Call to Perseverance, Faithfulness, and Discipline (10:19–12:29)

6. Rules for Christian Living (13:1–17)

7. Request for Prayer, Final Greetings, and Benediction (13:18–25)

Background

Author: The author of Hebrews is unknown. Some scholars suggest that the apostle Paul wrote Hebrews. However, Paul identified himself as the writer in his letters, and the author of Hebrews does not identify himself. Also, the difference in themes and style between Paul's letters and Hebrews argues against Paul as the author.

Date: Many scholars suggest a date from AD 60 to 69 for two main reasons: (1) The author of Hebrews mentions Timothy (13:23), and (2) the temple in Jerusalem, which was destroyed in AD 70, still appears to be standing. The author speaks of the temple in the present tense and doesn't reference the end of the Old Testament sacrificial system.

Audience: The author of Hebrews is writing to Jewish Christians. These converts appear to be tempted to resort back to Judaism or at least a hybrid version of Christianity mixed with Judaism. Some scholars suggest that the recipients of Hebrews were the large number of priests who converted to Christianity after the selection of the seven deacons in Acts 6:1–9. Because most people assumed that the audience of the book was Jewish, the book came to be called the letter to the Hebrews (or Jews).

Setting: The letter seems to address a group of Christians facing fierce persecution (10:32; 12:4). The persecution from the Roman government probably was not the only one. They might have experienced persecution from other Jews. During the first century, Judaism was a protected religion under Roman law; Christianity was not. The pressure of the persecution must have made it tempting for Christians to return to their Jewish roots in order to avoid persecution and possible death. Some scholars believe that in certain areas in the first century when Jews converted to Christianity, they were banned from the synagogue and their children couldn't attend the synagogue's schools.

Themes

The Superiority of Christ. Because of Jesus' superiority, what Christians have is superior to the old revelation. Jesus and the new covenant are superior to the old covenant, the old promises, the old sacrifices, the old "promised land," the old sanctuary, and the old priesthood.

Christ's Humanity. Christ became flesh to defeat the power of death, sin, and evil, and to give true freedom (2:14–15). Because Jesus became flesh, we know that Jesus understands our weakness and provides us with the grace to be faithful to him (4:15).

Faith, Perseverance, and Discipleship. Christ has given us a superior revelation and salvation. As a response in gratitude to him, we are called to endure persecution and suffering. We press on to our goal with faith in Christ: to rest in God's presence for all eternity.

Key Verses

For the word of God is alive and active. Sharper than any double-edged sword, it penetrates even to dividing soul and spirit, joints and marrow; it judges the thoughts and attitudes of the heart. Nothing in all creation is hidden from God's sight. Everything is uncovered and laid bare before the eyes of him to whom we must give account.—Heb. 4:12–13

Let us hold unswervingly to the hope we profess, for he who promised is faithful. And let us consider how we may spur one another on toward love and good deeds, not giving up meeting together, as some are in the habit of doing, but encouraging one another—and all the more as you see the Day approaching. —Heb. 10:23–25

Therefore, since we are surrounded by such a great cloud of witnesses, let us throw off everything that hinders and the sin that so easily entangles. And let us run with perseverance the race marked out for us, fixing our eyes on Jesus, the pioneer and perfecter of faith. For the joy set before him he endured the cross, scorning its shame, and sat down at the right hand of the throne of God.—Heb. 12:1–2

Heroes of the Faith in Hebrews 11

Abel (Gen. 4:2–10)

Enoch (Gen. 5:21–24)

Noah (Gen. 5:30–9:28)

Abraham (Gen. 11:26–25:11)

Isaac (Gen. 24:4–66; 25:9–11, 19; 26:1–40)

Jacob (Gen. 25:19–35:29; 49:1–28)

Sarah (Gen. 11:29–31; 12:5–17; 16:1–8; 17:15–18:15)

Joseph (Gen. 37:2–36; 39:1–23; 40:3–50:26; Ex. 1:5–8; 13:19)

Moses (Exodus, Leviticus, Numbers, and Deuteronomy)

Rahab (Josh. 2:1–24; 6:16–17, 22–25; James 2:25; Matt. 1:5)

Gideon (Judg. 6:11–8:35)

Barak (Judg. 4:1–5:15)

Samson (Judg. 13:1–16:31)

Jephthah (Judg. 11:1–12:7)

David (Ruth 4:17, 22; 1 Sam. 16:1–2 Sam. 24:25)

Samuel (1 Sam. 1:9–28:20; Ps. 99:6; Acts 3:24; 13:20)

Being God's People

God's promises of saving and transforming the world are made complete in Jesus Christ. Throughout the history of the Bible, heroes of faith have persevered through great trials and difficulties. These heroes provide us with insight into God's providence and faithfulness.

Throughout the book of Hebrews, the author gives five warnings to all believers:

1. Pay attention to everything you hear.

2. Fight against unfaithfulness and the hardening of your hearts.

3. Grow in spiritual maturity.

4. Persevere through trials and suffering.

5. Never refuse the Holy Spirit.

"Better Than"

The phrase "better than" occurs 13 times in the book of Hebrews—it is repeated in a couple of places:

- The prophets (1:1–3)
- Angels (1:4–2:18)
- Moses (3:1–18)
- Joshua (4:1–13)
- High priest (4:14–6:12)
- Abraham (6:13–7:10)
- Melchizedek (7:1–10)
- Aaron and priests (7:11–8:6)
- Sacrifices (8:7–10:39)

Jesus in Hebrews

Jesus Christ is the fulfillment of every promise that preceded him. Jesus Christ is superior to anything that came before him. In Jesus, we have a better hope, a better covenant, a better sanctuary, and a better inheritance. Jesus is the supreme and superior mediator, the sinless High Priest. There is no longer a need for repeated sacrifices because Jesus is the one and only sacrifice. Jesus' sacrifice provides all who believe in him access to the holy God.

Jesus Appearing to His Apostles by Duccio di Buoninsegna

JAMES

TEST OF A LIVING FAITH

Purpose

This letter emphasizes faith, testing, wisdom, and doing. The letter of James is concerned with helping readers see the importance of a living faith. The message of the book is clear: Go and do good things for others, rather than just talking about it.

The book of James was written to Christians who had become arrogant. Its message is different from Paul's letters. Paul dealt with one of the problems new Christians face: the belief that they can "earn" God's grace by being good enough. Paul concludes, "For it is by grace you have been saved, through faith—and this is not from yourselves, it is the gift of God—not by works, so that no one can boast" (Eph. 2:8–9). In this book, James deals with the other side of that problem: a misunderstanding about grace that results in an inactive faith. "In the same way, faith by itself, if it is not accompanied by action, is dead" (James 2:17).

Outline

1. Greetings (1:1)

2. Test of a Living Faith (1:2–18)

3. Faith Tested by Its Response to the Word of God (1:19–27)

4. Faith Tested by Its Reaction to Favoritism (2:1–13)

5. Faith Tested by Its Doing of Good Works (2:14–26)

6. Faith Tested by Its Production of Self-Control in Speech and Humility (3:1–18)

7. Faith Tested by Its Reaction to Quarreling, Judgmentalism, Arrogance, Selfishness, and Suffering (4:1–5:12)

8. Faith Tested by Its Resort to Prayer (5:13–18)

9. Conclusion (5:19–20)

Background

Author: Because of his prominent role in the church, many scholars agree that the author of the epistle was "James, the Lord's brother" (Gal. 1:19; Acts 15:13–29). According to an early tradition, James was martyred in Jerusalem in AD 62.

Date: The letter was likely written before the Jerusalem Council (Acts 15) in AD 49. The main reason to prefer this time is that the Gentile-Jewish controversies that caused the Jerusalem Council are not mentioned in the letter. In addition, the letter demonstrates a strong Jewish background, but with special familiarity with Jesus' teachings. For example, the letter uses the word "synagogue" (the NIV translates as "your meeting") (2:2), instead of using "church" (or "house church," as in the book of Acts).

Audience: Although impossible to say for sure, our best guess is that the letter was meant for Christian Jews. One of the reasons for this guess is found in the expression "to the twelve tribes scattered among the nations" (1:1). Scholars identify these "twelve tribes" with: (1) Christian Jews, (2) Gentiles, (3) all Christians, both Gentiles and Jews. Most scholars believe number one is most likely correct.

Themes

Temptation and Maturity. The Christian life is faced with many temptations in this world. However, for James, temptations are tests that strengthen our faith (1:2–8; 12–18).

Wealth and Poverty. The book of James does not condemn wealth. Rather, just like other biblical texts about riches, it condemns the abusive use of wealth. That is, James condemns two attitudes toward money: (1) an attitude that abuses or ignores the poor, and (2) when riches are substituted for God and become an idol (1:9–11; 2:1–13; 4:8–10, 13–16; 5:1–6).

Sins of Speech. Self-control is an important feature of true faith. Our speech can be a source of great goodness or great evil (1:26–27; 3:1–12; 4:11–12; 5:12).

Patience and Prayer. Prayer becomes a test of faith when it requires patience. The patience James writes about is born from a great dependence on God, which is born from wisdom (5:7–11, 13–20).

Faith and Actions. James writes about the faith of those who have already been saved. It is a visible faith, a faith shown in deeds rather than words (1:19–25; 2:14–26; 3:13–18; 4:1–7, 17).

Key Verses

Blessed is the one who perseveres under trial because, having stood the test, that person will receive the crown of life that the Lord has promised to those who love him. — James 1:12

Therefore, get rid of all moral filth and the evil that is so prevalent and humbly accept the word planted in you, which can save you. — James 1:21

As the body without the spirit is dead, so faith without deeds is dead. — James 2:26

Re-programming Our Minds

"Therefore, get rid of all moral filth and the evil that is so prevalent and humbly accept the word planted in you, which can save you" (James 1:21). Sin is pervasive and insidious; before we know it, we are slaves to our sin. Sin becomes second nature. However, the word of God, through the power of the Holy Spirit, transforms us and frees us from the slavery of sin. But like any "spring-cleaning project," it requires much work and is challenging. Yet the word of God can re-program our minds so we can "be made new in the attitude of your minds," and "put on the new self, created to be like God in true righteousness and holiness" (Eph. 4:23–24).

Being God's People

James is a strong reminder to all believers that faith must produce good fruit. With appealing images, a compassionate heart, and strong advice, James urges Christians to live out their faith. We must display a living, active faith. Faith without good deeds is constricted, unable to grow. Our faith must be visible in our self-control, maturity, treatment of weak people in society, and prayer.

Jesus in James

Although the letter of James mentions Jesus only twice (1:1; 2:1), Jesus' wonderful Sermon on the Mount in the Gospel of Matthew shines throughout the letter. James does not directly quote Jesus, but there are many important parallels.

James	Teaching	Matthew
1:2	Joy in the midst of trials	5:10–12
1:4	Exhortation to be perfect	5:48
1:5	Asking God for good things	7:7–11
1:17	God the giver of all good things	7:11
1:20	Warnings against anger	5:22
1:22	Becoming hearers and doers of the Word	7:24–27
2:5	The poor inherit the kingdom	5:3, 5
2:10	Keeping the whole law	5:19
2:13	Being merciful to receive mercy	5:7
3:12	To be known by our fruits	7:16
3:18	The blessings of peacemakers	5:9
4:2–3	Ask and you will receive	7:7–8
4:4	Serving God vs. friendship with the world	6:24
4:9–10	Comfort for mourners	5:4
4:11–12	Warnings against judging others	7:1–5
4:13–14	Living for today	6:34
5:2–5	Moth and rust spoiling earthly treasures	6:19
5:10	Prophets as examples	5:12
5:12	Warnings against making oaths	5:33–37

1 & 2 PETER

HOLY LIVING IN TIMES OF TRIALS

Purpose

The main focus of the first letter of Peter is the problem of suffering. As persecution against believers in the time of the apostles increased, this letter encourages faithfulness and Christ-like behavior in difficult circumstances. All other themes—the ministry of Jesus and the Holy Spirit, the people of God as God's flock, a life of holiness—come back to the issue of suffering. The letter teaches what it means to be God's people in times of suffering, persecution, and trials.

The second letter of Peter warns believers against false teachers, encourages them to grow in their faith, and instructs them regarding the return of Jesus.

Outline

1 Peter

1. Greeting (1:1–2)

2. The Nature of the Gospel (1:3–2:10)
   a. The blessings of the gospel (1:3–9)
   b. Anticipation of these blessings (1:10–12)
   c. Those who receive these blessings (1:13–2:10)

The Scribe

1 Peter, 1 and 2 Thessalonians, and the letter quoted in Acts 15:22–29 have a similar writing style. Some scholars have suggested that one writer/secretary was behind them all. The name Silas appears among all four works, making him the likely scribe behind these letters.

3. Holy Relationships (2:11–3:12)
   a. In a pagan world (2:11–12)
   b. With the government (2:13–17)
   c. With the family (2:18–3:7)
   d. In the church (3:8–12)

4. Christian Suffering and Service (3:13–4:19)
   a. Blessings in suffering (3:13–17)
   b. The example of Christ (3:18–4:6)
   c. Call to a holy life (4:7–11)
   d. Holiness in the midst of suffering (4:12–19)

5. Christian Discipline (5:1–11)
   a. Discipline of the body of Christ (5:1–6)
   b. Personal discipline (5:7–11)

6. Conclusion and Final Greeting (5:12–14)

Peter the Apostle by Giuseppe Nogari

2 Peter

1. Greeting (1:1–2)

2. God's Providence and Election Made Certain by a Godly Lifestyle (1:3–11)

3. Jesus is the Central Truth of the Testimony of the Apostles and Fulfillment of the Prophets (1:12–21)

4. A Warning Against False Prophets and Teachers (2:1–3:17)

5. Doxology (3:18)

Background

Author: The author identifies himself as Simon Peter, an apostle of Jesus Christ (1 Peter 1:1; 2 Peter 1:1).

However, authorship of the letters has been much debated. First Peter gained entrance into the New Testament canon quicker than 2 Peter. First and Second Peter are written in a different style, and the first letter uses an advanced level of Greek writing, while the second letter is written in simpler Greek. Some scholars argue that the level of Greek in the first letter is too high for a non-native speaker like Peter.

First Peter 5:12 suggests that Silas might have been involved in the first letter's composition. Silas was a partner and possibly a secretary to Paul (Acts 15:40; 1 Thess. 1:1). The Greek of 1 Peter could be explained as Silas' influence on the letter of 1 Peter. The lower Greek and stylistic differences in 2 Peter might be explained by the use of a different secretary, or even Peter actually writing the letter himself.

Date: The first letter was written late in Peter's life (AD 64–65). Peter seems to have written just before Nero's extreme persecution (AD 64–68). Although persecution is a main focus of the letter, it does not appear to be referring to the horrifying persecution under Nero. The second letter may well have been written soon after the first epistle.

Audience: Peter addresses his first letter to believers in parts of Asia Minor (modern-day Turkey) (1:1). If 2 Peter was the follow up letter (3:1), then the audience for both letters was the same group of believers. The many references to the Old Testament suggest an audience familiar with the Jewish Scriptures. On the other hand, Peter also seems to be writing to an audience with a pagan past (1 Peter 1:14; 2:10; 4:3; 2 Peter 3:15) suggesting a largely Gentile group of believers. Peter was probably writing to both Jewish and Gentile Christians.

Themes

1 Peter

- **Suffering.** Christians are called to suffer for the sake of Christ (2:19–25, 4:12–19).

- **Christian Testimony.** Holy living in the face of persecution and suffering is a testimony to the lost world (3:13–17).

2 Peter

- **Revelation.** The prophetic word and apostolic testimony are not human creations. They are reliable testimonies (1:16–21).

- **False Teaching.** False teaching is dangerous and destructive (2:1–3).

Key Verses

Though you have not seen him, you love him; and even though you do not see him now, you believe in him and are filled with an inexpressible and glorious joy, for you are receiving the goal of your faith, the salvation of your souls.—1 Peter 1:8–9

But you are a chosen people, a royal priesthood, a holy nation, a people belonging to God, that you may declare the praises of him who called you out of darkness into his wonderful light.—1 Peter 2:9

We did not follow cleverly invented stories when we told you about the power and coming of our Lord Jesus Christ, but we were eyewitnesses of his majesty.—2 Peter 1:16

Being God's People

God's people throughout the world continue to face persecution. God strengthens and is present with his people through times of suffering and the confusion of false teaching. The letters of Peter encourage all believers to hold on to Jesus, to be faithful and holy in the face of persecution, and to be on guard against false teachers.

Jesus in 1 & 2 Peter

Jesus gave his life for us; he knows suffering. God is with us, even in times when we feel alone and defeated. Knowing that Jesus will return gives us hope to continue being faithful and obedient to God. When Jesus returns, all our pain and suffering will be redeemed and we will be with him forever.

1, 2 & 3 JOHN

THE LOVE LETTERS

Purpose

1 John: John's first letter refutes false teachings that claimed that Jesus only appeared to be human. The letter affirms Christ's full humanity. This letter also stresses our adoption into God's eternal family and our brotherhood and sisterhood expressed in Christian love. The main focus of the letter is God's love through Christ. Because of God's love, we are called to love one another. The letter also assures believers of their salvation and corrects their beliefs regarding proper Christian discipline and morality.

2 John: Since false teachers were corrupting the gospel, John warned believers to use discernment when welcoming teachers into their homes. John also encouraged believers to seek love, hospitality, unity, and recognize the truth that Jesus came "in the flesh" (1:7).

3 John: The third letter of John—the shortest book in the Bible—was written to commend Gaius for his love, faithfulness, and hospitality, and also to denounce Diotrephes because of he was arrogant, gossiped maliciously about John and other leaders, and refused to welcome other Christians.

Outline

1 John

1. The Incarnation (1:1–4)

2. Living in the Light as God's Children (1:5–3:10)

3. Living in Love and in the Spirit (3:11–5:12)

4. Concluding Affirmations (5:13–21)

2 John

1. Greetings (1–3)

2. Love One Another (4–6)

3. Warning against False Teachings (7–11)

4. Final Greetings (12–13)

3 John

1. Greetings (1–2)

2. Commendation of Gaius (3–8)

3. Condemnation of Diotrephes (9–10)

4. Encouragement and Final Greetings (11–14)

Background

Author: The author of 1, 2, and 3 John, is John the son of Zebedee. John was an apostle, one of the twelve disciples of Jesus, and the author of the Gospel of John and Revelation. John was one of three disciples in Jesus' inner circle, and was called the "disciple whom Jesus loved" (John 13:23). In 2 and 3 John, he calls himself "the elder" (2 John 1:1; 3 John 1). Although some scholars think the name refers to a different John, the title of "elder" was common in the early church, even for the apostles (see 1 Peter 5:1 "To the elders among you, I appeal as a fellow elder").

Most scholars agree that the apostle John penned all three letters: 1, 2 and 3 John. The style within each letter has numerous similarities to the Gospel of John. They are all written in simple Greek and present contrasting terms such as light/darkness, love/hate, life/death, good/evil, and truth/lies.

Date: Most scholars agree that 1, 2, and 3 John were written at the same time as the Gospel of John, from AD 85 to 95. The late date is based on evidence from early church witnesses (Irenaeus and Clement of Alexandria), and the early stage of the Gnostic heresy.

Audience: John's first letter was a circular letter intended for several churches in Asia Minor—perhaps including, but not limited to, the seven churches of Revelation: Ephesus, Smyrna, Thyatira, Pergamum, Sardis, Philadelphia, and Laodicea.

John's second letter was addressed to "the chosen lady," who is unidentified. Some think that the expression stands for the church. The letter was probably sent to a house church in Asia Minor.

John's third letter was addressed to "Gaius," a Christian in one of the churches in Asia Minor. Gaius was a common Roman name at the time so it is difficult to identify who he was.

Ruins of the temple of Diana or Artemis in ancient Sardis

Setting: An early form of what became Gnosticism is an important background. It was a philosophy where all physical matter—including the human body—was considered evil and all spirit was good. According to early Gnostic beliefs, salvation was an escape from this evil flesh and was attained through a special knowledge (*gnosis*) and not by faith in Jesus' death and resurrection. Gnostics had two problematic views of Jesus: (1) Docetism—Jesus was 100% spirit and only *appeared* to have flesh, and (2) Cerinthianism—Jesus' spiritual divinity joined him at his baptism and left him before he died. Since Gnosticism taught that matter was evil, extreme asceticism (abstaining from all pleasure) and hedonism (indulging in pleasure) often developed. In their way of thinking, if the flesh has no consequence, then one can either mistreat the body or act immorally.

It was common practice for early believers to welcome itinerant missionaries and teachers into their homes. False teachers were taking advantage of this hospitality and spreading false beliefs among Christians.

Themes

- Jesus is the "Word made flesh." Jesus was not a ghost, nor did God's spirit latch on to the human Jesus at his baptism only to escape from that body prior to his crucifixion.

- The Christian life is an expression of love, obedience, and hospitality.

Key Verses

If we claim to be without sin, we deceive ourselves and the truth is not in us. If we confess our sins, he is faithful and just and will forgive us our sins and purify us from all unrighteousness.—1 John 1:8–9

This is how we know what love is: Jesus Christ laid down his life for us. And we ought to lay down our lives for our brothers and sisters.—1 John 3:16

Dear friends, let us love one another, for love comes from God. Everyone who loves has been born of God and knows God. Whoever does not love does not know God, because God is love.—1 John 4:7–8

And this is love: that we walk in obedience to his commands. As you have heard from the beginning, his command is that you walk in love.—2 John 6

I have no greater joy than to hear that my children are walking in the truth.—3 John 4

Being God's People

One of the greatest promises in John's letters is the promise of God's love and the assurance of our salvation in Christ. Everybody sins; the good news is that if we confess our sins, God will forgive us (1 John 1:8–9). We can't be perfect, no one can. Satan masquerades as an angel of light and his servants masquerade as servants of righteousness (1 Cor. 11:14–15). We must always be on the watch for those who wish to deceive us. Everything we encounter must be tested with Scripture.

The Apostle John

Jesus in 1, 2 & 3 John

Jesus came to this world in the flesh and he died for the forgiveness of sins and the salvation of those who believe in him. When we believe in Jesus we are adopted into God's family. We are God's beloved children. As God's children, we love and obey God our Father and we love our fellow brothers and sisters and treat them with kindness and hospitality.

JUDE

REMEMBER AND PERSEVERE

Michael Fights Rebel Angels by Sebastiano Ricci

Purpose

This short letter warns believers against false teachers and the dangers of their teachings. It encourages believers to remain faithful to the teachings of the apostles. Using examples from the history of God's people and God's judgment on apostates, Jude teaches that God will also judge all other false teachers. Finally, Jude urges believers to help others in danger of being misled.

Outline

1. Greetings (1–2)

2. Reason for the Letter (3–4)

3. Warning against False Teachers (5–19)
   a. Examples God's judgment against false teachers (5–13)
   b. Witness against the false teachers (14–19)

4. Exhortation to Believers (20–23)

5. Doxology (24–25)

Background

Author: The author identifies himself as Jude the brother of James (verse 1). Tradition holds that this is James the brother of Jesus who became the head of the Jerusalem church. This would make Jude ("Judas" in Greek) Jesus' brother mentioned in Matthew 13:55 and Mark 6:3. Jude might also have been a traveling missionary that Paul mentions in 1 Corinthians 9:5.

Date: Being so short a letter, it is difficult to determine when it was written as well as the false teachings the letter opposes. Any proposed date must be held tentatively. Thus, the date might vary from the AD 60s to the 80s. Some scholars suggest that Jude wrote his letter prior to AD 62 because if he wrote it after AD 62 when James was martyred, Jude would have used a word like "blessed," "good," or "just" to describe James (verse 1), which was the customary way to describe martyrs. However, it is still possible that Jude wrote much later in his life because in his letter he urges Christians to not forget what they had learned from the apostles (verses 17–18).

Audience: There is no specific audience mentioned in the letter. Jude may have been addressing a Jewish Christian audience—the use of the Old Testament suggests it. However, the letter applies just as well to Gentile believers.

Themes

Christ's Faithfulness. Christ is faithful and able to keep believers from falling (verses 1, 24).

God's Judgment. God is merciful. However, he judges evil, as the history that Jude reviews shows.

Key Verses

To him who is able to keep you from falling and to present you before his glorious presence without fault and with great joy – to the only God our Savior be glory, majesty, power and authority, through Jesus Christ our Lord, before all ages, now and forevermore! Amen.—Jude 24–25

Being God's People

God promises to keep us from falling into serious error if we trust in him. God challenges believers to stand up for the true faith and not be led astray.

Jesus in Jude

Jesus protects us and helps us reach the goal to be in his presence. While our task is to remain aware and cautious of false teachings, Christ gives us the strength to be faithful.

Jude's Strange Quotations

Jude quotes Michael the archangel and Enoch (Gen. 5:18–24; Jude 9, 14–15). Where did he get these quotations? It is possible that Jude obtained them from oral tradition handed down through the rabbis. More likely he is quoting from two books: *The Assumption of Moses* and the book of *1 Enoch*. These two books are not part of the Jewish or Christian Bibles. However, they are important for understanding the period between the Old and New Testaments. Jude's quotation of Enoch can be found in 1 Enoch 1:9, but his quotation of the archangel Michael no longer exists in the fragment left of the manuscript of *The Assumption of Moses*.

REVELATION

ALL GLORY AND PRAISE TO THE LAMB

Purpose

The book of Revelation describes the famous vision that the apostle John had while living on the island of Patmos in the Aegean Sea. We often think of Revelation as only focusing on the end of the world, but this book had a bigger purpose. Its message was to give hope to Christians who were going through several trials. They faced severe persecution, dealt with dangerous false teachers, and faced the temptations of immorality, idolatry, and spiritual complacency.

John wrote Revelation to instruct, guide, comfort, and reassure Christians in their journey through difficult times. It shows, with vivid images and powerful language, that even if evil seems too strong, God is in control of history. Although God's people suffer and can be in danger, God takes care of them. Even if evil seems to win the day, God will defeat Satan and his followers and show his justice and mercy to the entire creation. The book of Revelation speaks of the dearest longing of all believers: the return of the Lord as King and Savior. Then, God will renew creation, and his people will live with him forever. Until that day, all Christians join in with the final plea of the book: Come, Lord Jesus!

Outline

1. Introduction (1:1–19)
   a. Blessings (1:1–7)
   b. Vision of Christ (1:8–19)

2. Seven Messages to Churches (2:1–3:22)
   a. Ephesus (2:1–7)
   b. Smyrna (2:8–11)
   c. Pergamum (2:12–17)
   d. Thyatira (2:18–29)
   e. Sardis (3:1–6)
   f. Philadelphia (3:7–13)
   g. Laodicea (3:14–22)

3. Seven Seals (4:1–8:1)
   a. Interlude: Vision of heaven (4:1–11)
   b. Scroll with seven seals and the Lamb (5:1–14)
   c. Opening of the first six seals, including the four horsemen (6:1–17)
   d. Interlude: 144,000 sealed and the great multitude (7:1–17)
   e. The seventh seal (8:1)

4. Seven Trumpets (8:2–11:19)
   a. First four trumpets (8:2–12)
   b. Interlude: Woe! Woe! Woe! (8:13)
   c. Fifth and sixth trumpets (9:1–21)
   d. Interlude: The little scroll and the two witnesses (10:1–11:14)
   e. The seventh trumpet (11:15–19)

5. Seven Symbolic Histories (12:1–14:20)
   a. History of the dragon (12:7–12)
   b. History of the woman (12:13–17)
   c. The sea beast (13:1–10)
   d. The earth beast (13:11–18)
   e. The 144,000 (14:1–5)
   f. The angelic announcers (14:6–13)
   g. The harvest (14:14–20)

6. Seven Bowls (15:1–16:21)
   a. Commission of the angels (15:1–8)
   b. The Seven Bowls (16:1–21)

7. The Fall of Babylon (17:1–19:10)
   a. Judgment against Babylon (17:1–17)
   b. Announcement of the fall of Babylon (18:1–3)
   c. Call to God's people to leave Babylon (18:4–8)
   d. Lament for the fall of Babylon (18:9–20)
   e. Announcement of the fall of Babylon (18:21–24)
   f. Celebration of the coming of the King (19:1–10)

John the Apostle on Patmos
by Hieronymus Bosch

Apocalyptic Literature

The book of Revelation is unique in the New Testament. It is written in an apocalyptic style. Apocalyptic is a word derived from a Greek word meaning "to unveil, to uncover." Apocalyptic is a type of literature that reveals God's plans that had been hidden to humanity. The message is conveyed through signs, symbols, dreams, and visions.

8. Visions (19:11–22:5)
   a. The rider on a white horse (19:11–16)
   b. The defeat of the two beasts (19:17–21)
   c. The reign of the King for 1,000 years (20:1–6)
   d. The defeat of Satan (20:7–10)
   e. The last judgment (20:11–15)
   f. The new heaven and the new earth (21:1–22:5)

9. Epilogue (22:6–21)

Background

Author: John received the revelation from Jesus (1:1–2). Identifying who this John was, however, is not a simple task. An early tradition identified John with the beloved apostle, the author of the Gospel of John and the three letters of John. However, making a definite identification is difficult because the author did not write any details about himself in the book of Revelation—understandable, since the revelation is about Jesus and the events that would take place later. Another difficulty is that the name John—*Yohanan* in Hebrew—was the fifth most common name in first-century Jerusalem. Another difficulty is the vocabulary and writing style of the book. There is nothing like the book of Revelation in the New Testament.

Although these are important observations, the early, well-documented tradition among several church fathers, still makes John the disciple of Jesus the most likely author of the book.

Date: The content of the book suggests that the book was written during a time of severe persecution against Christians. Scholars have identified two possible periods when Christians suffered persecution under the Roman government: During the reign of Emperor Nero (AD 54–68) and the reign of Emperor Domitian (AD 81–96). Those arguing for the earlier date base their suggestions on some ancient versions of the book of Revelation that mention Nero's name, the severe persecution of believers during his reign, and the lack of references in the book about the destruction of the temple which occurred after Nero's reign in AD 70.

However, most scholars believe the later date is more likely correct. Significant testimony from early church fathers reports that John wrote the book during the reign of Domitian. An important argument for this date is what scholars call "emperor worship." Emperor worship was practiced since the time of Emperor Augustus (he ruled in Rome from 27 BC–AD 14). However, it was Emperor Domitian who required that he be addressed as *dominus et deus* ("lord and god"). Although there is little evidence of severe persecution of Christians during Domitian's reign, persecution increased steadily until it became terrible in a short time. Many scholars prefer the later date during Emperor Domitian's reign, somewhere around AD 90–96.

THE SEVEN CHURCHES OF REVELATION

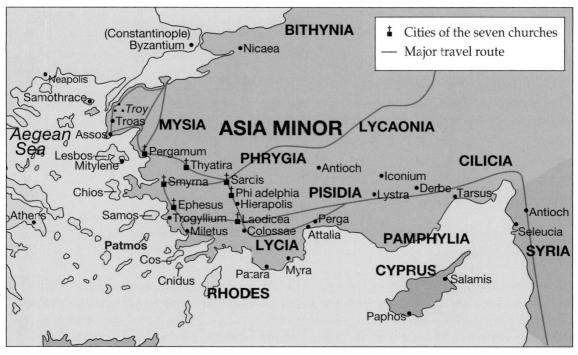

Audience: The author wrote primarily for the seven churches addressed in chapters two and three. Since these churches were located by widely traveled roads that connected them, the book of Revelation was meant to be a circular letter—a messenger would read the letter to Christians in one place, then take it to another place to read it to the believers there, and so on. However, the book of Revelation deals with essential issues for all believers. In this sense, the seven churches stand to represent all believers, in all parts of the world and throughout time.

Themes

The Trinity

1. **God, the Father**: God rules the universe. His power and authority rule over all areas of the universe, visible and invisible (4:11; 5:13; 11:17; 19:1–3). He is a good and compassionate God, who is deeply engaged with the world in general and his people in particular (7:12; 21:4).

2. **Jesus Christ**: He is the Lamb who is worthy of judging the nations and defeating evil (5:9–10). Jesus is the star of the book and all of history, from beginning to end (1:8). Before his death on the cross, Jesus promised his disciples that he would return and ordered them to be ready (22:7). The

Emperor Domitian, reigned AD 81–96

book of Revelation shows what it will be like when he returns. All the things that were prophesied, that have already happened and are still to happen, find their climax in this book (19:10). When Jesus returns, all things will be brought together, evil will be destroyed, justice will be done (20:7–15), and God will create a new heaven and a new earth where all believers will dwell forever (21:1).

3. **The Holy Spirit**: A crucial ministry of the Holy Spirit is to bring God's revelation to his servants.

The Agents of Evil. Evil is a reality, and the agents of evil are actively opposing God in the world. Even if evil seems to be winning the day, Revelation makes it clear that evil is under God's control and will be ultimately defeated.

1. The dragon
2. The beast from the land
3. The beast from the sea
4. The harlot
5. The Antichrist

Worship. Worship is central to the vision of God, the one sitting on the throne (ch. 4) and of the Lamb (ch. 5). Worship is the proper way for humans to approach and know God. Worship, which requires humility and trust in God, shows that the ultimate defeat of evil and the total transformation of the world is something God does. In his visions, John sees two realities: heaven and earth. What happens in heaven is the model of what should happen on earth—hence the prayer, "your kingdom come, your will be done, on earth as it is in heaven…" (Matt. 6:10). In heaven, God is worshiped as the true God and the Ruler of all: "You are worthy, our Lord and God, to receive glory and honor and power, for you created all things, and by your will they were created and have their being" (Rev. 4:11).

Key Verses

Blessed is the one who reads aloud the words of this prophecy, and blessed are those who hear it and take to heart what is written in it, because the time is near.
—Rev. 1:3

Worthy is the Lamb, who was slain, to receive power and wealth and wisdom and strength and honor and glory and praise!—Rev. 5:12

He [an angel] said in a loud voice, "Fear God and give him glory, because the hour of his judgment has come. Worship him who made the heavens, the earth, the sea and the springs of water."—Rev. 14:7

The Spirit and the bride say, "Come!" And let the one who hears say, "Come!" Let the one who is thirsty come; and let the one who wishes take the free gift of the water of life.—Rev. 22:17

Christ as King of Kings

Four Approaches to the Book of Revelation

Four Views	How Revelation is Viewed	More about This View	Example: The Trumpets Rev. 8:1–13
Futurist *Revelation is like a road map for the future.*	The book of Revelation is prophecy primarily about the future end of the world.	In the futurist view, all or nearly all of Revelation is yet to occur. Revelation is a prophecy that describes the end of time and the years leading immediately to the end.	The trumpets describe the events of the tribulation in the last days.
Historicist *Revelation is like a history textbook for the past, present, and future.*	The book of Revelation is prophecy about church history from the time of John to the end of the world.	Historicists view the events in Revelation as symbolic descriptions of historical events throughout church history. (Some futurists also understand the Seven Churches listed in Revelation 1–3 in a historical manner, treating each church as descriptive of a particular era of church history.)	The trumpets are the stages of church history, perhaps from about AD 400 until the fifteenth century (or to the present).
Idealist *Revelation is an allegory for all times and places.*	The book of Revelation is a non-historical and non-prophetic drama about spiritual realities.	This view treats the images, visions, and dreams as symbolic expressions of struggles between good and evil throughout history. These symbols represent the struggle between the kingdom of God and the powers of evil.	The trumpets are about the cycles of human sin, consequences, and God's salvation.
Preterist *Revelation is like an ancient newspaper.*	The book of Revelation is prophecy that was fulfilled primarily in the first century AD.	"Partial Preterism" views most of Revelation as prophecy fulfilled in the first century AD, though final chapters of Revelation describe future events to occur at the end of time. "Full Preterists" contend that the return of Jesus was spiritual and occurred in AD 70.	The trumpets represent a vision of the Roman war with the Jews in the first century AD and extend the seals' description in further detail.

The Four Horsemen of the Apocalypse (Rev. 6) by Victor Vasnetsov

Being God's People

The book of Revelation presents the climax of God's plans for the world. Evil, starting with Satan and all of his agents, will be destroyed. God will judge all who would set against him and claim glory and authority for themselves as if they were divine. Jesus, who died in humility for the sins of the world, resurrected with power, and ascended in glory, returns as the victorious King to claim what has always been his, judge all people, and restore his creation. The book of Revelation is not just a book of comfort for those who suffer; it is also a book of guidance. Like the North Star that guides ships, the book of Revelation guides us to the brightest star of all: Jesus, the Lamb who gave his life for us and the King who claims his throne in victory and righteousness.

Jesus in Revelation

In his visions of heaven, John sees Jesus as he is: the ascended and glorified Lord, who is worthy of all worship. Jesus has authority over all things, including Satan and death. His judgment is righteous and just. His promises to give rest and peace to his followers will be fulfilled in the new heavens and the new earth.

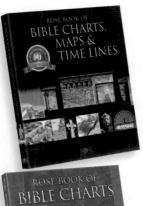

Rose Book of Bible Charts, Maps & Time Lines
– 10th Anniversary Edition
Dozens of popular Rose Publishing Bible charts, maps, and time lines in one spiral-bound book. Reproduce up to 300 copies of any chart free of charge.

- Christianity, Cults & Religions
- Jesus' Genealogy
- Islam and Christianity
- Denominations Comparison
- Bible Time Line
- Bible maps
- Christian History Time Line
- Bible Bookcase
- Trinity
- How We Got the Bible
- Bible Overview
- Temple and High Priest
- Tabernacle
- Ark of the Covenant

Includes MORE pages, 6 EXTRA topics, updated information, and a bonus 24" fold-out on Jesus' Family Tree.
Hardcover with a spine covering a spiral binding. 230 pages. ISBN: 9781596360228

Rose Book of Bible Charts Volume 2
Here are dozens of popular Rose charts in one book! Topics include • Bible Translations comparison chart • Why Trust the Bible • Heroes of the Old Testament • Women of the Bible • Life of Paul • Christ in the Old Testament • Christ in the Passover • Names of Jesus • Beatitudes • Lord's Prayer • Where to Find Favorite Bible Verses • Christianity and Eastern Religions • Worldviews Comparison • 10 Q & A on Mormonism/Jehovah's Witnesses/Magic/Atheism and many others!
Hardcover with a spine covering a spiral binding. 240 pages ISBN: 9781596362758

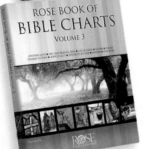

Rose Book of Bible Charts, Volume 3
Topics include • Who I Am in Christ (Assurance of Salvation) • What the Bible Says about Forgiveness • What the Bible Says about Money • What the Bible Says about Prayer • Spiritual Disciplines • Heaven • Attributes of God • How to Explain the Gospel • Parables of Jesus • Bible Character Studies and many more!
Hardcover with a spine covering a spiral binding. 240 pages. ISBN: 9781596368699

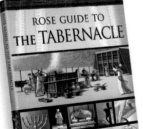

Rose Guide to the Tabernacle
Full color with clear overlays and reproducible pages. The Tabernacle was the place where the Israelites worshiped God after the Exodus. Learn how the sacrifices, utensils, and even the structure of the tabernacle were designed to show us something about God. See the parallels between the Old Testament sacrifices and priests' duties, and Jesus' service as the perfect sacrifice and perfect high priest. See how:
• The Tabernacle was built • The sacrifices pointed Jesus Christ • The design of the tent revealed God's holiness and humanity's need for God • The Ark of the Covenant was at the center of worship. Clear plastic overlays show inside/outside of the tabernacle.
Hardcover with a spine covering a spiral binding. 128 pages. ISBN: 9781596362765

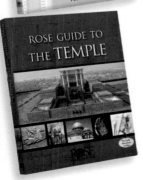

Rose Guide to the Temple
Simply the best book on the Temple in Jerusalem. It is the only full-color book from a Christian viewpoint that has clear plastic overlays showing the interior and exterior of Solomon's Temple, Herod's Temple, and the Tabernacle. Contains more than 100 color diagrams, photos, illustrations, maps, and time lines of more than 100 key events from the time of King David to modern day. It also includes two full-color posters: the Temple of Jesus' time and the stunning National Geographic poster on the Temple Mount through time. You will understand how the Temple looked, its history, and its biblical importance.
Hardcover with a spine covering a spiral binding. 144 pages. ISBN: 9781596364684

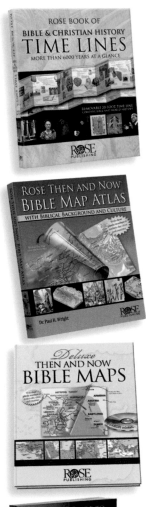

Rose Book of Bible & Christian History Time Lines

Six thousand years and 20 feet of time lines in one hard-bound cover! This unique resource allows you to easily store and reference two time lines in book form. These gorgeous time lines printed on heavy chart paper, can also be slipped out of their binding and posted in a hallway or large room for full effect.
• The 10-foot Bible Time Line compares Scriptural events with world history and Middle East history. Shows hundreds of facts; includes dates of kings, prophets, battles, and key events.
• The 10-foot Christian History Time Line begins with the life of Jesus and continues to the present day. Includes key people and events that all Christians should know.
Hardcover. ISBN: 9781596360846

Rose Then and Now® Bible Map Atlas with Biblical
Background and Culture

It is the only Bible atlas with a combination of:
• 120 stunning detailed Bible maps
• Clear plastic overlays of modern cities and countries so you know where Bible places are today.
• Incredible insights into the lives of 30 important Bible characters.
This Bible atlas focuses on people—not regions—and how the Middle East geography affected their lives and decisions.
Hardcover. 272 pages. ISBN: 9781596365346

Deluxe Then and Now® Bible Maps Book with CD-ROM!

See where Bible places are today with Then and Now® Bible maps with clear plastic overlays of modern cities and countries. This deluxe edition comes with a CD-ROM that gives you a JPG of each map to use in your own Bible material as well as PDFs of each map and overlay to create your own handouts or overhead transparencies. PowerPoint® fans can create their own presentations with these digitized maps.
Hardcover with a spine covering a spiral binding. ISBN: 9781596361638

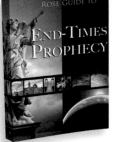

Rose Guide to End-Times Prophecy

An easy-to-understand overview of Bible prophecy from several viewpoints. Jesus talked a lot about the end of time and his second coming. These are key teachings that every Christian should know. So why don't they? Perhaps the topic seems too complex or too confusing. And that's a shame because it doesn't have to be.
The Rose Guide to End-Times Prophecy is an easy-to-understand overview that examines key portions of Scripture and explains different ways that Christians have interpreted end-times prophecy. Simple charts and illustrations help you see the whole picture.
Paperback. ISBN: 9781596364196

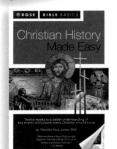

Christian History Made Easy

Summarizes the most important events in the history of the church, from the time of Jesus to modern day. *Christian History Made Easy* explains early church history, the Church Councils, the Great Schism, the Crusades, Francis of Assisi, John Wycliffe, Martin Luther, the Protestant Reformation, and more. *Christian History Made Easy* presents key church history events and great Christian leaders everyone should know, along with full-color church history timelines, photos, pictures, and maps.
Paperback. 224 pages, ISBN: 9781596363281